LOCOMOTIVE

PORTFOLIOS

THE

PRINCESS ROYAL

PACIFICS

THE

PRINCESS ROYAL
PACIFICS

PEN & SWORD
TRANSPORT

First published in Great Britain in 2018 by
Pen & Sword Transport

An imprint of Pen & Sword Books Ltd
47 Church Street, Barnsley, South Yorkshire S70 2AS

ISBN 9781473885783

Pen & Sword Books Ltd incorporates the imprints of Pen & Sword
Archaeology, Atlas, Aviation, Battleground, Discovery, Family History,
History, Maritime, Military, Naval, Politics, Railways, Select, Social History,
Transport, True Crime, and Claymore Press, Frontline Books, Leo Cooper,
Praetorian Press, Remember When, Seaforth Publishing and Wharncliffe.

For a complete list of Pen & Sword titles please contact:
Pen & Sword Books Limited
47 Church Street, Barnsley, South Yorkshire S70 2AS, England
E-mail: enquiries@pen-and-sword.co.uk
Website: www.pen-and-sword.co.uk

Design and typesetting
by Juliet Arthur, www.stimula.co.uk

Printed and bound in India by Replika Press Pvt. Ltd

CONTENTS

Cover Photo: 6201 shortly after preservation and restored to her former glory with a Royal Scot headboard (RO).

Back cover Top Left: Another arrival for 46206 unobserved except for a lone photographer (THG).

Back cover Top Right: 46200 barely run in and preparing for her first run to Euston to meet her public (LMS PR/AE).

Back cover lower: 46200, towards the end of her life, in her usual habitat working up the steep inclines to the North of England and Scotland (THG).

ACKNOWLEDGEMENTS

This book has its roots in an inheritance. During 1984, my uncle, Ronald Hillier, died and I acquired his lifelong railway collection: models, books, documents, magazines, photographs and correspondence. Due to time constraints I was unable to go through all of this material in any depth until I retired in 2010. When I did it became apparent that my uncle had been fascinated by the work of Sir Nigel Gresley and Sir William Stanier. It was a fascination I shared and wished to explore. And so a seed was sown that has grown into this book; my uncle must take credit for this, with his collection providing the primary and unique reference source.

To his efforts must be added the invaluable work of the National Railway Museum (NRM) and the National Archives (NA), plus the endeavours of many individuals who, as steam was dying, saved invaluable records from destruction and recorded the day-to-day lives of steam engines. Without the NRM, the NA and these forward-thinking individuals, much would have been lost and this and many other books would have remained unwritten. I thank these two institutions and the holders of personal collections for permission to quote from material they hold or the books they have written.

Where would we be without our parents? I was blessed with a mother and father who were loving, always supportive and greatly influenced my life. However, they probably wished their son had aspired to greater things than being an avid devotee of railways, the Royal Navy and Tottenham Hotspur. So in fact they are the chief culprits in allowing me to write this book. As always we blame the parents!

INTRODUCTION

46200 in her prime, but with only a few years of life left before withdrawal. (THG)

I was lucky to be born in the post-war years; it seemed a gentler, more ordered world. The Second World War was not long over, but the sense of peace and stability were strong, and many people returning from the conflict wanted to build a better world and a better life. The 1930s had seen similar hopes, once the effects of the Great Depression eased, but dictators put paid to ideals of greater security and prosperity.

So, my parents' generation and mine grew up in periods where hope and recovery were common threads. Expectations rose and a feeling of possibility encouraged greater effort.

But development of this potential has to be sustained by something more substantial than hope. Investment in business and people was essential. In the 1930s Britain was still heavily industrialised with engineering at its core. It was, perhaps, the last decade when we could boast that we could manufacture anything, defeat competition and sell it to the world. While it lasted, companies both large and small prospered, none more so than our railway builders, who developed locomotives for home and export in vast numbers.

Steam was still the driving force, with coal cheap and plentiful. Locomotive engineers hoped to wring the last few improvements from this ageing technology, before new forms of traction were exploited and as the country recovered from the First World War, and investment increased, the railways were encouraged to develop and build. Steam locomotive engineers seized the opportunity to push ahead with new designs, ignoring, for the most part, emerging technologies. They lived in a world where engineering had a glamour and status that today IT has inherited, attracting the brightest minds. It dominated society and drove the country

forward. The dramatic impact of their products were exploited by the many new outlets for news and propaganda that became available in this fast-moving decade.

It was in this atmosphere that four new railway companies, formed in 1922/23, plied their trade. Each pushed ahead with developments to make their service better. Hard selling was essential to make sure railways attracted customers, particularly on the lines from London to the North and Scotland, where the London, Midland and Scottish Railway (LMS) and the London and North Eastern Railway (LNER) competed for lucrative trade. A fast, cost-effective service was essential, but an illusion of glamour was also key to selling the trains to an emerging business class eager for such a service. As the economy improved, holiday traffic added to this growing demand for rail transport.

The LMS and LNER looked to improve their locomotives and rolling stock, and recruited two of the best locomotive engineers of all time. William Stanier, at the LMS, and Nigel Gresley, at the LNER, were encouraged to be bold and inventive. But Gresley had been given a head start of many years and, by the time Stanier arrived at Euston in 1932, was well into a massive building programme. Undeterred, he launched a locomotive modernisation plan to rival, if not surpass, the LMS's main rivals.

Any competitive transport fleet needs glamour to attract publicity and trade. Goods engines are the core, suburban trains pull in

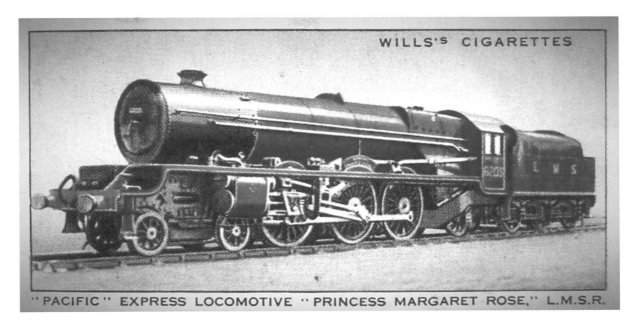

WILLS'S CIGARETTES

"PACIFIC" EXPRESS LOCOMOTIVE "PRINCESS MARGARET ROSE," L.M.S.R.

essential commuting traffic and second-string express trains provide a good basic service, but it is the frontline express trains, operating over the main routes, that sell a company. The *Golden Arrow*, the *Flying Scotsman*, the *Cornish Riviera Express* and others gave each business allure, but each needed something extra to meet aspirational demands. Comfort, a sense of modernism and looks were essential. The LNER responded with a fleet of powerful Pacific locomotives, but, until Stanier's arrival, the LMS built good engines without any making such a strong impact.

There were also concerns on the LMS about the power and stamina of its express locomotives. With long runs, on arduous routes north, their 4-6-0 designs lacked endurance and often relied on double-heading to do

their duties. Cost and efficiency seemed compromised by the design policies of the many organisations that had been drawn together to form the Company. Stanier needed to break with this past to truly modernise the LMS, and a new class of express engine was central to this need. And so the first two Princess Royal Class locomotives appeared in 1933 and steam power entered its last, dramatic phase.

As a child I was imbued with a love of steam locomotives. I appreciated their majesty and elegance, and was captivated by their energy and movement. And I was born into a world where these engines supported so much of our lives: trade, travel, work, leisure and the opportunities they offered. Even now, when this country relies so heavily on its roads for survival,

PR in the 1930s tapped many sources. (RH)

46200 late in her career. (RH)

the railways still meet many of our needs.

My family encouraged my passion. My father, uncle and grandfather made sure I saw many wonderful scenes at London`s main line stations, from a very early age. Visits to engine sheds and works were not uncommon, and gradually, an understanding of this world, and the engineering that supported it,

grew and provoked a sense of history, which I felt necessary to record. In the years until steam locomotion disappeared, I followed its dying embers, remembering and recording all I saw, armed with my Kodak Brownie 44A camera and endless curiosity.

Being a North London boy, I found the old LMS and LNER locomotives, now operating under

British Rail's banner, fascinating. Accompanied by my father and uncle, Euston and King's Cross became our regular stomping grounds, and, when I was old enough, I spent much time at each place on my own, drawn by Stanier and Gresley's Pacifics as they reached the end of their lives. Hoping to be invited onto the footplate remained my constant, but unfulfilled hope. The closest I came was an unplanned ride in the first carriage behind 46245 *City of London*, with my head and shoulders hanging out the window, breathing in smoke and steam.

In 1961 I was taken to a railway exhibition at Marylebone to see a mixture of steam, gas, electric and diesel locomotives. My uncle pointed out Sir William Stanier, mingling with the crowd. He seemed very old, but stood erect and happily talked to people. I would love to say that I was one of them, but I was more interested in clambering onto the footplate of 71000 *Duke of Gloucester*, too young to fully understand the importance of this proud and dignified man. Later, of course, I regretted this missed opportunity. But as the fascination fostered by my family grew, I understood the complexities of these engines and the men who built them. Great designers and engineers experience defining moments in their lives when they exploit an opportunity that comes their way. For Stanier, it was his promotion to Chief Mechanical Engineer (CME) with the LMS and being given free rein to build what could be the ultimate steam locomotive. His design team produced a fine series of engines of all types, but it was his Princess Royal Class that drew the most attention and turned him into a hugely significant figure.

Many see this class as a stepping stone in a programme that led to the Coronation Pacifics, and these later engines did surpass the Princesses in terms of power, performance and

number. But with a little modification the Princesses could have become even better. They also better represent Stanier's ideas and standing as an engineer, since the Coronations were largely designed while he was on duty in India. With the Princesses he had to lead a team he inherited, coping with any prejudices or well-established working principles and practices.

Many accounts of Stanier's work focus on locomotive design and performance. These are essential in understanding how his mind worked, but we need a broader approach to gain a true understanding of the problems he and the railways faced in bringing these expensive projects to fruition, and then sustaining them. Social, political, economic, operational and engineering issues all played significant parts.

I saw Princesses frequently in their final years of service and rode

An unidentified Princess taking water while at speed, passing Newbold Troughs near Rugby. (RH)

46204, grimy and neglected, near the end of her life. (THG)

behind them twice. I can still hear and see them pounding up Camden Bank, and always look forward to viewing the two that have survived into preservation. My father and uncle travelled with them in their prime when steam seemed an unchanging part of their lives.Sadly, so much information about our railway history was lost or destroyed when steam locomotion was discarded in the 1950s and 1960s.

Some far-sighted people did gather material, sometimes just before its destruction, and this now rests in many public and private collections. My uncle was one of these concerned individuals and preserved many items – photographic and documentary – and recorded the memories of those who were there. It is the basis of this book, supplemented by the wonderful work of the National

Railway Museum and many more like-minded people.

This is not the first and won't be the last book about the Princess Royal Class, but I hope it will be a fitting memorial to those who designed, built, maintained and crewed these elegant locomotives. I also hope it will do justice to the many souls who took the time to record and preserve traces of their history for me to follow.

SKILLS, OPPORTUNITIES, INFLUENCES AND EXPERIENCES

William Stanier could have been a nearly man. Born, raised and absorbed into the traditions of the Great Western Railway (GWR), his unique skills should have seen him become the Company's Chief Mechanical Engineer (CME), but his age and the timing were wrong. Charles Collett, another talented engineer of a similar age to Stanier, was ahead in the pecking order and became CME in 1921. By 1931 Stanier, with Collett unlikely to relinquish the post, seemed destined to remain a good deputy and never experience the true engineering freedom that came with this promotion. As a man of some reserve he did not seek publicity as a reward, but he needed to be stretched professionally and lead a team of like-minded people towards engineering perfection.

Undeniably there were opportunities at Swindon, even as a deputy, but some felt the GWR was no longer moving forward, instead relying on the success of established locomotives and concepts. Some also believed their dynamism and desire to experiment stopped when George Churchward, their most influential leader and a significant influence on Stanier,

Charles Collett, George Churchward's successor and a man who fostered Stanier's career. He also drew heavily upon Stanier's goodwill and skills when grief consumed him following the death of his wife. (WS/RH)

retired. Stanier must have felt that a great opportunity was passing him by.

Despite this likely hiatus in his career, it had still been one of rapid promotion and achievement, supported by Churchward's patronage and admiration for his young protégé, and then fostered by his successor, Charles Collett. Each man gave him the freedom to think broadly, to observe and then develop

Stanier as a young man at Swindon, self-assured and ready for the challenges that lay ahead. (GWR)

William Stanier Senior. A strong, resourceful man who rose to senior rank in the Great Western Railway (GWR) and was a huge influence on all of his children, but particularly his eldest son. (GWR)

training was stiff and expensive, the Works seemed to be a place where he could develop his skills. In the late nineteenth century, apprenticeships were a good alternative to an expensive university education. In due course, when promotion might see them rise to senior positions, they would come face to face with university graduates better versed in scientific research and practice. As a result, some felt as though they were second-class citizens, unable to embark upon true scientific exploration and reach equal status. A social and educational glass ceiling, perhaps, and one that many found hard to break through. Education was a difficult and time-consuming route, especially when employed full time and possibly with family commitments.

William's father, who in 1892 was the GWR's Stores Superintendent and a man of great influence in the Company, might have considered other options for his son. Although Stanier passed his Cambridge Local Exams, university might have seemed a step too far. Stanier senior had also started his working life with the GWR as an office clerk and knew the benefits from following such a well-established path.

With the introduction of a series of factory and education acts in late Victorian Britain, forward-thinking people put in place two essential building blocks in improving and regulating the lives of those sucked into the often unsympathetic world of industry. Exploitation was rife and remained so for many more years,

but society was changing and demands for a better quality of life found a voice in these ground-breaking new laws. The railways, in particular, applied standards common to the age and only slowly embraced liberal change, but, by the time William Stanier entered the Works, new rules applying to the employment and training of apprentices at Swindon were coming into force and he had to wait until his sixteenth birthday, in May 1892, before beginning his technical education. Supported by his father, he managed to join the Company a few months earlier as an office boy, absorbing the atmosphere of life on this pre-eminent railway. Others were not so lucky; even as late as the early 1900s the GWR risked prosecution by employing boys under 14 years old in its workshops, where working conditions were extremely harsh and unsafe.

Apprenticeships had to end by an individual's twenty-first birthday, when they reached the age of majority and had to be paid as men, not boys. These training schemes also created a large and cheap workforce. In 1891 the GWR Swindon Works employed nearly 1,700 apprentices, usually at five shillings a week, in a workforce of 12,200, according to returns submitted to the Board of Trade. And the working conditions were often as bad as any in industrial Britain at that time. People were a cheap and easily manipulated commodity, and most employers only gave a passing nod to their health and welfare. Alfred Williams,

as a leader as well as a designer. From his earliest days as an apprentice, something in Stanier's approach and desire to learn impressed his tutors at Swindon, raising him above those of his and other generations.

From childhood he displayed a keen interest in engineering and seemed destined for a career in this field. Having a father who was a long-term employee of the GWR, and with the good opportunities for young men at Swindon, at a time when competition for professional in his autobiography *Life in a Railway Factory*, which coincided with Stanier's early years at Swindon, captured the brutal way in which these young lives were transformed:

'Southward the shed faces a yard of about 10 acres in extent. This is bounded on every side by other workshops and premises, all built of the same dingy materials blackened with smoke, dust and steam. To view it from the interior is like looking around the inner walls of a fortress. It is ugly; and the sense of confinement within the prison-like walls of the factory renders it still more dismal. There is no escape, he accepts the conditions and is swallowed up by his environment.

'A great alteration, physically and morally, usually takes place in the man or boy newly arrived from the country into the workshop. His fresh complexion and generally healthy appearance soon disappear. In a few weeks' time he becomes thin and pale, or blue and hollow-eyed. His appetite fails; he is always tired and weary.

'The change in character and morals is often pronounced as is the physical transformation: the newcomer, especially if he is a juvenile, is speedily initiated into the vices prevalent in the factory. Some of the workmen are greatly to blame in respect of this, and are guilty of almost criminal behaviour in their dealings with young boys.

'While the men are inside the walls of the factory, they are under the most severe laws and restrictions, many of which are utterly ridiculous and out of all reason considering the general circumstances of the toil and conditions in vogue; they are indeed prisoners in every sense of the term. There is little or

Swindon Works in the 1920s. (GWR)

no thought taken for the future, no knowledge of the value of life.'

It was into this strange environment that young Stanier entered at a very tender age, from a genteel, middle-class background, to begin an apprenticeship that would see him labour in a number of workshops accumulating a wide range of skills. It was on-the-job training to develop a practical understanding of the railway, but in his case, better education and a wealthier background than the majority meant Stanier's future was considerably brighter than many other new apprentices. Even so, he faced the same tough, continuous assessment to make sure he was progressing, and each year many were 'given up' as being unsuitable. In 1892, 76 were weeded out, 119 in 1893 and an average of 100 in each

successive year. To survive such a system, and such daunting working conditions, each apprentice had to develop inner steel and resourcefulness. It seems that Stanier absorbed many hard knocks along the way from which even his influential father could not protect him. He undoubtedly learnt valuable lessons that stood him in good stead when facing many daunting challenges in later life.

In 1901, when Stanier applied for associate membership of the Institution of Mechanical Engineers, his submission detailed the elements of his workshop training he thought most valuable: 'Served an apprenticeship to engine fitting, turning and erecting, and pattern making at the GWR Locomotive and Carriage Works, Swindon.' He added separately: 'Received

The centre of Stanier's life at Swindon. A typical GWR workshop in the early part of the twentieth century. (GWR)

instructions in technical subjects at the Swindon and North Wilts Technical School.' For most apprentices their time in the Works was solely to fit them for a single trade and learning by example achieved this. In these cases there was no need to attend college or receive a more formal education. But the brightest and the best needed a broader tutoring in engineering theory, which was provided by Swindon's Mechanics' Institute. This body began life in the mid-nineteenth century when a group of GWR workers identified a need to improve educational standards. From occasional meetings this grew to become an all-encompassing training facility with its own building and a clearly

defined philosophy: 'to disseminate useful knowledge' for railway workers and their families. With its links to the GWR, a great deal of effort was put into giving technical and engineering training and support. By the time Stanier began work at Swindon the Institute had grown considerably and its Chairman, Sir Daniel Gooch, then also the GWR's Chairman, had set specific educational goals for apprentices: 'I urge upon those young mechanics of the Works the importance not only of making themselves acquainted with the mere mechanical work of their profession, but of attaining a knowledge of the sciences of their profession by which they would be enabled to demonstrate to others, on

paper, any theory or invention which had presented itself to their minds.'

Gooch and the GWR placed great emphasis on personal responsibility for accomplishing this training, but stressed its extracurricular nature. They could have shown themselves to be progressive and responsible employees by improving apprentice training in the Works, but capital and labour were still imbued with a master and slave mentality. Compulsory attendance came in time, driven by the needs of technology and a requirement for a better-trained workforce to meet these needs, but this did not happen while Stanier was an apprentice. Gooch was at least reflecting a slightly enlightened spirit and he complemented this by establishing an annual prize for the best engineering student. It was awarded for the first time in 1891, two years after his death.

By the time Stanier began his training, the Institute had more than 500 students attending technical classes, creating an overspill into the town's other schools. The demand was so great that the education authority set up a coordinating body to oversee these developing needs, resulting in the creation of the Swindon and North Wiltshire Technical Institute in Victoria Road. Many apprentices, like Stanier, seized the opportunity and attended classes including geometry, technical drawing, machine construction, theoretical mechanics, magnetism and electricity, arithmetic and mensuration, carriage building, steam and steam engines. The college also offered broader, more aesthetic classes in the arts.

Stanier, being a committed and ambitious man, realised that practical and theoretical work had to be combined from the first. So during his five-year apprenticeship, and throughout his life, he read and studied all he could find to increase his engineering knowledge, supplementing this with evening classes at the Technical Institute.

For the first nineteen months of his apprenticeship, Stanier was assigned to the Carriage Works where he learnt carpentry skills, preparing timber for carriage building and repair. The tasks allocated to him would have been relatively simple, since the craftsmen carpenters would have jealously guarded the more complex work.

In the Carriage Works, Stanier came under the influence of Frank Marillier, son of the Vicar of St Pauls, Bristol, a civil engineer who was working for the Bristol and Exeter Railway when it became part of the GWR in 1876. Marillier was an expert in the design and repair of rolling stock, and workshop production techniques. He was also an innovator, producing a number of new engineering concepts and patents. Such was his standing that in 1902 he was promoted, by George Churchward, to Carriage Works Superintendent, holding this post until 1920, a year or so before Churchward retired. Marillier was a great admirer of the 'old man' and sought to emulate all that he did, especially in encouraging apprentices to develop beyond the

boundaries of their immediate working environment. He was directly involved in the Mechanics' Institution, particularly its Junior Engineering Society, and became its Vice President. He involved Stanier and in time saw the younger man become its Chairman.

From his writings it is clear Marillier was greatly impressed by Stanier. As a man who encouraged the development of professional skills while pursuing technical innovation, his example would not have been lost on Stanier.

Passing successfully through this training, Stanier moved to the Locomotive Works, spending twenty-one months in the fitting and machine shops, learning how to handle machine tools so as to make metal components. The workshop foremen soon noticed his natural ability, allowing him to take on tasks other less-talented apprentices were denied. By mid-1895 Stanier had progressed so far that he was moved into the erecting shop, where for four months he was involved in building new engines. Four more months were then spent on locomotive repair, before his final year saw him learning millwright and pattern-making skills, where another natural ability emerged.

When his Certificate of Apprenticeship was awarded in June 1897, William Dean, the Locomotive and Carriage Works Chief Superintendent, added a short summary: 'William A. Stanier has satisfactorily completed a term of 5 years apprenticeship at these Works. He has always borne a very good

Frank Marillier shortly after being awarded the CBE for his services during the First World War. A man of great significance on the GWR carriage and wagon side of the business, but also of interest because of his influence on the young Stanier. (RH)

character, has been punctual and diligent in attention to his duties, and the foremen under whom he has been employed report that he is a very good workman.'

Although Dean's words are understated, it was unusual for such a senior man to write any comments beyond a short summary. Clearly Stanier had made a strong impression. A year later Charles Stanier, William's younger brother, was awarded the coveted Gooch-inaugurated Chairman's Prize for apprentices. However, as their careers developed, the older sibling would pass his brother and move far ahead.

Armed with such good references and highly-developed engineering skills, William was selected for full employment with the Company. But his next step was an interesting one, spending six months in the shop producing patterns for castings, working alongside more experienced employees. Throughout his life many fellow engineers and scientists would point to his understanding of

the workshop, production techniques and machine tools as his greatest talents. Two abilities had yet to be demonstrated: managing complex organisations and producing new designs. Sir Harold Hartley, his colleague in the LMS days, best summed him up when writing:

'He was a devoted intuitive engineer whose strength lay in his lifelong study and practice of production techniques rather than in outstanding originality or scientific research. Much of his leisure was spent in studying literature to keep himself up to date and to absorb the work of other engineers around the World as they sought to advance steam locomotive design. This was a time and a field of experimentation restricted by the scope of advance in such a limited, old technology.

He, like many other engineers of that time, would have benefited greatly from the wider education and research facilities available at university. Apprenticeships were valuable, but great minds like Stanier's needed the freedom higher education offered to truly develop their skills and reach into the unexplored worlds of science.'

It is interesting to compare Stanier's apprenticeship with those of close associates. Many followed this common route with varying degrees of success and it produced some exceptional engineers. And each apprenticeship could be different, reflecting the needs of the Company and, one hopes, the needs of the individual. Frederick Hawksworth, who became Charles

Collett's successor as CME and a designer of some note, entered the Works in 1899. His apprenticeship saw him working in the tool shop, before specialising in locomotive work, finally spending a year or so in the Drawing Office honing his design skills. His potential was identified early by Churchward and his career directed down this specific route. He was so successful that the GWR supported him in applying for a Whitworth Scholarship, set up by Sir Joseph Whitworth to provide support for the highest-calibre apprentices pursuing an academic engineering degree. As a result, he attended the Royal College of Science in South Kensington, London, and received a first-class honours degree in machine design.

Stanier and Hawksworth were both engineers of great skill, but one would follow a production route and the other became a design engineer. Stanier specialised in combining manufacturing technology with management science to create a product, whereas Hawksworth and his team developed concepts and detailed designs. Each looked to the other's field hoping to gain experience of wider engineering needs. Later, Stanier's fertile mind was drawn by the complexities and the unique challenges design offered. With the examples of Churchward and Dean at Swindon, this route became even more attractive. In time his move to the LMS was the catalyst for this change and offered him the challenge he sought. But, for the moment, his career followed a different path, directed largely by the needs of the GWR and the skills he had clearly demonstrated.

In November 1897, when his time in the pattern shop came to an end, Stanier began a two-year period in the Drawing Office. He had taken technical drawing and mathematics classes at the Mechanics' Institution during his apprenticeship so already had some skills in this area. Here, for the next two years, his time was divided between carriages and wagons on a broad range of tasks designed to expand his knowledge and technical skills. More importantly, it placed him in close proximity to Churchward, soon to replace Dean as Locomotive Superintendent.

Stanier always referred to Churchward in the most flattering terms and it is not difficult to see why: a young man eager to learn, and an older man eager to lead and impart his knowledge. Their personalities matched and each could see in the other the same strengths and ambitions; beyond that lay the most profound, lasting friendship. Of all the people who influenced Stanier professionally, Churchward stands head and shoulders above them.

It is difficult to assess when this relationship began, but Churchward might have known the young Stanier from an early age through his father. Two such senior officers in the GWR would have had the closest contact and this seems to have resulted in an almost paternal interest in William. A similar relationship developed with Frederick Hawksworth, aided no doubt by his father, who was a draughtsman working under Churchward. With Churchward eager to have the best and brightest around him, these apprentices were obvious candidates for his patronage. Hawksworth, perhaps more than Stanier, benefited from this interest much earlier in his career; Stanier moved around on the periphery of the central team, expanding his knowledge of the wider railway and locomotive worlds.

During his last few months in the Drawing Office, Stanier focused on locomotive and experimental tasks working for Collett, who had recently been promoted to Chief Draughtsman. His performance was deemed so good that it led to his appointment as an inspector of materials with the Birmingham and Manchester Districts of the GWR in March 1900, then as a mechanical inspector of locomotives at Swindon nine months later. In his biography of Stanier, John Chacksfield believes this move might have been influenced by conversations between Stanier's father and William Dean. If so, a paternal interest in his son's career remained strong, as did a natural desire to support his child's ambitions.

This posting was a major step up, especially for someone who had qualified so recently. He worked for the Divisional Locomotive Superintendent, W. Williams, at the Swindon Shed, which stabled some 100 engines, and oversaw work at many other depots, including Gloucester, Oxford, Reading and Weymouth.

Professional recognition through one's work is essential in building a

Frederick Hawksworth in the mid-1920s. (GWR)

good career. For an engineer, improving qualifications and becoming a member of professional bodies are equally important in sustaining an emerging talent. The Institution of Mechanical Engineers (IME) was formed in 1847 as the Industrial Revolution took hold across Britain and the development of engineering skills became even more important. Founded by George Stephenson, who became its first President, the IME achieved great status by the beginning of the twentieth century and became a

Offices at Swindon. The scene of much of Stanier's early career. (RH)

The Mechanics Institute in Swindon opened the door to learning for many people who would otherwise have been denied the opportunity to develop new skills. Stanier became a chief beneficiary of this unequalled facility. (RH)

major focus for engineers worldwide. Membership was seen as essential to aspiring specialists and, encouraged by Dean and Churchward who supported his application, Stanier applied and was accepted in July 1901. He remained an active member all his life and became its President in 1941, one of only a small number of railway figures to do so. In time the Institution of Locomotive Engineers was formed and Stanier played a major role in its activities as well.

Stanier always stressed the importance of these professional bodies, and they influenced his own development and ideas. Each year the Institution's members presented learned papers highlighting new developments or the results of their own research. From these discussion followed and, such is the nature of science, other experiments developed, and research and discovery expanded as a result. The railways especially benefited from the Institution's work and also became a major contributor. Stanier's fertile mind grasped all

that these bodies produced, and learnt much from their proceedings and through meeting fellow members. If, as Hartley believes, he was not an innovative engineer, then he was at least open to new ideas and capable of developing them in a practical way. His membership, and the work he did, also reveals his ability to encourage others to develop their skills and to lead a team towards better solutions. When he became CME of the LMS this knowledge, and his capacity to adapt and learn, reached their peak, resulting in developments that exceeded all expectations.

As a 'coming man' more promotions followed swiftly. In 1904 he became Assistant Divisional Locomotive Superintendent at Westbourne Park Shed, near Paddington, then two years later he moved back to Swindon as assistant to the Works Manager for six months. This was followed by

another promotion, aged just 30, to Divisional Locomotive, Carriage and Wagon Superintendent. Each move increased his knowledge of the railway and in particular the vagaries of managing both a large pool of locomotives, technically and operationally, and a large team of workers. Stanier might not have been getting exposed to design work like Hawksworth, but his day-to-day involvement in the practical aspects of locomotive management, including testing and the response of different designs to the effects of hard running, was of equal value. And he observed, first hand, the way Churchward shaped the locomotive fleet, trying new ideas and developing designs that changed the way the GWR did its business. He was setting an example that other railway companies followed in time.

Even before he formally succeeded Dean in 1902, Churchward had begun his revolution. No part of

Mechanics Institute, Swindon

the GWR would be unaffected by his desire to move forward, embrace change and make the Company more successful. His locomotive strategy was key to the whole programme. Under Dean many successful engines had been designed and built, but by the early 1900s Churchward argued they had reached the limits of their engineering. New designs with better performance were essential to meet growing business needs and grow the Company further.

Dean had focused on 4-4-2 and 4-4-0 designs, whereas Churchward believed 4-6-0 engines would produce a far superior performance. Just before the older man's retirement the first engine of this type appeared, with two outside cylinders and inside frames. It was an experiment and many commented on the apparent crudity of its design, but testing new concepts was essential and led to greater refinement. This engine, *William Dean*, became a test bed to analyse design.

Churchward always looked across the engineering world for new ideas or refinements of older ones. In this he was not alone. The railway community was tight knit and many engineers who worked within it believed in a collective, inclusive approach to design. Their employers might be in direct competition, but science demanded a more pragmatic approach. Professional institutions were a catalyst for this process and became a primary forum for sharing knowledge. In a paper presented to the IME in 1906, Churchward touched upon his main design theme

and the ideas being developed elsewhere that he had noted:

'The modern locomotive problem is principally a question of boiler. The increase in the size of boilers and in the pressures carried, which has taken place during the last few years, has necessitated the reconsideration of the principles of design which had been worked out and settled during many years' experience with comparatively small boilers carrying low pressures. In America the great power of engines now employed renders the wide firebox a necessity, but in Great Britain few boilers of this kind have been built. On the Great Northern Railway Mr Ivatt has provided his fine "Atlantic" Class with wide fireboxes and they are undoubtedly proving successful. The employment of a superheater is having an extended trial in Germany and also in Canada. This affords the prospect of obtaining the same steam efficiency by the use of, say, 175lbs. pressure, as by employing the pressures of, say, 200lbs. to 225lbs. This no doubt offers some prospect of success. The Great Western Railway are fitting one of their standard boilers with the Schmidt arrangement, with a view to see what advantage can be gained.'

Watching, absorbing, analysing and then producing good engineering solutions was key to Churchward's success, along with a good team of designers around him. He constantly encouraged others to take this broader view and seek the best solutions possible, no matter from where they came. This approach suited Stanier, and he adopted it for the rest of his career.

Although Stanier was not part of the locomotive design team, he sat on the edge of this activity as

In 1904 Stanier was appointed to Westbourne Park Shed, Paddington, as Assistant Divisional Loco Superintendent. This photo captures a brief scene from his everyday life. (THG)

Divisional Locomotive Superintendent at Swindon. He was therefore aware of each development, and participated in trials and tests of new engines as they appeared. As a rising star he was in close contact with Churchward and become a sounding board for his chief, giving opinions on a wide range of technical issues involving engine performance, workshop operation and other areas in which he had become a specialist. Both men benefited from this contact and a close friendship grew, with Stanier frequently visiting Churchward's house adjoining the Works. During these years, as Churchward reformed many aspects of the GWR's operations, he established and put into practice theories that underpinned his view of the future. In 1950 Kenneth Cook, an ex-GWR employee, by then Vice President of the Institution of Locomotive Engineers, summarised the ideas his late leader had promoted:

'The stages by which these (developments) matured were characterised by rapid, intensive scheming and sectional experimentation, so that the first full-scale trial either met his desires or clearly indicated any minor modifications necessary.

'Standard Locomotives. The conception of the Churchward series of main-line engines appears on a drawing dated January 1901, which provides the foundation for a most comprehensive locomotive development. The drawing outlined six projected engines and indicated a number of common components. It was but a small step

from this to the development of his famous standard locomotives.'

For Churchward standardisation of locomotives, with commonality of parts, was a key objective. Many railways had suffered because they had built a plethora of engines requiring excessive and expensive quantities of spare parts. There was a need for different types of locomotives to meet a variety of needs, but the number of classes to achieve this could be much smaller and be better managed with common parts and fewer differences. Cook continues:

'Boiler Development. The development of the standard boilers appears to have commenced with the steam generator for the new "Bulldogs", which coincided with his appointment to the locomotive works in 1898, very soon after which he devoted great attention to the standardisation of boiler-flanged plates and mountings.

'In June 1903 his standard No 1 boiler with the rear barrel tapered and at 200lbs. pressure was used on the first of the 2-8-0 engines, on account of weight restrictions Churchward had to produce a lighter edition and this became known as the standard 2. It was used on the 2-6-2 tank engine.'

Development of standard boilers was a natural extension of Churchward's locomotive policy. As they evolved, three types of boiler (standards 1, 2 and 4) met the needs of the soon to be built 4-6-0 'Saints', 2-8-0 mineral engines, a 4-4-2 tank, light and heavy versions of the 2-6-2 tank engines, the 4-4-0 'Counties' and the 2-6-0 43xx class, 2-8-0 tank engines, plus Dean's

'Bulldogs', 'Atbaras', 'Cities' and 'Aberdares', when being modified under Churchward's stewardship. Cook explains:

'Superheating. Churchward gave early attention to the principle of superheating and the first engine to be fitted with this was No 2910 in 1906 (the Schmidt superheater with 3 rows of 8 elements). In 1907 a 4-cylinder "Star" class engine was fitted with a Cole superheater, having 3 rows of 6 units. Subsequently, three designs of Swindon superheater were fitted in 1907 and 1909. The third became the standard Swindon superheater.

'Churchward did not favour a high superheat, and he decided that this requirement was met with a low degree of superheat which was sufficient to ensure the absence of condensation in the cylinders.'

A superheater that reheated steam and increased an engine's thermal efficiency was attractive, and Churchward placed great trust in it, after successful trials. Wilhelm Schmidt developed the first practical model in the last decade of the nineteenth century and it appeared in the German Prussian S4 series of 1902. Churchward procured a unit and then developed it for GWR use. A superheater became a basic part of locomotive building until the demise of steam. Cook notes:

'Smokebox. The Swindon testing plant was installed in 1903 and amongst other uses to which it was put was the obtaining of data in connection with smokebox design, and the even distribution of the gases to ensure a uniform flow through the bank of tubes. Smokebox proportions were regarded as

of great importance (by Churchward and his designers), and Great Western engines during their development were fitted with smokeboxes larger than the dimensions prevailing elsewhere. Amongst the features which were investigated were the relationships between the blast pipe tip, chimney height and choke diameter, and as a result of the experiments made, a standard formula embracing these dimensions was evolved.

'**Piston Size.** Two sizes of piston valves were utilised (by Churchward) throughout the standard range of engines, viz., 8in and 10in. nominal diameter, and these went up in oversize steps of 1/16 in up to 3/8 in oversize. Churchward indicated a wear figure of .030in at which the steam chest should be re-bored and it is interesting to note that research into piston valves some years later confirmed both the angles of the snap rings and the limit of wear which he had laid down were in fact ideal.

'**Cylinder Lubrication.** The system (Churchward) adopted was that of a hydrostatic lubricator with sight feed, controlled from the regulator handle, supplying atomised oil into the steam pipes between the regulator valves and the steam chest.

'Churchward had undoubtedly struck a most important factor for reducing the rise of temperature and reduction of wear in the cylinders when drifting with steam off.'

Cook went on to describe other key engineering ideas Churchward developed – a top-feed system, vacuum braking and axlebox bearings – then added a note about his meticulous attention to standards of workmanship and accuracy of

the items produced. Finally, he summarised the contribution Churchward made and the impact of his work:

'During his reign, 888 of his standard locomotives were produced of which 583 are still in service today, and since his retirement 862 more of them (including the "Hall" class and those to be built during 1950) have been added and compose a range conceived nearly 50 years ago, still capable of competing on level terms with any standard range of modern British locomotives.'

Stanier was in the audience, on 22 March, when this paper was read and was the first to comment, in the discussions that followed:

'As members probably know, I served my time under Dean, but worked all my active life, until 1922, under

Churchward. I have a great regard and affection for his memory. As Mr Cook has said, "His soul goes marching on." That is true because all his engines, which are still of the most modern type, were built before 1910. Those who have come after Churchward have tried to follow in his steps ever since.'

None more so than Stanier himself, who followed his late leader's example with, perhaps, even greater success in a company presenting an even more severe challenge. But in the early 1900s this test was far in the future and for the moment Stanier continued developing his skills under the guiding hands of Churchward and his successor, Collett.

From the start of his apprenticeship Stanier's rare talents had been

Social functions formed a key part of life within the Swindon Institute. Today we would call it networking, a skill Stanier quickly learned and exploited as his stature as an engineer grew. (GWR/RH)

_ 4-CYLINDER ENGINES _

_ PACIFIC CLASS _ 6-S WHEELS _

_ 4000 CLASS _ 6-S WHEELS _

_ 2-CYLINDER ENGINES _

_ 2900 CLASS _ 6-S WHEELS _

_ 3800 CLASS _ 6-S WHEELS _

_ 4300 CLASS _ 5-S WHEELS _

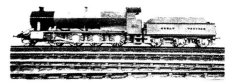

_ 4700 CLASS _ 5-S WHEELS _

_ 2800 CLASS _ 4-S WHEELS _

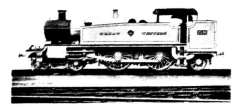

_ 2200 CLASS _ 6-S WHEELS _

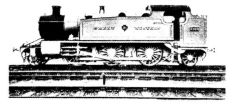

_ 3100 CLASS _ 5-S WHEELS _

_ 4200 CLASS _ 4-S WHEELS _

The result of Churchward's standardisation work. Stanier, his disciple, was deeply influenced by this impressive body of work, and his task with the London, Midland and Scottish Railway (LMS) was clearly inspired by these developments. (GWR/RH)

identified and nurtured by men of considerable skill and ability, predominantly Churchward. Thanks to their support, his own deep understanding of engineering concepts, hard work and a clear sense of direction, he had, during the first decade of the nineteenth century, moved swiftly from apprentice to the edge of the greatest part of his career.

Stanier was Churchward's disciple, and held his working principles and ideas close to his heart. But like his leader, he was always open to new ideas and broader thinking. Neither were scientists or innovators in the true sense, but they were much more than engineers simply following well-established design paths. Their minds were open and inquisitive, and each sought excellence. And they had the drive and determination to make sure their voices were heard, and their ideas pursued relentlessly. They were great engineers, but also great managers of organisations and change. With such skills Stanier would move seamlessly forward in the years ahead to design and build his own standard locomotives. At their core would be his Pacific Class, the clearest statement he made of his search for engineering perfection.

CHAPTER 2

FROM A BEAR TO CASTLES AND KINGS

William Stanier spent four years as Divisional Superintendent at Swindon studying all elements of locomotive building, testing and operation. Charles Collett, meanwhile, had, in 1912, been promoted to Works Manager, in lieu of Henry King, who had become assistant to George Churchward. Eager to have Stanier beside him in this demanding post, he sought agreement for his promotion and, on 1 January 1913, he became Assistant Locomotive Works Manager. Churchward knew the workshops needed modernising so as to improve productivity, and his new Works Manager and assistant were given this project.

This was an ideal role for Stanier, because it allowed him to exercise his considerable knowledge of workshop processes. Although he tackled the project with great skill and determination, he must have cast envious looks at his locomotive-design colleagues and wondered if he would ever get the chance to participate more directly in their work.

Although Churchward surrounded himself with very able men and gave them opportunities to develop, he was also a realist and recognised the need to exploit their skills for the good of the Company. Stanier was a proven workshop man and that is where his skills were best used at a time of great change. The declaration of war, eighteen months later, threw even more jobs his way and much of Swindon's workshop capacity was converted to the manufacture of munitions, often to the detriment of other tasks. While hostilities lasted, wartime production took over life at Swindon and most other engineering establishments around the country. Peace, when it came, was dominated by repairing the damage war's changed priorities had caused to men and machinery.

This difficult time stretched each railway company to their limit. Some looked back at pre-war days as a halycon time, sprinkled with experimentation and great advances. Socially the world was also changing. Having sacrificed so much for their country, men returning from the war demanded better working conditions and a greater say in the way their lives were regulated. Austere, hardnosed Victorian-

Stanier: austere and severe in looks, but dynamic and capable as a leader. (GWR)

principled management across all industries found it difficult to adjust to this change, none more so than at Swindon. A clash was inevitable and not long in coming. Small wonder that the pre-war period was seen as a golden age for the GWR. But at least now, unhindered by wartime restrictions, locomotive designers could continue development, hoping this would restore prestige and pride in the Company.

Much had happened since Churchward succeeded William Dean in 1902 and standard-class locomotives were now the mainstay

Churchward's Star Class engine No.4000, *North Star*. Built with four cylinders, it included many design features that influenced Stanier and led to his work on the Princess Class. (RH)

of the railway. But greater power output was always desirable and all possibilities were examined to see if improvements were feasible. 4-6-0 engines had become fashionable and continued to be the main focus, but the potential benefits of the 4-6-2 Pacific design were also being explored.

Evolution, and the combining of ideas to create new areas of research and discovery, is the cornerstone of science. This was nowhere more apparent than on the railways where each advance often suggested other possibilities. It is believed that the Pacifics grew from the 4-4-2 Atlantic Classes and the 4-6-0 configuration, with the two earliest examples being developed in the USA. During 1887, the *Lehigh Valley Railroad* discovered that mounting a new firebox onto a 4-6-0 design meant the extra weight

could only be carried if the frames were extended. To give balance and stability the designers hit upon the idea of adding two trailing wheels. In 1897 the Chicago, Milwaukee and St Paul Railway also found it necessary to add a set of trailing wheels when developing a 4-6-0 design so that axle loading would be reduced. However, neither design found favour and were not continued.

In 1901 the New Zealand Railway Department commissioned the Baldwin Locomotive Works of Philadelphia, Pennsylvania, to design and build thirteen new engines. The specification called for fireboxes capable of burning poor-grade lignite coal. As design work proceeded Baldwins realised the engine required a much larger firebox than normal and the extra support this needed could be best provided by a 4-6-2-configured locomotive, rather than a 4-6-0.

The success of this work soon reached the attention of engineers around the World and the model began to be explored in depth.

Designers were intrigued by the concept's potential to offer greater stability at speed and higher tractive effort. It also encouraged the addition of bigger, wider fireboxes and larger boilers to improve an engine's efficiency and output. And so a massive building programme got underway, particularly in the USA and Canada, where more than 6,500 Pacific locomotives were in service by the 1930s. They were a global phenomena and appeared on railways across all continents as the century progressed. In Europe, the

first prototypes appeared in France during 1907, designed by the Compagnie du Chemin as an improvement to their 4-4-2 Atlantic locomotives. This was followed by an example being built in Germany, although design work had begun two years earlier.

Ever watchful, Churchward and his team read the limited material available describing these early developments and showed interest. Although their new standard engines were meeting the Railway's needs, there was always room for improvement. The Pacific configuration seemed to offer more power and speed, but any advantages needed to be assessed and proven before a change of locomotive policy could be sanctioned. The decision to build one example was taken, but it is unclear if it was pursued by Churchward alone, eager to prove or disprove a theory, or the GWR Board, seeing some advantage in the development of a high-profile, unique engine. Considering Churchward's power and authority within the Company, the former is more likely. Either way the project went ahead and during January 1907 the Drawing Office prepared their designs, using elements of existing locomotives wherever possible. Many developments seemed to have been inspired by the recently-produced Star Class 4-6-0 locomotives.

In many ways this worked towards the targets Churchward had described in his 1905 paper to the Institution of Mechanical Engineers and his hypothesis that the 'modern

locomotive problem is principally a question of boiler'. Greater capacity was a primary aim and the Pacific design could achieve this, but would the greater weight and length be a disadvantage on the GWR's railway system, and would it perform better than their 4-6-0 engines on fast passenger duties?

Investing an agreed £4,400 in the project, the designers soon decided the boiler should be 23 feet in length, built in three rings, with the middle section coned. It would contain 141 x 2.5-inch fire tubes, against 176 x 2-inch tubes in the 'Stars', but with the same number of superheater flues

(eighteen), though 3/8-inch wider. To improve the engine's performance significantly, the firebox, a Belpaire type, had to produce greater heat, so the firegrate was built proportionally larger, with greater capacity than those attached to the Star Class. When completed this new boiler was designated Swindon Standard No.6.

The remainder of the locomotive drew heavily on the Star Class design. There were four cylinders: two middle ones set well forward between the frames, and the outer ones covering the tops of the rear wheels of the leading truck.

Harold Holcroft, the draughtsman responsible for producing the cylinder design for this engine, described in his book *Locomotive Adventure* how Churchward was involved in each stage of development, often disagreeing with the draughtsman's proposals:

'Churchward insisted that the "Star" class arrangement should be adopted without modification, other than in cylinder diameter, and the only point outstanding was as to how the diameter could be increased above the 14 ¼ inches of the "Stars". The longer wheelbase increased the bogie side movement and the angle taken by the trailing wheels of the

The Great Bear, Churchward's only Pacific experiment, appeared in 1908, numbered 111. Although Stanier was not involved directly in its development, its production clearly influenced his thinking when designing a Pacific locomotive for the LMS. (WS/RH)

GWR 111 passing between her regular haunts of Paddington and Bristol. It was ill-balanced and ungainly in looks, and its performance was no great improvement on the Company's 4-6-0 designs. She was rebuilt into this form in 1924. (BR/RH)

leading truck behind the cylinders. For this reason, a 15-inch diameter was the largest predictable in the limited space.

'This was explained on Churchward's next visit. I pointed out that GWR tyres were 5 ¾ inches wide, and that if narrower tyres were used the increased clearance behind the cylinders would allow a diameter of 16 inches. The Chief would not agree to departure from the standard width of tyre, and seemed quite satisfied with 15-inch cylinders.'

With only a small increase in diameter size, the tractive effort produced was marginally better than the 'Star' Class. Consequently, many of the potential gains from adopting the Pacific design were not fully exploited. Hawksworth, who was the other leading draughtsman involved in the design, also found any ideas that moved the engine away from the standard concept met a similar response from Churchward. He allowed his team great freedom, but was quick to rein them in when he suspected the end result might be costly or unnecessary. It was an

approach Stanier adopted when he managed similar projects: encourage individuals to think broadly, be open to new ideas and debate, but keep developments within a clearly established framework.

Although on the sidelines of this new development, Stanier was only too aware of this new Pacific taking shape in the workshops and followed each stage closely. He was intrigued and impressed by every element of the design. There is little doubt that this first British Pacific locomotive influenced him considerably, and would have featured in his regular conversations with Churchward; conversations that went on even after Stanier moved to the LMS.

The GWR's Pacific emerged from the workshops in 1908, named *The Great Bear*, and began a series of trials. It seems likely that Churchward never had any intention of building more than a prototype, so he might have regarded the engine less as a means of testing a new concept than as a means of developing a larger boiler. He was also aware that the total weight of engine and tender, which was more than 140 tons, created a coupled axle loading of 20 tons and 9 cwt, and this placed a severe restriction on its use over many GWR lines. The limits changed in time, but in the years leading to the First World War it was only sanctioned for use between Paddington and Bristol. On this line she did pull all sorts of loads, from express trains to fast goods. On one noteworthy occasion she was recorded pulling 2,375 tons non-stop from Swindon to Acton, at an average speed of 24.5mph.

As befitting an experimental engine, she was prone to problems, and spent long periods undergoing maintenance and repair. There were complaints about her steaming quality, which improved when the firemen got used to the wide firebox, and she was prone to derail on tight curves in shed yards. But with modifications, and as understanding of the design grew, she became a

successful engine and saw service until 1924 when a decision was made to convert her to 4-6-0 configuration. She was facing a general repair, and needed a new boiler and cylinders, so Collett took the opportunity to bring this singular engine in line with other designs and turn her into something 'similar to one of the "Castle" types'.

In 1921 Churchward retired and Collett became CME for the Railway, with Stanier promoted to be his principal assistant a year later. Although the new CME was reputedly a difficult man to work for, he and Stanier had forged a good working relationship over many years. This would now prove hugely beneficial for both men, especially when Collett's wife died suddenly in 1923. Grief took hold and he became more isolated, losing himself in studying unanswerable questions posed by metaphysics, such as 'what is the fundamental nature of being?'. Distracted by sorrow, he found the pressing needs of his job almost impossible to bear for many months and relied upon his assistant to act on his behalf. This allowed Stanier to improve his professional skills and become more directly involved in locomotive development at a very important time. The next GWR class of 4-6-0s was being designed and built; the first, 4073 *Caerphilly Castle*, appeared in August that year. With Collett grieving, responsibility for completing this work fell on Stanier's shoulders, the first time he had carried such a burden.

The Castle Class was essentially an improved Star, designed to

supplement and then replace them on the heaviest expresses. The years following the First World War had seen a sharp rise in traffic as the country recovered from the conflict and the 'Castles' were designed to meet this need. Collett's aim was to take the basic layout of the Star, extend the frames, add a new boiler that was larger, but lighter (to be called the No.8), and enlarge the four cylinders to take advantage of the increased amount of steam created. As building proceeded, the editor of

Collett with Queen Mary during a royal visit to Swindon in 1924. Although withdrawing from many aspects of life following his wife's death, he occasionally displayed a more sociable side. But more often than not, Stanier stepped into the breach to manage matters. (GWR)

Officers of the Great Western Railway Chief Mechanical Engineers' Department

Mr B. Giles
Wolverhampton

Mr C.T.H. Riches
Cardiff Valleys

Mr E.G. Ireland
Newport

M. J.W.A Kislingbury
Old Oak Common

Mr E.G. Wainwright
Newton Abbot

Mr C.B. Collett
Chief Mechanical Engineer

Mr W.A. Stanier
Works Assistant

Mr J. Auld
Docks Assistant

Mr C. Crump
Loco Running Superintendent & Outdoor Assistant

Mr G.H. Burrows
Chief Draughtsman & Personal Assistant

Mr A.J.L. White
Chief Clerk

Mr R.A.G. Hannington
Manager, Loco Works

Mr E.T.J. Evans
Manager Carriage & Wagon Works

Mr O. Barker
Central Wales

Mr R.J. Armstrong
Bristol

Mr J. Kelynack
Assistant Chief Clerk

Mr C.J.T. Billingham
Cardiff

Mr H.J. Roberts
Barry

M. F.C. Hall
Neath

Mr A.T. Rodda
Worcester

Mr E.W. Green
Newport

Mr T.R. Herbert
Port Talbot

the *Railway Gazette* was invited to witness 4073 and the engines that followed:

'Whilst retaining the special features of the GWR standard boilers, the dimensions have been increased, the barrel having a diameter at the front end of 5ft 1 13/16ths, and 5ft 9 at the throat plate, the length remaining at 14ft 10ins, as in the case of the No 1 standard boiler. The firebox is of the same design as that fitted to the No 7 standard and has the same grate area. The inside cylinders are supplied with steam through the passages in the saddle supporting the smokebox, the steam pipes for the outside cylinders being brought through the side of the smokebox and connected directly to the steam chests.

'The provision of larger cylinders brings the tractive effort up to 31,626 lbs, at 85% of the boiler pressure, as compared with 27,800 lbs of the present 4-cylinder class, thus making the new engine the most powerful used on passenger services in the British Isles, the nearest approach to it being the 4-6-2 3-cylinder engines of the LNER. These latter develop a tractive force of 29,800 lbs, and in that of the Darlington-built engine of 29,918lbs, an important factor in this connection being the GWR locomotive carries a much higher working boiler pressure than the other locomotives, namely, 225 lbs per sq inch, as compared with 180 lbs per sq inch and 220 lbs per sq inch respectively.

'In these new GWR locomotives the adhesion weight is distributed almost equally on the 6 coupled wheels, the

The GWR's senior management team during the 1920s. (GWR)

aggregate being 58 tons and 17cwt, whilst the leading bogie supports 21 tons, a total for the engine in working order, without tender, of 79 tons 17cwt. Advantage has been taken of the increased length of the frames to provide a longer cab having side windows, and an extended pattern roof. Incidentally, this, in our opinion, improves the general appearance of the locomotive. Owing to the fact that no fittings in the cab project beyond the regulator handle, greatly increased space for the driver and fireman is afforded.'

Churchward's influence was unmistakable, but so was the Collett/Stanier partnership, which not only pushed the boundaries of what was possible in engine capacity and performance, but also improved the ergonomics of footplate design, for greater efficiency and crew comfort. A roomier, better-laid-out footplate became a fundamental part of all Stanier's locomotives, to the great benefit of their crew. Seeing the world in an unrestricted way, accepting and considering new ideas, and producing something better on many different levels was one of Stanier's great strengths.

The Castle Class was very successful and came into being when the UK's railways were undergoing profound change. The country was served by many different, sometimes competing companies. The inefficiency of this system was only too obvious in the war when the Government was seeking to support military needs with an infrastructure often creaking under the strain of extra traffic, but also a myriad number of managers in each

company. To provide an adequate service the railways were brought under state control, which continued until 1921. Full nationalisation was considered, but rejected in favour of drawing all of these companies together into regional groups. Debate raged over the number, which was eventually set at four, and in 1923 the bulk of the major companies became part of this new structure: the London, Midland and Scottish Railway, the London and North Eastern Railway, the Southern Railway and the Great Western Railway. The GWR underwent the least change and its historic unification meant it was well ahead of the other three groups in many areas when the new system came into force. Their management was settled, the standardisation policy continued to bear fruit, its main centres of activity were clearly defined and many other issues were capably managed. Not so the other

regions, where new structures had to develop and old rivalries continued, often to the detriment of the new businesses.

The LNER were lucky in that they had an experienced CME. Nigel Gresley, already a successful manager of the Great Nothern Railway (GNR), took the top job when grouping came into being, the ageing John Robinson declining the post. A man of considerable gifts in both engineering and management, Gresley came to the LNER with a reputation for innovation and technical excellence. Like Stanier, he was a disciple of Churchward, and had brought these and other principles to bear when developing engines and rolling stock for the GNR. He was also fascinated by the potential of 4-6-2 tender engines, seeing them as the way forward for fast, long-distance express services. The GNR and the North Eastern Railway, now combined under the

Stanier played a pivotal role in the production of the King Class in his last years at Swindon. Many, looking at the outline of this class and then seeing a Princess, would see a hereditary chain. (RH/THG)

The Chief Mechanical Engineer's (CME) Department in the late 1920s. Even in this large group photograph Stanier draws the eye and dominates the scene. Collett is a shadowy figure in comparison. (GWR)

LNER banner, had already produced two Pacifics each in 1922 and on grouping this development continued; strangely at a time when the GWR was abandoning its well-established Pacific locomotive.

By 1924, when the 'Castles' appeared in number, the LNER had advanced their work even further and twelve Gresley three-cylinder Pacific engines were in service, with the next ten in production. One of the first of these, No.1472, was named *Flying Scotsman* and was selected by the Company to represent it at the Empire Exhibition at Wembley that year. Nearby the

GWR had *Caerphilly Castle* on display, asserting that it was 'Britain's most powerful passenger locomotive'. The LNER challenged the claim when exchange trials were agreed the following year. Many suspected this to be a publicity stunt rather than an attempt to further locomotive development, but each company treated the exercise very seriously and their engines were prepared carefully for the trials.

In April 1925 the LNER's 4474 worked the *Cornish Riviera Express* from Paddington to Plymouth and back, with the GWR's 4074 following the same route. The Castle

ran well, but the Gresley engine underperformed, with poor-quality coal and an unfamiliar road cited as reasons. In simple coal consumption terms the Castle used 42lbs per mile and the LNER engine burnt 48lbs per mile. When working over the LNER system, *Pendennis Castle* used rather more coal, at 53.4lbs per mile, but so did the other engine, consuming 57.1lbs. In June the LNER produced a summary of the trials:

'The higher boiler pressure of the GW engine tends to economy in coal, but involved higher cost in boiler maintenance. Although the tractive effort of the GWR engine is higher than

that of the LNE engine, the boiler power is considerably less. Fast running was therefore made by the GW engine on short rising gradients, such as London to Finsbury Park, but on the long hill grades of the GW system, the Pacific engine ran faster. As to high-speed running on the flat and down the grades, there is nothing to choose between the two engines, which are both free running and capable of running at high speeds.

'The trials show that the road bed of the LNE is superior to that of the Great Western. The Pacific engine could not be safely run at such high speeds on falling grades on the Great Western road as their own engines, probably due to the greater length, weight and height of the Pacific engine. Strict observation had to be observed on the speed limits on the curves and crossings by the Pacific engine, and consequently higher speeds were required on the upgrades to maintain the schedules. The higher coal consumption is partially consequent upon this.

'It was arranged, before the trials were started, that no results should be published without our mutual consent: this agreement has not been kept. The Great Western Publicity Department have obtained all the data and furnished them to the Press for advertising purposes.

'When it is remembered that the trials over the Great Western system consisted of only three trips by the LNE engine, it will be realised that no conclusive results could be arrived at.'

Stung by the trials, and the free publicity gained by the GWR, Gresley was persuaded by his assistant Bert Spencer of the benefits of the long-travel valve gear fitted to the 'Castles'

and the economies in coal this could achieve. The system was fitted to Pacific No.2559. In trials coal consumption reduced from about 50lbs to 40lbs per mile. It demonstrates how engineers, although in competition, could still learn from one another and absorb new or better practice from professional or business rivals. For the most part, all of these engineers were members of the Institution of Locomotive Engineers and some belonged to the Mechanical Engineers as well. Through these professional bodies, they would have met occasionally to discuss the research and probably compare notes.

It is difficult to explain such an apparent contradiction. On the one hand they fought for an advantage, even when two companies were not business rivals, as was the case with the GWR and LNER; on the other hand, they freely exchanged information, allowing 'rivals' to improve performance. It was something Stanier practised himself. He clearly took huge pride in what the GWR had achieved and one wonders if he saw these trials as vindicating their decision to end their own Pacific experiment. 4-6-0s had proved better than the 4-6-2s. Had he been a supporter of the experiment or simply a witness to something with which he did not agree? Either way, within a few short years he embraced the concept and arguably produced the most outstanding engines of this class.

Under Collett's guiding hand locomotive development continued apace on the GWR. For many years

there had been a limitation imposed by the effect of an engine's hammer blow, as it passed through the driving wheels onto the track below. This, coupled with weight restrictions imposed by a number of bridges, meant that axle loading had been kept to a maximum of 20 tons. The problem had reduced *The Great Bear*'s usefulness, and meant the Castle Class design had been restricted in size and power to avoid damaging the permanent way. Bridge strengthening and a better understanding of the effects of

A picture that captures a stern and determined character. This is clearly a man chosen to lead, and a natural choice for the misfiring LMS when looking for someone to bring order and advance the Company. (RH)

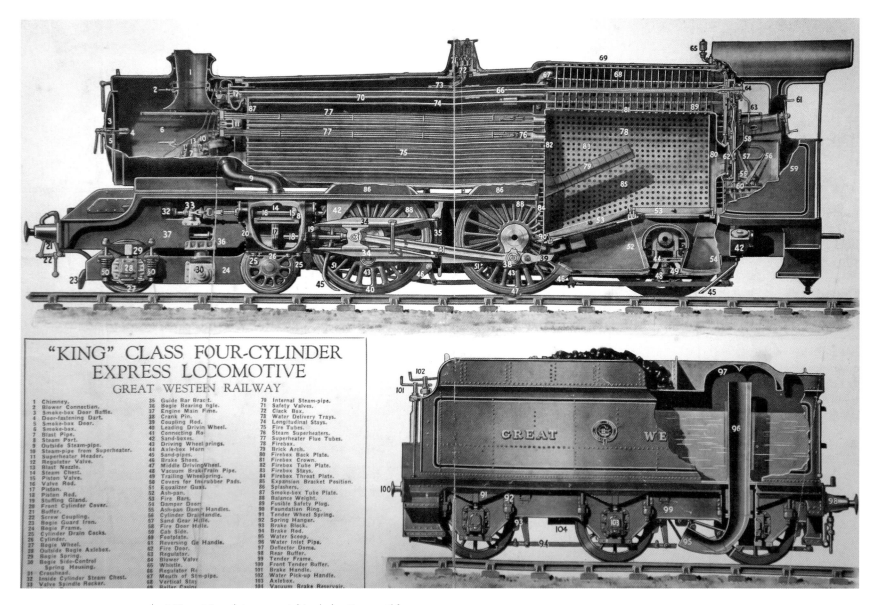

A King stripped. An eye-catching 'advertisement' for their products by the GWR PR Department. This was part of a pamphlet produced by the Company and sold to the public. (THG)

hammer blow eventually led to the restrictions being relaxed, allowing Collett and Stanier to consider building bigger, more powerful locomotives. They were concerned that the 'Castles', although exceptional engines, might struggle to pull the heaviest expresses, especially if the types of coal they relied on were in short or restricted supply. In May 1926 this had been the case, when the General Strike shut much of Britain's industry, including the Works at Swindon, for nine days. This major challenge to authority changed many people's perspective and led them to consider contingency plans should these disputes become a regular part of life.

At Swindon, managers seem to have displayed little understanding of the causes of the strike or the strength of feeling among a workforce rebelling against poor labour practices. Even Stanier, an understanding man, was caught up in the dispute as Angela Tuckett, a solicitor and great advocate of workers' rights, recorded:

"The morning of Tuesday, 4 May, pickets went on all the gates, but they were not needed. The unions agreed to allow apprentices to clock in if they wished that first morning and issued instructions accordingly. One of these was L.V. Parker, a vehicle builder. He described what happened next, "We let them through, but we took their names and noted which shop they worked in. But there was no work done by them as the men were out and the machinery stopped. After they had gone inside they organised meetings during the morning, gathering their fellow apprentices

together from all over the works. They decided they would go out. When they reached the Tunnel entrance in London Street, the manager, W.A. Stanier, was there. To prevent them leaving he had a hose turned on them. For a time they held back. Then a tall ginger-haired chap decided that he was not going to put up with that. He got amongst the boys and they decided to rush the exit in a body. And they did. Some got soaked through, but the manager was swept aside, his hat knocked off his head, and the boys swept out to the cheering of the men. It was a sight to see the manager treated like that." By 12.30 pm a notice appeared signed by C.B. Collett, the CME: "In view of the of the large number of men who have failed to report themselves for duty, these works are hereby closed until further notice." There was no doubt, the battle was on.'

The strength of the dispute in the Works and across the industries supporting the railways, particularly the mines, must have come as a great surprise to managers more used to obedience and deference. Small wonder that the CME looked to nullify the effects of future strike action, even in the design of engines. But Tuckett's account of the strike also demonstrated the strength of Stanier's style of management. A lesser man might have let the apprentices leave unchallenged. The CME's assistant was made of sterner stuff, holding his ground and demonstrating the force of his convictions. Such a man would not be discouraged by setbacks, but continue pushing forward no matter what the odds. When he became the

LMS' CME, these characteristics carried him through many difficult times, gathering support and achieving great things.

Late in 1926 the Drawing Office took Collett and Stanier's new specification, and created a design that would deliver 39,700lbs of tractive effort, with four 16-inch bore by 28-inch stroke cylinders and a 250lbs per sq inch boiler. At the instigation of Sir Felix Pole, the GWR's General Manager, ever aware of the prestige in developing the biggest and best locomotives, it was suggested that this limit be raised to 40,000lbs. If achieved, it would place the new King Class well ahead of any other locomotives in Great Britain and secure much-needed publicity. Pole also insisted the first engine be ready to haul heavier trains on the main line in 1927.

Collett and Stanier saw little need to deviate from the Castle Class design, and perceived the 'Kings' as enlarged versions, principally with a bigger boiler, offering a relatively high pressure and reasonable levels of superheat. But even with a larger boiler and firebox, a longer wheelbase and connecting rods, extended frames and bigger cylinders, the new design could only produce 39,000lbs of tractive effort. It was decided that the new specification could best be met if the engine's driving wheels were reduced in size from the standard 6ft 8 ½ ins to 6ft 6 ins. This solution worked and 40,300lbs was achieved, although any practical improvements to performance were difficult to quantify. However, the

Publicity took many forms, including this book sold at news outlets on stations. (THG)

22.5 tons, considerably heavier than the 'Castles'.

Publicity was essential, especially when heralding the arrival of a new locomotive. National newspapers, railway periodicals and scientific journals were fed information, and encouraged to visit the workshops. *The Engineer* magazine led the way in supplying influential commentaries that the railways could transmit more broadly, if deemed complimentary, but it also set new developments in a wider, more critical context. Comparison is only good if your product is deemed the best. When it came to the 'Kings' the GWR had two serious rivals, which *The Engineer's* editor was quick to include in his evaluation. After describing Collett's latest locomotive he added:

'The new locomotives now being placed on the LMS by Sir Henry Fowler (the Royal Scot Class) have the distinction of being the most powerful ever employed on any of the several lines which go to form Britain's largest railway system: furthermore, the engines of the class to which they belong, together with Mr C.B. Collett's new engine and Mr Maunsell's Lord Nelson, probably mark the limit of size and power for the particular wheel arrangement employed - the 10-wheeled type. The six-coupled bogie locomotive has now been with us for some years and a number of notable designs have been built.

'In looking over these three notable designs, one is struck with the similarity which exists. Actually in power output there is little to choose, for the reason that, given equal cylinder efficiencies,

reduced wheel size did offer the potential for higher average speeds on steep gradients. Smaller-diameter wheels might also have been necessary to make sure a larger boiler could be fitted, thus keeping the engine within weight limits. Even so, the loading on each of the driving-wheel axles reached

power will be dependent upon evaporation, and all three boilers are in this respect much alike. As would be expected, the three-cylinder engine (the Royal Scot) is lighter for a given amount of heating surface than either of the four-cylinder types, but of these, although Mr Maunsell employs four sets of valve gear as against but two for the GW locomotive, his engine is rather the lighter of the two. We hope as time goes on to hear something as to the performance of these interesting examples of modern construction. Tests which show how the fuel burned compares with the power developed at the draw-bar would be valuable. All three engines are examples of good well-tried practice, but they in truth contain nothing that is new. It would be, therefore, a mistake to assert that any real move has been made to obtain by means of new ideas, either in the shape of boiler design or valve motions, superior results which could not be had by common-sense application of well-proved machinery.'

The tone is dry and even slightly bored in noting that the 4-6-0 design had reached the limit of its development, as far as express trains were concerned. Whereas the railway press might herald the 'King' Class as a big step forward, professional engineers were less impressed by their reliance on well-established design principles. The editor seems to be asking where is the innovation and experimentation, both key to moving science and the railways forward. But the GWR maintained their engines met the needs of the Company more than adequately and radical change to its steam-engine policy was unnecessary. And business insisted that any advances be risk averse and cost effective. Innovation was expensive and failure a likely result.

Many have argued the GWR stood still in developing its engines, and much more was possible if only they had been braver and pushed forward. The LNER and LMS were less cautious, possibly because they had not enjoyed the GWR's long history of sound development and security. They were disrupted, to different degrees, by the malignant in-fighting still taking place between their constituent companies, some still loath to admit that amalgamation had taken place. Gresley was overcoming resistance and taking the LNER forward, but the LMS seemed unable to break free. As the 1920s came to an end their Chairman, Josiah Stamp, was searching for solutions. His admiration for the GWR was well known and he must have looked enviously at Swindon, where all he sought to achieve was already well established.

With the first engine of the class, *King George V*, soon ready for service, the GWR's Chairman announced the locomotive would be shipped to the USA for exhibition. One of the country's oldest railroads, the Baltimore and Ohio, was celebrating its centenary and wished to display a number of engines to run alongside their own. Perhaps not the most prestigious event as far as British railways were concerned, but still an opportunity for publicity. In August 1927 the engine began its

Swindon Works. A confusion of engine types showing the diversity needed to run a railway in the 1920s. This was an everyday scene for Stanier during that decade. (GWR)

voyage to America, accompanied by a small team led by Stanier. Collett's continued remoteness from many aspects of GWR life, during which Stanier provided effective cover, along with the latter being instrumental in getting the new engine through the Works and ready for service, meant the younger man went instead.

The trip went well and Stanier viewed many other locomotive designs on show at the 'Fair of the Iron Horse', and afterwards when *King George V* toured North America. The GWR engine was the only

foreign visitor to the show and had the honour of leading the procession of modern machines during each daily cavalcade, run from 27 September to 15 October. Before departing for America the locomotive had had only limited operating time on GWR metals, so was barely run in when asked to pull demonstration trains on American track. The most impressive performance took place on 17 October, when it successfully hauled a VIP train weighing 543 tons, about 150 tons heavier than the loads for which she was designed, between

GREAT WESTERN RAILWAY OF ENGLAND
1837 · · · · 1927

The Quickest Route
NEW YORK TO LONDON
via PLYMOUTH

A brochure produced to commemorate Stanier and *King George V*'s tour of the USA in 1927. (THG)

souvenirs in great quantity. The journey back to Britain in November, followed by a short period in the workshops before returning to service, must have seemed an anti-climax to Stanier and his team.

For the remainder of the decade the 'Kings' gradually increased in number and, through a programme of hard running and testing, proved themselves sturdy engines. Meanwhile, Stanier slipped back into his usual working routine, and soon became involved in the design and building of a two-cylinder general-purpose 4-6-0 locomotive, which became known as the Hall Class. This was followed, during 1929, by the 5700 Class Pannier tanks, the first fifty being built, under contract, by the North British Locomotive Company in Glasgow. And so life went on. The GWR continued to absorb all Stanier's effort, but his role in supporting Collett and covering his many tasks must have been irksome. Any ambitious person wishes for a top job in their chosen professions, especially one for which they are so well suited. This was nowhere more apparent than the GWR, where Collett was unlikely to retire in a timescale suiting Stanier, being only a few years younger. As it was, the CME did not leave until 1941, just short of his 70th birthday, when his principal assistant was 65. But with only four main railway companies of note, and only four CME posts, opportunities for promotion were few and far between.

Any organisation worth its salt keeps track of professionals in their field, hoping to attract the most

Baltimore and Washington, via Philadelphia. A return trip the following day was equally impressive. The publicity machine moved as smoothly as the engine, and soon heralded these achievements far and wide, producing booklets and other

talented people. Sometimes companies already had the right people, but lacked the vision to fully engage the talents that help the business grow. Sometimes they let existing staff take the company forward, but attitudes, working practices and old enmities are so entrenched that progress is impossible.

Solutions have to be found and a ruthless edge employed to avoid collapse. After grouping, the GWR, the LNER and Southern Railway had found a way forward, but the LMS was afflicted with many ills and struggled to make progress. The recruitment of Sir (later Baron) Josiah Stamp, a noted economist and industrialist, as President and Chairman, was a belated attempt to shake up the organisation after four years of stagnation. He realised an injection of new blood was necessary to move the Company forward. Stamp was a man of great intellect, with business experience that allowed him to look more broadly for effective solutions. He upset many established practices and ways of doing business, evoking the often-heard criticism that, 'he's not a railwayman so cannot possibly understand what we do!' But he did understand a balance sheet and the modern world, and intended making the LMS a sound and progressive industry.

Stamp recruited senior managers from many fields, principal among them Sir Harold Hartley, a distinguished chemist, and late Fellow and tutor at Balliol College, Oxford. He was appointed

Vice President and Director of Scientific Research. In these roles Hartley became an astute observer of Stamp's efforts to modernise the Company. In 1965 he described the key steps taken:

'The LMS had a very different post-amalgamation history to the Great Western, as it was formed by combining 8 main-line companies and 27 subsidiary companies, and there was an immediate struggle for power amongst the constituent partners in which one then another was in the ascendant, until Stamp arrived in 1927. As each CME of the constituent companies had his own ideas about the appropriate locomotive designs for particular tasks, the LMS found itself with no less than 393 types and 10,316 locomotives it inherited on amalgamation. By the end of 1931 this had been reduced to 9032 of 261 types,

Frederick Hawksworth. Like Stanier his career was held up by Collett's wish to carry on as CME until into his seventies. (GWR)

A Castle Class locomotive under test. The GWR was well ahead of its rivals in its testing regime, adopting on-the-road as well as 'static' workshop processes to gauge and improve performance. Stanier followed their practices, but his, and Nigel Gresley's, efforts only bore fruit after both had departed the scene. (GWR)

Mr and Mrs Stanier presenting prizes on the eve of his departure to Euston. His 1,000-yard stare suggests he had other things on his mind. (GWR)

most of them of considerable age. When I went to Euston in 1930 to replace the late Mr R.W. Reid, who had died during an operation, the rationalisation of the locomotive stock was obviously one of the most urgent problems.

'Individual costing of each engine class had made it possible to discard the least efficient, but there was an urgent need for a range of standard locomotives, such as Churchward, Collett and Stanier had built for the Great Western. Stamp had sent me in the summer of 1930 on a three-month tour of the American railways, with my five chief officers, to study conditions and practices in the USA, and to give me a chance to get to know my staff more intimately. In

January 1931 Sir Henry Fowler, the CME, moved over to research and Ernest Lemon took his place. However, by the summer Stamp had decided that Lemon was to become Vice President Operations and Commercial, and told me to find a new CME. Both Fowler and Lemon advised me that Stanier was the best man for the job. He had the advantage of not belonging to one of the constituent companies of the LMS and therefore was in a neutral position to sort out the differences between rival practices.

'Stamp agreed with our recommendation and, as usual, left the approach to me to give me the opportunity of making up my mind. So

in October Lemon asked Stanier to lunch with us at The Athenaeum and we discussed water softening, among other things. Stanier then lunched with me at the Travellers when I pointed out to him that he was 55 and that Collett showed no signs of making way for him on the GWR, while, if he came to Euston, he would have a wonderful opportunity to modernise our locomotive stock. Stanier was surprised that the invitation had not come from Stamp to his General Manager, but when his Chairman made it clear that he would not displace Collett and when due formalities had been observed, Stanier decided to come to Euston and took over on 1 January 1932.

'For 40 years Stanier had been gaining experience in every aspect of the steam locomotive, in its design, its fabrication and erection, and in its operation, and the day had come when he could put that wealth of experience and judgement into independent action.'

One can only imagine the frustration Stanier felt at seeing the CME job at Swindon staying beyond his reach. He might also have realised that if Collett did retire, he might not be the chosen successor anyway, with Hawksworth being carefully groomed as a future leader. No doubt his heart remained with the Company – a lifetime's association is difficult to break – but his head saw the benefits of moving to a company so clearly in need of his great skills. And so he stepped into the most challenging role of his career, but one where he could develop the many ideas he had nurtured at Swindon. His sense of release must have been enormous.

CHAPTER 3

FREE TO MANAGE

During a speech in early 1928, Josiah Stamp described the London, Midland and Scottish Railway (LMS) as a 'sprawling giant barely awake, and riven by internal conflict and lack of cohesion'. For a company formed only five years earlier, this was a sad indictment of its management and hardly encapsulated the spirit of optimism that accompanied its creation. Politicians and industry experts who had sought to improve the railways, with their grouping initiative, were not impressed by the rate of progress either. But they failed to understand, as legislators often do, the depth of economic depression and social unrest that still hung over Europe. Add to that the sprawling nature of the LMS and the lack of unity among its constituent parts, and the picture Stamp describes is understandable. Shortly before his untimely death, during a bombing raid in 1941, he reflected on the problems faced by the LMS, the business principles he had applied and reviewed performance against the many daunting targets he had set the Company:

'The railway service has to work through thousands of servants touching the millions of the travelling and commercial public at hundreds of different points. It has to preserve uniformity of treatment and yet keep individuality alive. Every cog has to be sentient as the whole machine. From the highest officer to the lowest ranks, the staff has to be made into one team working for the good of the industry.

'But organisation for standardised performance is one thing – organisation to absorb, control and utilise a constant stream of change, both human and technical, is far more difficult and important. The pace of change does not slacken. And it is not merely a question of fitting in an alteration at an appropriate point and time. The railway evolves, partly consciously, partly empirically, as a co-ordinated whole – touch one part and all the other parts are affected and require adjustment. A change of speed in the locomotive may mean an overhaul of signal distances, of braking power, of permanent-way alignments, and a score of other factors.

'During the passage of years-railway equipment has had to be adjusted to the needs of the community and also to its "wants" – not always the same thing – and has had to be kept in line with industrial movements as they have gradually evolved, and with all the shifts of industrial life. More so than ever has this been necessary since the amalgamation of 1923, when standardisation of equipment and practices became imperative if

economical management were to be effected and costs reduced.

'Modernised methods have evolved largely through the medium of an engineering outlook on non-engineering problems. Measurement and close analysis are no longer the tools of the engineer alone, for they have been

Sir (later Baron) Josiah Stamp, the colossus who bestrode the LMS and many government functions in the 1920s and 1930s. (LMS PR/RH)

LEFT: The impressive centre of Stamp's empire. The LMS' HQ at Euston, built in the early 1930s. (LMS PR/RH)

RIGHT: The opposition – the London and North Eastern Railway under Gresley). (THG)

brought to the service of departments not primarily associated with machines; the principles underlying modernisation of factories, such as line or "belt" operation (where the same detailed function is specialised at the same spot and the 'subject' is moved to successive spots), are being applied to the practice of motive-power sheds, and to the movement of traffic and operating work of all descriptions.

'During the past few years such methods have been applied for three ends – namely to reduce costs, to diminish fatigue, and to increase operating efficiency and service.

'This brings me to the locomotive – the chief actor in the railway drama. The demand for higher speeds, and heavier trains, have put the ingenuity of locomotive engineers to the test, made so much more severe by the difficult physical contours, the limits of height and width of tunnels, bridges and platforms. They have risen to the challenge, and in the past decade the steam locomotive has made greater developments than for many previous years.

'On amalgamation in 1923, it was apparent to us that the multiplicity of types of engines of the various constituent and subsidiary companies forming the LMS would be a bar to economical progress unless some standardisation were carried out. This policy, coupled with the construction of more powerful types, has been followed.

'In coming to the decisions about the right types on which to concentrate new *capital expenditure, the most elaborate and detailed methods of individual working costs have been adopted, A much greater practical use of a given number of locomotives has been obtained by various methods; improvements in repair methods in the shops and interavailability of standardised parts have released them more quickly; improvements in motive-power sheds and stimulation of the workers' interest have recently increased the average number of miles between "breakdowns" to a most remarkable extent. The stock is more effective for its task and more economical in use. Our policy is to lose no opportunity of learning locomotive lessons.*

'Scientific research is also important. Instead of our links being intermittent or non-comprehensive, we are, through our new laboratory, our own research department, our defined contacts with the great research organisations, and our advisory committee of highest experts, tackling each problem systematically and bringing to bear upon it the most recent resources.'

In January 1932, when Stanier took up his new appointment, the situation he faced was complex and volatile. The position described by Stamp and Harold Hartley, many years later when they knew the outcome, probably understated the problems. There was a lack of cohesion at all levels and many new initiatives struggled to find a willing audience, among a set of employees who were, for the most part, still floundering in the comfort of their pre-grouping worlds. After the comparative calm and order of life at Swindon, the future, based within the LMS's HQ at Euston, must have seemed daunting even to Stanier.

Even the changes introduced by Stamp, in an effort to streamline processes, increase accountability and establish best practice, had the potential to multiply the problems if professional support and goodwill were not forthcoming. The GWR's CME had had a wide brief, which included managing the running department and oversight of all locomotive development programmes. The LMS gave its new CME a more restricted brief in comparison. Ernest Lemon, in his new role as Vice President in charge of Railway Traffic Operations and Commercial matters, oversaw day-to-day operational management of the railway, including its locomotive department. He and his team defined motive power needs and set targets for the CME to meet. Stanier could, in theory, simply be made to respond to a requirement instead of using his well-honed engineering skills to assess need and produce the best solutions possible. One wonders whether Lemon engineered this position to retain control of locomotive policy, seeing in Stanier a man used to being second in command and therefore offering little opposition. If so, he would be surprised.

As part of a reorganisation the CME post became answerable, in the first instance, to Harold Hartley, Vice President for Works and Ancillary Undertakings, and Director of Scientific Research. Hartley's appointment, in 1930, laid down a marker by Stamp in establishing his new working principles and methods. A scientist and an academic of great substance, he was also a well-versed advocate of the new business techniques being rolled out across the Company by its Chairman. Having selected Stanier, he was likely to be a strong supporter of the new CME, but as a leading scientist he inevitably saw a need for greater research and experimentation in all railway matters. In setting up a research directorate, from the small research team already in existence, he denuded the CME post of some authority, and potentially laid the

SIR JOSIAH C. STAMP

CHAIRMAN
AND
PRESIDENT

Stamp's Board at the time of Stanier's arrival.
(LMS PR/RH)

MR. W. V. WOOD

VICE-PRESIDENT
(Finance and Services)

SIR HAROLD HARTLEY

VICE-PRESIDENT
(Work and Ancillary Undertakings)

MR. E. J. H. LEMON

VICE-PRESIDENT
(Operating and Commercial)

Ernest Lemon in 1932. A man of considerable talent with whom Stanier forged a working alliance, having replaced him as CME. (LMS PR/RH)

diligently sought and worked towards well-constructed, productive relationships. As Stanier sat at his desk at Euston, in January 1932, for the first time, he must have seen all the obstacles and considered how to negotiate them. He needed to seek allies, confront opposition, establish a clear path for his department and build strong working relationships. His long apprenticeship with the GWR had developed all the skills he now needed to achieve these goals.

Many of those now working under him felt a natural reticence often created by the arrival of a new leader, especially one so heavily infused with the culture and philosophies of a rival company. And many were already struggling to understand and implement the changes introduced by Stamp. A good, experienced leader, such as Stanier, should understand all of this and recognise that change is best managed when a team is set clear targets, fully involved, given responsibility for delivery and managed with a strong, but responsive hand. Some would call this the George Churchward way, but Stanier was his own master and these techniques came naturally to him. It was what the LMS needed more than anything at this stage in its evolution.

In reality, the state of the LMS was not as bad as some thought. There had been progress in aligning so many disparate companies and bringing in new ways of working. For example, under Lemon, as CME, assembly-line methods for producing and maintaining rolling stock had

seeds of future discontent and confrontation if relationships were handled badly.

There is no organisation, then or now, where the ambitious do not jockey for position or play political games to gain advantage. These are basic tenets of life in any competitive industry. Despite Stamp's wish to build a unified, supportive structure, many played these self-serving games, using past allegiances or firmly-held beliefs as excuses. At the same time others, with a broader, more balanced view of the future,

been introduced. This had increased efficiency and availability, allowing a significant reduction of numbers, as well as achieving financial savings. A major review of locomotives, which set out to establish types and capacity, and match these to future need, had been completed and had already led to a substantial drop in numbers. This important work established a baseline on which Stanier could build.

But elsewhere the picture was not so rosy, particularly in areas important to Stanier as the new CME. Standardisation had barely begun. The locomotive fleet, although substantial in number, was, for the most part, outdated, inefficient, and not deemed fit for purpose by Stamp, Lemon and Hartley. And these problems were exacerbated by the lack of cohesion between the main centres of locomotive production – Derby, Crewe, Horwich and St Rollox – and their entrenched attitudes towards design and construction.

The ability to transform all of this overnight was extremely limited. Too much change too soon could be counterproductive and undermine the Railway's ability to perform. Stanier had to gain acceptance, then gradually modify the organisation. At the same time, he was under great pressure from his Board to significantly enhance the stock of locomotives available to the running department. His starting point had to be the continued rationalisation of the fleet, modification of existing engines where possible, standardisation and the production of new, higher-

LEFT: Stanier in 1932 on arrival at Euston. Although spreading a little around the middle, his expression suggests the fire inside still burns strongly. (LMS PR/RH)

RIGHT: James Anderson, Chief Motive Power Superintendent, who dictated locomotive policy to two previous CMEs: George Hughes and Henry Fowler. His wings were firmly clipped by Lemon and he departed the scene on forced retirement. (LMS/RH)

performance locomotives to take the Company forward.

With Collett's agreement, Stanier left Swindon armed with documents, drawings and reference books. Stamp and Hartley actively encouraged this, seeing in the GWR's strategies the seeds of what they hoped to achieve with the LMS. The more astute and far-seeing members of Stanier's new team read up all they could find on GWR developments, and considered how these ideas might be incorporated into their work. The LMS papers that have survived from this period, in public and private hands, are dotted with examples of GWR documents and drawings, often with scribbled comments or modifications added by

staff at Derby and Crewe. Some might have been concerned that all they knew and valued would be swept aside by this GWR influence. But Stanier always took a broad view and sought to absorb good ideas no matter from where they came. In due course, his staff did this too.

The need for allies, especially in challenging circumstances, is always important. Relationships soon developed in his new post, but Stanier maintained contact with old friends and colleagues at Swindon. The need to talk through new ideas and find an independent, but knowledgeable 'sounding board' was important. Churchward, now long retired, but still living in his 'grace and favour' house within yards of the Works,

provided this sounding board. Although now aged 76, hard of hearing and sight, Churchward's mind was still sharp and his interest in locomotive design undiminished. There seems little doubt Stanier would have discussed the LMS post with his old mentor before accepting and then sought his advice once appointed. But he was not alone. In a letter, surviving in private hands, written by Josiah Stamp in 1931, he expressed his admiration for Churchward's views on railway management and design. Being a sound and progressive industrialist, he would have been attracted by the GWR's policies and record of success. As a company the GWR was far in advance of its competitors and Stamp was not slow

George Hughes, CME (1923–25). (LMS/RH)

in identifying the main architect of this work. It may well be that Churchward recommended one of his 'disciples' to Stamp to take on this work, especially as he saw Stanier's path to the CME post at Swindon blocked by Collett. We shall probably never know, but it is an intriguing possibility.

Stanier's first step was to get to know the organisation and establish good working relationships, but at the same time take the survey of locomotives prepared by Lemon and determine the best way forward. He had to engage with James Anderson, Chief Motive Power Superintendent, who believed that it was for him to decide types and numbers of engines needed. In his biography of Stanier, John Chacksfield relates how the CME disabused him of this view:

'Stanier and Anderson took to each other from the start, but sometimes did not see eye to eye. Anderson would specify so many engines of an existing type when asked for future needs, and the memorandum containing this request was put in Stanier's "pending" tray. When asked why no reply was forthcoming, William replied firmly: "I am trying to decide what new locomotives are needed, and can only do this if you specify the numbers and the duties they perform." Anderson got the message and co-operated.'

Anderson had worked for Henry Fowler for many years and been recommended by him, and Vice President J.H. Follows, as his successor. In the debate that followed, led by Hartley, this option was rejected and Lemon took the post instead. In time, Follows' resignation led to Lemon's next promotion as his replacement and heralded Stanier's arrival. Despite this history, Anderson and the new CME might have established a working relationship of sorts, but the signs were not promising that old and new methods could be combined successfully. In October 1932 Lemon, clearly unimpressed by Anderson, 'relieved him of his duties with immediate effect as it is desirable that his successor should take office concurrently with pending changes.' By all accounts Anderson was a staunch advocate of Derby practices and, rightly or wrongly, was associated with the pre-grouping, partisan ways of doing business.

Stanier next had to determine what the locomotive requirement was, how best to meet it, then design, cost and justify his proposals. Building and testing would then follow. All in all, the process set very challenging targets for an organisation struggling to adapt to change, especially if there was opposition. Although backing from the Board was a certainty, and their authority carried much weight, delays could occur naturally or be created by dissident elements withholding their support. The workshops and drawing offices were working hard to keep existing locomotives running, so fitting a substantial new construction programme into the schedule could strain it beyond working limits.

Two key requirements of the LMS locomotive-development programme were the production of new classes of heavy-freight and mixed-traffic engines. They were the life blood of any railway, providing, as they did, the guts of any motive-power fleet. Strong and effective engines in these categories were essential for commercial success and, as proven by the GWR, standardised designs, drawn from best practice, provided this essential operating base. The third key need was for a class of heavy-express engines capable of pulling 400 tons plus loads at high speed, unaided, over very demanding routes to the north. During the 1920s, LMS designers had debated how to meet this need. But it was a debate often afflicted by past loyalties and the strongly-held beliefs fostered by the Company's constituent elements. If moderate, far-thinking men sought a new path, their voices were often crushed by these entrenched attitudes. So a policy of underpowered engines, frequently forced into the added expense of double-heading, became the norm.

The LMS's two previous CMEs before Lemon, George Hughes and Henry Fowler, had looked more broadly at locomotive design. But either through lack of imagination or lack of control over selection, they had fallen short of providing engines better suited to company needs. The Royal Scot and Patriot Class engines failed to deliver the hoped-for improvement. Hughes and Fowler had also watched as other railways produced and successfully ran Pacific designs, and they, in turn, produced outline plans of 4-6-2 locomotives for Anderson to consider, as an alternative to the 4-6-0 or 4-4-0 configured engines he preferred. In fact, the Chief Locomotive Superintendent exerted a level of control over new construction that the CMEs found hard to control. He even went to the extreme of ordering a new class of 2-6-0+0-6-2 freight engines directly from Beyer, Peacock of Manchester. This act contradicted the advice given to him by Hughes shortly before he left the Company.

Such a restrictive attitude afflicted the Organisation. Who is to say what might have been achieved if Hughes and Fowler had been encouraged to develop their ideas for a Pacific Class in the mid-1920s?

In his book *Locomotive Panorama*, Ernest Cox, a talented engineer who rose through the ranks of the LMS and eventually became British Rail's Deputy CME, witnessed Hughes, and Fowler's efforts to develop a Pacific locomotive:

'The need for a more powerful express-passenger engine for the West Coast main line was self evident. It was natural that the appearance of Gresley's first Pacific in 1922, followed by Raven's version on the NER, should turn the CME's mind towards something similar for the LMS. As a result, early in 1923 a tentative diagram was produced and some calculations made as to possible performance. Thereafter a long silence followed, and it became apparent that a quite different solution was being contemplated. The Midland had always followed a policy of small engines and light train loads, its whole passenger philosophy based upon "little and often". The new operating hierarchy therefore visualised splitting up the West Coast services into separate portions, each capable of being worked by a Midland-type 4-4-0 compound.

'It was due to the growing interest in a heavy-freight engine for the Toton to Brent coal traffic that the next step towards a Pacific was taken. It seemed sensible to develop the 2-8-2 which was the current thinking for the freight job, side by side with the passenger engine in order that a common boiler and other components could be worked out for both. In June 1924 a serious proposal was submitted. The centrepiece of this exercise was to use 4 cylinders and two sets of valve gear following the design of
the rebuilt Hughes 4-6-0 as closely as possible. By the end of the year the 2-8-2, having changed to a 3-cylinder proposal, necessitated the 4-6-2 diagram being altered accordingly, but no work was done on scheming arrangements in any detail. That was the end of the Hughes' Pacific.'*

Although dropped in 1924, the principle of building 2-8-2 and 4-6-2 engines did not go away entirely. During 1925, the idea was revived following an information-gathering visit to railway companies in France led by Fowler, shortly after Hughes had retired. Their French counterparts had developed compound engines, but there was

Sir Henry Fowler, CME (1925–30). (LMS/RH)

Crewe in the mid-1930s. A Pacific Class locomotive takes shape. (LMS PR/RH)

not complete acceptance of the savings achievable or the effectiveness of the design. But Fowler returned with a positive view of its potential and, as Cox relates, revived Hughes' 1923 proposals:

'The evidence was thought sufficiently encouraging to go ahead, and a design team was organised forthwith to progress the matter. Gass took the lead at Horwich with cylinders and valve gear, Chambers tackled the boiler at Derby and Grover, Chief Draughtsman at Crewe, came in on the detail work. A meeting at Derby on 23 October 1925, settled the main details, which were set out in one of the last schemes I worked upon before leaving Horwich. Apart from what is indicated on the diagram, 9"- diameter piston valves were proposed for HP and 11" for LP. The drive was divided and two outside Walschaert gear operated the four valves. Separate HP and LP gears were ruled out because it was felt that both by training and temperament it was unlikely that British drivers would make full use of independent cut offs.

'Whilst this work was proceeding in the three offices, it was also decided to convert one of the Hughes 4-6-0s to compound expansion following the same principles and number 10456 was turned out of Horwich in July 1926.

'This engine spent its life on the Crewe-Carlisle line, was very free running, and was liked by the drivers. On test with 350-ton trains it showed 26% coal savings over similar locomotives as built, but only 9% over the same engine ultimately fitted with valve heads having six narrow rings. On the other hand its best efficiency was nearly 20% below that ultimately attained by the Royal Scots.

'The big engines might have done better than this because of their higher pressure. Pre-Chapelon, as they were, they could not exploit compound expansion to the full. Design work was well advanced with a lot of material ordered before the dramatic order came to stop everything. No trace now remains of all this activity excepting the four-ply frame construction at the back end over the trailing truck which principle was incorporated into the eventual Stanier Pacifics.'

Cox then detailed the problems each CME faced in developing locomotives for the LMS they thought would best meet the Company's needs and why these two attempts to build a Pacific Class failed:

'Consider what befell Sir Henry Fowler – the two largest prestige locomotive designs which he had *sponsored to the hilt, and on which work was proceeding at full bore in three drawing offices was halted, and alternatives were proposed by others (Anderson principally), accepted by Management, and brought to fulfilment, which owed nothing to Fowler himself or his people.'*

Even when writing this account nearly forty years later, the sense of frustration and consternation Cox and others must have felt is still palpable. In a letter written in February 1982 he added an interesting postscript to this story:

'We would probably have found that the Hughes/Fowler Pacific and 2-8-2 would have required many modifications before they were successful, but all designs underwent change, especially during an experimental stage. But, it seems fairly certain to me, that they would have met our needs far better than anything proposed by Anderson, supported by his overlord, Follows.

'However, they were forced to acknowledge that 4-4-0 Midland Compounds simply would not suffice for the Anglo-Scottish service, but they would not see the 4-6-2s as a suitable alternative, despite evidence to the contrary. Rather than follow this path they preferred to investigate the construction or procurement of a suitable 4-6-0 and hit upon the GWR's Castle Class as a suitable engine to copy. It was an excellent design, and Anderson and Follows evidently convinced Management to apply for a loan of one of these engines.

'So, in September 1926, while the design of Fowler's Pacific was in full flight, No 5000 "Launceston Castle" arrived. It performed with quiet mastery

all the work on which our own comparable engines struggled. So successful was it that the LM Board expressed a wish to build 50, but this was changed when difficulties with the loading gauge were identified. A 3-cylinder 4-6-0 having a maximum-size boiler, high steam pressure, high-degree superheat and long-travel valve gear was quickly substituted. With the Derby drawing office committed to other work, including the Pacific, and the need to have the new 4-6-0 ready for the following summer, the design and construct contract for these new engines was placed with the North British Locomotive Company. Thus was born the Royal Scot Class.

'When Stanier arrived in January 1932, armed with many drawings from Swindon, including the "Great Bear" and the King Class, Chambers (his Chief Draughtsman) brought the earlier work on Pacifics to his attention. Many discussions followed as Stanier's Pacific took shape and he, with Hartley and Lemon's support, managed to suppress any opposition from Anderson, now no longer backed by Follows.

'When the Princess Royals appeared in 1933 I felt that their lineage could be traced back to the work of Hughes and Fowler, as much as GWR developments. They had tried to change the culture imbedded at Derby and Crewe, and in doing this laid the base on which Stanier could develop his "big engines".'

The saying 'hitting the ground running' applied to Stanier during his first few months with the LMS. With considerable patience and great energy, he gathered information, studied the teams under his control, built a rapport with many elements

within the Company and quickly put together a massive construction programme. As the months passed this huge effort resulted in specifications reaching the drawing offices for detailed work to begin, including a new Pacific Class. By July 1932 the first stage of Stanier's locomotive renewal programme was ready for assessment by the Mechanical and Electrical Engineering Committee. The main points of the submission were:

'In a review of the short-term programme authorised for 1932, the

The argumentative, but hugely talented Herbert Chambers. He was Stanier's Chief Draughtsman during the crucial phase of the CME's tenure. He successfully translated often sparse initial outlines into effective and outstanding locomotives. In this he was ably assisted by Tom Coleman. (LMS PR/RH)

Passenger Tender		
4-6-2 Superheated	3	£27,630
4-6-0 Superheated	-	
Converted Claughtons	25	£165,000
4-6-0 Superrheated	-	
Converted P of W	10	£65,000
Freight Tender		
2-8-0 Superheated	5	£31,500
2-6-0 Superheated	-	
Mixed	40	£208,000
Passenger Tank		
2-6-4 Superheated	45	£229,500
Tenders already Authorised	-	£14,805
Totals	**128**	**£741,435**

The result of long years of learning and managing – the first Princess emerges at Crewe. (HH/RH)

completion of which was to coincide with the Company's financial year, the report explained that the work of building the 75 new locomotives and the breaking up of the 172 engines was proceeding according to programme, with the exception that as a result of experience gained with the No 7 0-8-0 standard freight tender engine, it was considered that material advantages in reliability and haulage capacity would be obtained by introducing a standard locomotive of the 2-8-0 type. In addition it was considered that, in view of the work performed by the five 0-4-0 that a simple saddle tank would meet requirements. The total estimated cost of

the 1932 programme would therefore be reduced by £29,266.

'Consideration had been given to the 1933 requirement in order to maintain the economic continuity of new work in the Company's workshops and having regard to the elimination of old and uneconomic types of locomotives, and the standardisation of the Company's stock, it was recommended that during 1933 the following 128 new locomotives be constructed in the Company's workshops:

'The 128 locomotives to be constructed will replace 152 to be broken up, and in addition, it is proposed to break up a further 250 engines, a total of

402, at a total replacement cost of £1,295,775.

'Based on the annual mileage, the average cost per engine mile of the new locomotives, as compared with the locomotives to be displaced, would show an estimated saving of £32,611 per annum, and in addition there would be a further estimated saving of £30,357 per annum in interest at 5% on the decreased cost of the 128 new engines compared with the estimated replacement cost of the 402 engines to be displaced.'

In a very brief and succinct document Stanier had precised complex proposals, shown achievable savings, highlighted operational efficiencies to be gained and given a clear plan of action. He carefully constructed this and other papers to gain the support of Stamp, Hartley and Lemon, so in many ways the backing from this and other committees became straightforward. By August approval had been given and the building programme could begin in earnest, with a new 4-6-2 Pacific at its core.

CHAPTER 4

DESIGN AND BUILD

The LMS, with so many operational problems, came late to the hard-selling world of advertising and public relations. Being so large a commercial concern, surviving only if growing its trade year on year, this was a remarkable oversight. The emerging economy of America and, sadly, the growing strength of dictators in Europe were showing the power of advertising and image projection. By 1932, propaganda was a weapon few could ignore. Once started, the LMS displayed an unerring knack of hitting the right note and selling itself very effectively.

It was not only speed, comfort and value for money that featured in its glossy adverts, but also the way it functioned and the technical advances in many areas: better station and catering facilities, development of new rolling stock and improved, more glamorous locomotives. They revelled in the advances that followed William Stanier's arrival. The Royal Scot Class, introduced in the late 1920s, had been exploited, but nothing like the introduction of Stanier's Pacifics had been seen before. In many ways the Company followed the example set by its main competitor, the LNER, and its alluring, headline-grabbing trains and locomotives. But the LMS was a bigger company and needed to fight to dominate all competition – on the railways, at sea and the roads.

It is unclear who was the main supporter for selling the technical side of the business. The launch of new engines and trains was a pure PR topic that could easily be sold to newspapers, and make an excellent addition to the newsreels shown regularly in cinemas between the main features. But the less glamorous side of the design and building process also became a significant part of the 'hard sell'. And it was the development of Stanier's first Pacific that was used to demonstrate what the Company hoped to achieve.

Films with sound were still something of a novelty in 1933. The first 'talkie', *The Jazz Singer*, had been shown in 1928, but it was well into the 1930s before the medium became commonplace. The LMS grasped this new technology, under the auspices of its head of PR, George Loftus-Allen, and produced its own films. One of the first released recorded the development of the seventh Pacific, entitled *A Study in Steel*, made by the Commercial and Educational Film Department of the Topical Press Agency. It opened with a short sequence showing the engine pulling the *Royal Scot* away from Euston. Then, in a series of 'flashbacks', the

Stanier a few years into his career as CME for the LMS. (LMS PR/RH)

film follows the engine through its design, to construction. In just seventeen minutes this vivid account captured all the work and the extreme industrial effort that went into the Pacific's assembly.

Industry had come some way from the blighted awfulness of

Members of Stanier's senior team in 1933: (l to r) Herbert Chambers, Chief Draughtsman; Robert Riddles, Deputy Works Superintendent at Crewe; Sandham Symes, Personal Assistant to CME William Stanier; Hewitt Beames, Deputy CME; and Fred Lemon, Works Superintendent at Crewe. Photo taken at Crewe with the first Princess, 6200, behind.
(LMS PR/RH)

Victorian factories that existed by bedevilling the lives of those unfortunate enough to work within them. But the work was still hard, mostly manual, undertaken in polluted, highly dangerous environments that, even when sanitised by the remoteness of an audience watching a film in a comfortable cinema, seemed precarious. The commentary was clipped in speech and bounced along on a wave of optimism belying the harshness captured by the images flickering on the screen:

"In Britain many thousands of men are working all the year round just turning out new locomotives. The demand of today is speed and still more speed. Longer trains call for bigger and better engines. Exacting requirements for an exacting task, but Britain's engineers are equal to it. Every new engine has to make its appearance on paper. More than 370 drawings of the various parts have to be worked out and prepared. When plans have been approved a specification is prepared. This is a volume that runs to 361 pages and contains more than 2500 items. The specification is broken up and each department receives details of its particular share in the job ahead. Industries all over the country benefit and in due course materials start arriving at the Works. The main frames, which may be called the foundation of the engine, arrive in the form of flat steel plates weighing 3 tons."

The commentary extracted the key parts of a complicated and demanding process. For Stanier and his team, as they set out to design and build a new fleet of standard locomotives of many different classes, the view was much more complex and fraught with problems. The new Pacific was the glamorous core of the programme, but construction still had to be fitted into the tightest of schedules and compete with other equally pressing demands on the Drawing Office, the supply organisation and workshops. Here, Stanier's great skill as a manager came into play. He knew how to condense ideas, explain them clearly, lead a team no matter how difficult they were, direct and delegate, set standards and then make sure they were applied

consistently to the tightest of
schedules. And when he looked
around the large, diverse organisation
under his control, he must have
wondered whether it was capable of
delivering all that would be
demanded. It soon became apparent
that he had inherited a great deal of
talent and experience, even if many
of those now working for him had
slipped into dubious practices due to
poor or confused leadership.

Although Stanier might have
been able to tinker around the edges
of the structure and move those who
were too disruptive, the bulk would
remain; the problems surrounding
new locomotive construction made
any other course impossible. His mix
of strong leadership, engineering
excellence, understanding and the
ability to create a robust, resourceful
team drove the programme forward.

Around him at Euston, Crewe,
Derby, Horwich and St Rollox, he
found a varied team, in many cases
eager to impress. But the senior
posts were his main concern in his
first twelve months. By their
support, or otherwise, he might
stand or fall. James Anderson, on the
running side, offered backing, once
he realised Stanier would not be
bullied or cajoled, but soon left at
Ernest Lemon's instigation, to be
replaced by 46-year-old David Urie.
Urie had the potential to be a thorn
in Stanier's side. Small of stature and
described as dour, he was not a man
to court popularity. Ernest Cox later
described him in most unflattering
terms: 'Whereas Anderson used to
chastise our department with whips,
Urie was apt to chastise us with

A cylinder being cast
for a Pacific at Crewe.
This photo captures
the extreme working
conditions in a steam
locomotive workshop,
and very little in the
way of health and
safety to restrain poor
or dangerous
working practices.
(LMS PR/AE)

Boiler plate for a
Princess being pressed.
(LMS PR/AE/RH)

A middle cylinder block for a Princess undergoing final preparation before installation. (LMS PR/AE/RH)

scorpions.' It was recorded that he was called an 'Irish Blackguard', although of Scottish descent. He had spent part of his career, before the First World War, with the Midland Great Western Railway of Ireland, hence the origins of this unappealing nickname. It seems he was no ally of Stanier's, although much of his excessive and occasionally corrosive zeal was tempered by Lemon's controlling hands. He remained Locomotive Superintendent until retirement in 1943 and so had to be dealt with diplomatically or forcefully as the need dictated.

As his Deputy CME, Stanier had Hewitt Beames, a man of considerable experience and skill. Before the GWR man was selected, Beames seemed likely to become the next Chief. He had been deputy to George Hughes, Henry Fowler and Lemon, so he must have expected this promotion. He showed great equanimity and diplomacy in accepting this let-down, writing to Stanier to congratulate him on his success and adding, 'You will understand how disappointed I am, but I may say there is no one I would rather work under than you.' Beames supported Stanier until his retirement in 1934 and served him with all the skill he could muster.

Directly supporting Stanier at Euston was Sandham Symes. He had been appointed Fowler's Technical Assistant in April 1928 and remained in post when Stanier became CME four years later. Born in 1877, Symes served his apprenticeship at the Inchincore Works of the Great Southern and Western Railway Company in Dublin. By 1903 he was responsible for new engine construction, before moving to the North British Railway Company in Glasgow to broaden his experience. After only five months he found employment with the Midland Railway and became their Chief Draughtsman at Derby in July 1913, and then Works Manager in October 1925. As assistant to both Fowler and

The work goes on.
(LMS PR/AE/RH)

Stanier he tended to be a neutral observer of the changes taking place. He was not a difficult person and tended to acquiesce or show diplomacy when challenged. Ernest Cox described him as a delightful and courteous person, but one who lacked strong convictions about the direction new designs should take. In many ways his approach, during Stanier's early days at Euston, was ideal. At a time of great change and uncertainty, a diplomatic and understanding deputy could smooth the passage for the new CME and a concerned workforce. But in time Stanier needed stronger, more innovative support and Symes moved on, although not before the first new Pacific rolled off the production line.

The position of Chief Draughtsman to the LMS was held by Herbert Chambers at Derby. His was a pivotal role. Today the title of draughtsman suggests someone who simply takes a designer's ideas and turns them into drawings. But

Frames for 6200 assembled. (LMS PR/AE/RH)

Driving wheels for a Princess being assembled. (LMS PR/AE/RH)

in the 1930s the role focused on the design, drawing, estimating and quantification.

Chambers was appointed to this role in January 1927, aged 42, and had a good reputation as an engineer and manager. He coped with design work through many difficult years, as requirements changed depending upon whose views or preferences were in the ascendency. He also held very strong views himself about design, driven to some extent by his allegiance to the old Midland Railway and the type of engines it espoused. This did not make him a natural ally for Stanier, particularly when 'his' radical programme of change was dominant. There were, it

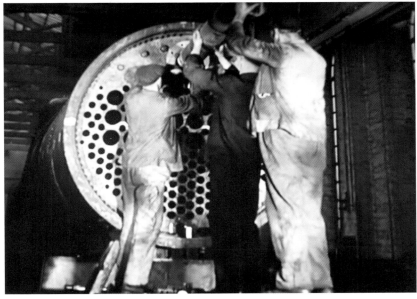

seems, arguments and disagreements over design. Not in itself a bad thing, because the creative process is often best served by debate, but this cannot go on indefinitely and eventually the person taking final responsibility for a development has to hold sway.

In his book *Master Builders of Steam*, H.A.V. Bulleid, who spoke at length to Stanier before writing, summarised the problem Chambers presented:

'He argued with Stanier about all those innovations which he could not readily accept. A good Chief and a good assistant both know that a nice balance between querying orders and blindly following them is essential, but Stanier and Chambers were unable to find this balance with Chambers as Chief Draughtsman.'

Chambers only relinquished the role in March 1935 when promoted to become Stanier's Locomotive and Personal Assistant at Euston. A strange move considering the differences that existed, but perhaps a true reflection of Stanier's admiration for his skills. Sadly, Chambers died in 1937, aged just 52, and left no account of these years. Undoubtedly he would have argued that he always had the best interests of the Company at heart and felt that some innovations were wrong or could be improved. He could also point to the fact that, during his time as Chief Draughtsman, the bulk of the rebuilding programme was effectively handled by him and his team, including the design of the Pacific. By any standards a considerable achievement.

If Chambers was unnecessarily argumentative, one of his immediate deputies, Tom Coleman, was more pragmatic. After serving an apprenticeship with Kerr, Stuart of Stoke, he became Chief Draughtsman to the North Staffordshire Railway, before moving to Horwich in 1927 to fulfil the same role there. During 1933, he transferred to Crewe, without relinquishing the Horwich post, where he principally worked on the design of the new Class 5, 4-6-0, and Class 8F, 2-8-0. In many ways he was the antithesis of Chambers and found promotion under Stanier because of his undoubted design and leadership skills, but also to counterbalance the more senior draughtsman. When Chambers was promoted to become Stanier's Technical Assistant in 1935 Coleman replaced him, remaining in this post until retirement in 1949. He, more than anyone else, could justifiably be given the title of chief designer of the LMS' locomotive redevelopment programme.

LEFT: The fabricated left-hand side cylinder in a jig ready for final assembly in the Tinsmith Shop. (LMS PR/AE/RH)

RIGHT: Boiler tubes being inserted. (LMS PR/AE/RH)

More work on the frames, but now the outside cylinders are in position. (LMS PR/AE/RH)

The Pacific Class was built in the workshops at Crewe. Whereas other elements of the new building programme were contracted out to external manufacturers, principally some of the new Class 5s to the Vulcan Works. But it was felt that the new, prestigious locomotives should be built at Crewe. These tasks placed an extreme burden on the workshops there and particularly the Works Superintendent, Frederick Lemon. A Somerset man by birth, he took up this post when it was simply known as Works Manager. By 1933

his reputation for good work and organisation was made, having overseen a massive reorganisation programme that introduced new techniques to locomotive production and maintenance. Quality control remained an issue, as Stanier soon discovered. But in Lemon he had a man of great determination, who pulled out many stops to make sure the engines Stanier wanted were produced on time, although not always to budget. New ideas, or poorly prepared specifications, could often stretch careful estimates to the

limit and beyond, and much that the CME proposed fell into this category.

In many ways Stanier and Lemon were similar. Both were experienced production engineers rather than designers. They knew, understood and could resolve the problems associated with manufacturing. They could make organisations work effectively and could both stand firm in the face of opposition, especially when they knew they were right. Lemon remained as Superintendent until 1941 when deafness, caused by the noise in the workshops, led to his

The frames completed.
(LMS PR/AE/RH)

retirement, but for nine years he faithfully and effectively supported Stanier, and produced many of the masterpiece locomotives that graced the LMS and then British Rail. The bond between the two men was a close one. They kept in touch until Lemon's death in a nursing home in Watford on 23 October 1961.

In any organisation as close knit as the LMS, family connections were common. Lemon and Tom Coleman shared one of these links. In 1939

Lemon's son George and Coleman's daughter, Helena, married in Derby, cementing a friendship that had grown over many years.

Although many people played significant parts in the Stanier revolution, there was one, Robert Riddles, whose star was rising and who would play an ever more important role. Born in Chippenham in 1892 and brought up in Worthing, where his father was a contract manager, Riddles was still only 39-

years-old when Stanier took up office in 1932. By then rapid promotion had seen him advance from being a fitter at Rugby, to Frederick Lemon's assistant at Crewe, where he led on workshop reorganisation, to become Assistant Works Superintendent at Derby. In a glittering career, which began as a premium apprentice at Crewe in 1909, he quickly acquired a superb reputation and Stanier was swift to mark him out as a leading player in his reforms. In 1933 he

Frames and cylinders complete, trailing and leading bogie wheels installed, plus rear coupled wheels.
(LMS PR/AE/RH)

became the CME's Locomotive Assistant at Euston, where his political acumen and great skill supported many projects, particularly the development of the 4-6-2s.

As the design and construction of the new Pacific got underway, members of Stanier's senior team faced a colossal workload, and some felt thwarted or sidelined by his appointment. Only Coleman and Riddles benefited from his arrival, and they faced demanding challenges themselves at Crewe and Derby. Forging a good working relationship with an inherited team is never easy. In this case, where so many substantial targets were introduced, the problems were significantly greater. At best, Stanier must have hoped for co-operation and professional support, even grudging acceptance, but he, ever the realist, probably planned for confrontation and disagreements. At Board level, support was almost guaranteed. They had selected and recruited him, and if he successfully met their targets he would retain their backing. But it was a hard, competitive world, where any lapse or lack of success was soon questioned and punished. Cox, an astute observer of these first months of Stanier's tenancy, gave a telling portrait of the man and his approach:

'*Stanier was big in stature and in mind, and we quickly realised that he was no doctrinaire; he did not immediately or blindly graft Swindon practice as a whole on to his new charge. His other outstanding characteristic was that when he found he had made a mistake, he would never seek to cover up bad engineering or worse, but would change direction quickly and completely, without wasting a moment of further time on what had proved unsatisfactory. In keeping with this trait he was not a man of many words. He gave his instructions in brief terms; when the resulting schemes were put before him, he was apt to accept or reject with a minimum of comment. He was the antithesis of the committee type. Above all he was human and kindly, and could talk to a tool fitter, the draughtsman or the engine driver in language they understood.'*

During April 1932, line drawings and brief specifications of each proposed new type of locomotive arrived in the Drawing Offices under Stanier's control. The short period since his arrival had been very busy. He was eager to get the draughtsman working on the many design details and costings, but also allow the workshop teams to consider how the programme could fit into their production schedules. Armed with their estimates, Stanier took his proposals to the Board for their approval, which was duly given in autumn 1932. Three Pacifics were authorised, but only two proceeded as conventional locomotives. The third was an experimental model designed to create a test bed to prove the worth of non-condensing turbine technology. Such a radical departure, at such a critical stage of the locomotive development programme, was unusual, especially for someone appearing as cautious and measured

as Stanier. His 'great experiment' created much interest, but proved a distraction at a time when other projects demanded attention.

The Drawing Office at Derby became the centre of activity for the first three Pacifics. In his book *Under 10 CMEs*, Eric Langridge, a draughtsman in the team, gave a rare glimpse of how the design of these engines was managed:

'Jack Francis, who had been brought back to Derby earlier, was given a copy of E9, the 4-6-2. As we were together again next to each other in the drawing office, we discussed things together naturally. It has been stated that Stanier brought a box of Swindon drawings with him, but, if so, only their top-feed and regulator came our way. For the rest Dudley Sanford (then senior technical draughtsman) gave us a copy of the Railway Engineer dated July 1919 which became well thumbed, containing an article and details of GWR boilers, which we assumed to be current; and a copy of the general arrangement of Gresley's 4-6-2 from a Railway Gazette, useful for the wide firebox design.

'The frame for the 4-6-2 was given to Willie Armin, the outside motion to Percy Lucas; I cannot remember who did the rest. I suspect Frank Carrier, being next to Percy, did most of the motion; it looks as if they had a copy of the GWR motion, otherwise they would not have driven the expansion link by a projection on its side, very near the loading-gauge line. Of course, there were four separate gears, but a divided drive to the coupled wheels rather spoiled the perfection presumably aimed at. I doubt if Euston had thought much about the strength of frame passing under the firebox front;

6200's boiler.
(LMS PR/AE/RH)

Armin had a job to get enough plate there. The so called "breathing plate" at the rear had a persistent way of shearing off its fixing bolts, giving rise to thumps under the footplate which made some crews refuse to take the locomotive out. The pony truck design came from the Fowler-rejected Compound; it was a thing of many plates, gussets, spittoons and fussy control gear – and heavy.

'It seems that Stanier opted for the GWR style of staggered cylinders and

The boiler now in the frames and 6200 is nearly complete.
(LMS PR/AE/RH)

equal length connecting rods. Each cylinder, having its own valve gear, would produce the identical indicator diagrams, outward and inward strokes, although the inward ones would differ from the outward due to the effect of the angularity of the connecting rods. So far as torque was concerned, it would then be like a 4-cylinder vertical steam engine.

'The boilers on Numbers 6200 and 6201 (the numbering sequence of this new class) had tubes 20ft 9in long – reminiscent of Vincent Raven and the old NER where his Pacifics had tubes 21ft between the tubeplates – and 16ft flue tubes, each carrying two individual flow and return superheater elements, ie the steam made one pass down and back to the header. This design was detailed by Jack Francis from a Euston engine diagram. We were told to shorten the tube length to 19ft 6in; we were also told to make the tubes parallel, no reduced ends, to screw the large flue tubes into the firebox tubeplate – no copper ends as on the LMS hitherto – and to provide two rows of these. As to weights, Euston were a bit short of experienced designers. If they based them on former Horwich sketches they would be "chancing their arm" on an unknown quantity, so presumably they used the "King" weights with a pony truck behind. As the job grew, Chambers could see the locomotive would come out very heavy, but got no help from Euston, the boys there had done their jobs and departed into the wings – riding on footplates, and inspecting etc.'

Langridge was a seasoned draughtsman, and well used to taking outline concepts and proposals and turning them into working designs. But even he seemed surprised by the sparse nature of Stanier's 'plans' that arrived from Euston, writing: 'Later I came to the conclusion that he [Stanier] was no designer as such.'

A copy of the original specification does not seem to have survived, so we have no way of knowing how accurate Langridge was in his assessment. But in June 1933 the LMS published a short booklet that described how the project evolved and the key requirements, dimensions and capacity of the first two, conventional locomotives:

'As a result of about six years' experience with the "Royal Scot" locomotives, which have given very satisfactory service for the loads for which they were designed, it has been considered desirable to experiment with a still more powerful type of locomotive capable of hauling heavier trains of 500 tons loading between Euston and Glasgow. Previous experience has shown it desirable to provide an improved boiler with a grate area of 45sq ft. to ensure satisfactory combustion during such long through runs. This large grate calls for a wide firebox to permit efficient firing and also a trailing truck of the Bissel type to carry the heavier weight at the trailing end of the (Pacific) engine.

'The tenders for these engines have been increased in both coal and water capacity to meet heavy requirements; 4000 gallons of water and 9 tons of coal being provided.

'The standard type water pick-up has, of course, been arranged on the tender, and in addition "Timken" roller bearings are fitted to the six tender wheels.

6200 being positioned over her main coupled wheels. (LMS PR/AE/RH)

Fitting out continues within a timescale so tight that Fred Lemon was concerned that 'corners might be cut'. (LMS PR/AE/RH)

'The leading dimensions are as follows:-

4 simple cylinders	16 ¼ "diameter x 28" stroke.
Valve gear	Walschaerts long travel 7 ¼"
Coupled Wheels	6' 6" diameter
Boiler Pressure	250lbs. per sq. inch
Firebox Heating Surface	190 sq.ft
Tractive Effort	40,300 lbs at 85% boiler pressure
Total Weight of Engine and Tender	158 tons 12 cwt
Wheelbase (engine and tender)	63' 10"

Even before design work was completed, Order No 371 had been placed on Crewe Works and the process of planning, ordering material from sub-contractors and scheduling the work began. Derby Order No 8254 was issued shortly afterwards, in November 1932, authorising construction of some Pacific parts there.

The key to any successful locomotive design is an effective boiler. Impressed by the use of tapered boilers, matched to Belpaire fireboxes, on GWR engines, Stanier adopted this practice when he came to the LMS. And it became a standard part of his engine-building programme. The LMS needed engines with boilers of greater capacity to pull heavier trains over longer distances, often non-stop, and this match of boiler and firebox met this need.

In 1935 Coleman, at Stanier's instigation, wrote a brief paper on the benefits of tapered boilers for the running department. He emphasised that the gases produced by combustion are hottest near the firebox and rapid cooling takes place as they pass away down the boiler

Finally ready for inspection at Crewe. Stanier was unhappy with the finish and there was some last-minute work to 'fettle' the engine properly.
(LMS PR/AE/RH)

tubes. Most evaporation, which is key to the process, takes place where the gases are hottest. So a tapered boiler, coupled to the greater surface area of a Belpaire box, focuses and improves heat transfer where most effective, and increases steam production as a result.

No doubt the change met opposition. Inevitably some old hands hoped that established practice would prove more successful. And such a pressured development programme unsurprisingly hit teething problems, generating a lot of 'I told you so' comments. In time change was accepted and the steaming qualities of these new engines, with tapered boilers and wide fireboxes, was fully appreciated by most.

As the design process continued, the draughtsmen gradually teased out a fuller picture of what was needed and completed all the drawings necessary to allow building to begin.

Throughout this challenging programme a stream of senior officers visited Derby to discuss the new engines, much to Chambers' obvious frustration. Debates often turned to argument, especially when the Chief Draughtsman felt his advice was being ignored. The importance of the work could not be diminished, and Stanier, Harold Hartley and Beames called in regularly to monitor progress. They gradually hammered out all the details and decided priorities so that the first engine would appear on time. There was much to be resolved, as Tom Coleman later

Painted in grey and ready for her first trip to Euston for a very public inspection. (LMS PR/AE/RH)

Euston, 28 June 1933. (LMS PR/AE/RH)

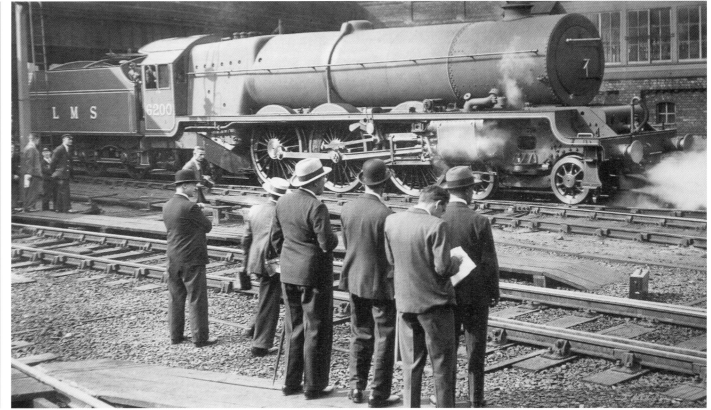

6200 drawing interested gazes from railway workers, journalists and the public (28 June 1933). (LMS PR/AE/RH)

recalled in a letter to an old friend who was preparing to write about this work:

'There were two sticking points – fitting Great Western ideas into what Derby did and producing a new class of engine in a short timescale; with so much else going on. Herbert Chambers was a considerate and thoughtful man, but the pressure he was under was immense and he felt that the task would have been managed better if he had been left alone to get on with it. Stanier would not have allowed that. Keeping his hands on the tiller in uncertain waters was his way, and who can blame him for that. He had not established his position in the LMS at that stage and much rested on his shoulders.

'For a while there were disagreements over the number of cylinders – 3 or 4 – and the boiler. There was no doubt Stanier wanted to go with GW practice and have four cylinders, a tapered boiler and a wide firebox, and that's what we did, although Chambers did favour something closer to the Scots. The discussions, I am told, became quite heated and it was about this time that I became involved in this work at Derby. I also regularly visited Stanier at Euston, where we discussed with Mr Lemon and his deputy the best way of managing the new Pacifics in service. There were concerns that the crew would need special training and the engines might be too large for many of the stations – where platform clearance might not be sufficient.

'One of my tasks was to review the main drawings of the engine as Chambers was concerned over its weight and wanted to get it down a bit. Two

things struck me – the GW appearance of the engine; it looked like a King converted into a Pacific – and the fact that the design had been taken so far without a clear idea that it could run on our system. The cart before the horse!

'In looks it was handsome, but to my mind the frames were too long and the outside cylinders seemed badly positioned. This gave it a slightly unbalanced look.

'You asked about technical details. I have looked through the papers I have retained and found two which you might find interesting. A copy of a presentation I was asked to prepare explaining to drivers and firemen how the Princess Royals worked and how these bigger engines will change how they do their jobs. The second is the technical specification that Derby produced detailing the main parts of the engines.

As it is a rather a large book I won't send it to you, but will list here some of the main features:

'**Boiler** – you know about this already. The tapered boiler created the maximum water space around the firebox and this maximised evaporation. The heat transfer at the front end, where the water space was more restricted and so evaporation less, was not so important. With such a large engine as this, a tapered boiler carried less weight and it did not affect the amount of steam produced, so kept the engine within loading limits. It was also believed that this type of boiler would require less maintenance. This had proved the case on the Great Western. However, the Type 1 tapered boiler proved troublesome in service – it had poor steaming qualities due, in part, to Stanier's insistence on a low degree of superheat

A photograph of 6200, still painted grey and unnamed, apparently at Lime Street Station, Liverpool. (LMS PR/AE/RH)

As with all new locomotives 6200 is photographed in Crewe Yard, the background cut out to give a clear view of her shape.
(LMS PR/AE/RH)

and too few superheater elements; another GWR practice. Chambers tried to persuade the Chief to consider modifications and in time this happened. But, more about that later.

'**Frames** – with the weight of that large boiler, there were concerns that the frames might become distorted with time. To eliminate this possibility, the frames were constructed from 1 ¼ inch steel plate, which were then spaced 4ft 1 ½ in. apart. The thickness of the metal meant that the amount of staying could be reduced. The main frames finished just forward of the firebox throatplate, at the rear of the trailing coupled wheels. The cab was then mounted on upswept splice frames. I'm told that the rear frames were based on the LMS's earlier work on a Pacific design. A few years later some cylinder movement was discovered and problems with the

crosshead had to be corrected. These were thought to be due to some flexing in the frames and required attention. By the time I retired this problem still affected the engines, though various modifications had been carried out.

'**Cylinders** - I thought 4 cylinders a far better solution than 3. The outside cylinders and valve chests were set at a sloping angle and made of cast-iron. They provided drive to the middle coupled axle. The inside cylinders and chests were set in a horizontal position forward of the outside cylinders and drove the leading axle. Each valve was driven by its own Walschaerts gear, as an alternative to two sets of valve gear and rocking shafts. By splitting the tractive effort of the four cylinders between the two axles, rather than one axle, it was hoped that there would be a better balance and a more even steam

distribution. It was also believed that this would greatly reduce wear overall, as well as lessen the stress pressures on those long frames. In the light of experience, we later reconsidered these ideas and looked for other solutions.

'**Wheels and trucks** – the main driving wheels were 6' 6" in diameter, which followed the pattern set by the GW Kings. I thought that 6' 9" would have been better, but Stanier and Riddles believed that the smaller wheels would be more effective in achieving maximum power and better free running. We did not repeat this mistake with the Coronations, which benefitted greatly by having the larger wheels, but were more prone to slipping.

'The bogie and pony trucks adopted the principles used by the Great Western, following trials with the De Glehn 4-cylinder compound Atlantic, *which had been imported from France just after the turn of the Century.*

'I could go into greater detail about these locomotives, but I think this will give you sufficient for your purposes. I enclose a number of articles that have appeared over the years concerning the "Princesses". They were good locomotives, but could have been much better if Stanier had been allowed more time to consider other ideas. We learnt much from studying their design when building the "Coronations". I will write again with my views on this later.'

The building programme was given the highest priority in the workshops at Crewe. The LNER had stolen a march on their rivals in the mid-1920s with their premier express services, pulled by a large fleet of new Pacific locomotives, seemingly more advanced than anything the LMS could offer. Commercial necessity was a merciless driver and gave little time for an organisation creaking under the strain of rebuilding to plan and produce new locomotives in a realistic timescale. But a deadline of June 1933 had been set for 6200, the first new Pacific, to appear and the PR team publicised this event as Easter approached. Stanier, by all accounts, was loath to give too much away. The engine when it left the workshops was an experimental machine, although based on well-established principles. It was also untested and so an unknown quantity. Recent experience on the LMS and the LNER with other locomotives in this evolving state demonstrated the folly of promising too much. Both Fowler and Nigel Gresley had experimented

with high-pressure boilers as the decade came to an end, and achieved little success, but their 'failures' took place in the full glare of publicity. Stanier would have been aware of this and preferred to get the engine running, with as many teething problems as possible resolved, before risking public scrutiny.

Two periodicals, the *Railway Gazette* and *The Engineer*, showed great interest in the engine taking shape at Crewe. As specialist publications their reputation was well established among railway professionals, which gave them easier access to the companies and their work. In the months before the

engine's launch they were allowed to see the work in progress and begin their critiques, ready for publication during the summer. But the first engine had to be completed before this could happen and Stanier was not prepared to sanction anything until he felt sure the engine was presentable. Here he faced a major problem. During a visit to Crewe in May to inspect the first locomotive, he found evidence of poor workmanship. Years later, when speaking to H.A.V. Bulleid, as he prepared his book *Master Builders of Steam*, the story found a voice:

'… and soon Stanier was asked along to give his final blessing before

After her initial 'running in' turns, 6200 sits ready for painting red.
(LMS PR/AE/RH)

Finally painted red and named. (LMS PR/AE/RH)

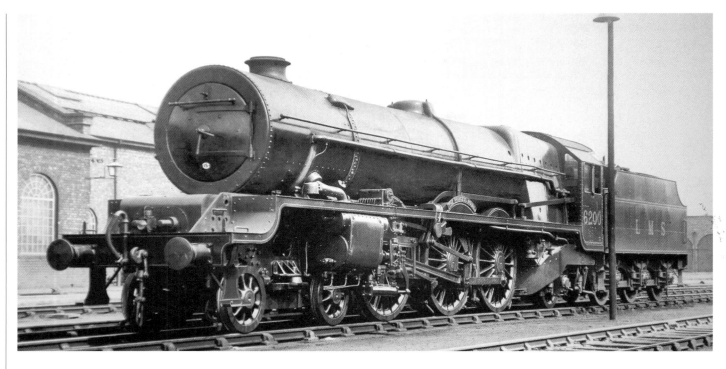

unveiling. *This he at first refused, finding the engine decidedly rusty here and there, several fittings left in an aggressively "as cast" condition, and other minor blemishes. These he rather testily blamed on Crewe's lack of finesse, and provocatively asked whether they would not rather turn out a job to Swindon standards: but to be fair it was a symptom of Crewe economy pushed over by the cheese-paring Stamp regime. Two weeks later the engine, now looking resplendent and rather expensive, was driven to Euston for inspection by the Board.'*

The work continued until 26 June, the day before the engine's journey to Euston, when a final inspection was carried out by Stanier and Symes in the morning, with Lemon, Riddles and Chambers in attendance. But she had to appear in grey primer, with no time remaining to get her into her red topcoat. This was not unusual, since railway companies traditionally outshopped their engines in this guise for official photographs, then preliminary testing. But it was usual when formally launching an engine at press parties, and before Board members, for painting to have been completed.

Riddles later recalled the scramble to get the locomotive moving and the risks of running an untested, brand-new engine on the mainline. His memories were then written up by Colonel H. Rogers in his biography of Riddles:

'At 5 am (on the day of launch) the Pacific left the Works, without any previous trial in steam, to run the 158 miles to Euston "light engine" in the gentle time of 10 hours – none too long a time for an untried engine which was the first of a new class. It had been arranged that Riddles should ride on the footplate as far as Rugby where he would hand over to the Works Superintendent, F.A. Lemon. Buckets of oil were carried on the footplate and frequent stops were made "just in case", whilst examinations were carried out and much more oil was poured on. The news of the new engine had got around and even at that early hour they were accorded something of a triumph.

'From Rugby, Riddles returned to Crewe, and there he saw at the top of the station the materials van "with lots of pieces in it". This turned out to be the special tackle drawing the crosshead of the Princess Royal and he wondered what on earth had gone wrong. He soon

found out that the crosshead had overheated and the metal run out 12 miles beyond Rugby. It was a design fault that was corrected eventually, but the engine had to go back to Rugby to have the slide block re-metalled – a task which entailed a hectic night for all concerned. Nevertheless, the engine was on view at Euston the following day.'

The problems encountered by Lemon, after Riddles returned to Crewe, needed slightly more work than he described. Re-metalling of the slide block was insufficient to get her going, and Lemon's solution was to remove the crosshead, piston rod and head, then replace them with parts from 6201, the second, partly-assembled Pacific at Crewe. Being Works Superintendent and a man of considerable skill, he was able to martial the organisation to get the work completed quickly and remained beside the engine to make sure it happened. By the evening she was running again and on her way to Euston, this time with a pilot engine to make sure she reached her destination should any other fault occur.

Frederick Lemon is a man largely overlooked in most accounts of the LMS in this period. Yet it is most unlikely that the massive programme the Company began on Stanier's arrival could have been completed so successfully without him or men of this type. Lemon occupied a pivotal position where he had the power, should he wish to exercise it, to disrupt production or throw obstacles in the way of the CME or anyone else he disagreed with. He chose not to and instead worked tirelessly at Crewe to bring

these ambitious plans to fruition. Roland Bond, who replaced Riddles to become Lemon's deputy in late 1933, caught the essence of this largely forgotten man in a letter written many years later:

'I knew my new chief, F.A. Lemon, both personally and by reputation. Each time we met he greeted me with kindness and an old-world courtesy. He had a reputation for irascibility, caused in part by a determination to get things done, but also a rising frustration resulting from an increasing deafness, which was threatening to isolate him from his surroundings. He had a sharp tongue and did not mince his words or hold back in dressing down anyone who displeased him, as they did on many occasions. But a large and hardy industrial workforce, with many demanding targets, needed someone like this at its head.

'More than once in the years that followed, senior foremen were to come into my office, white faced and shaking with anger after being dressed down by Lemon. They received some comfort, if they deserved it, but knew that he was right, and went back to work clear on what they had to do and the consequences if they did not. He remained in post for a long time under Stanier because he had undoubted skills. He would have gone long before if he had fallen short of the CME's demands.'

Thanks to Lemon's efforts, and those of his men, the engine arrived

6200 at Euston.
(LMS PR/AE/RH)

6200 on another running-in turn, apparently. (LMS PR/AE/RH)

at Euston in time to be viewed by interested parties from within the LMS and the wider world. The full Board were there, including Ernest Lemon, just returned from a goodwill visit to the USA with the *Royal Scot*, Stanier and his wife, and many other notables. Although barely operational, the engine made a fine sight, even in her primered, slightly dowdy condition, and received a number of accolades. Her appearance only seventeen months since Stanier's arrival was a remarkable achievement, reflecting his supreme efforts to modernise the locomotive fleet and overcome dissenting voices. If Stamp and Hartley had harboured doubts about their choice of Stanier as CME, this surely must have overcome them.

Strangely enough, 6200's presentation at Euston did not include a naming ceremony. One assumes the locomotive's arrival had been so speculative and uncertain that such a formal event was difficult to plan. Also, adding a name to something untested and untried could prove a PR fiasco. In time, Royal approval was sought to name the engines after Princesses, but in the weeks after 6200's appearance, the Company engaged the press in a mild attempt at public involvement in naming the first two locomotives. Suggestions received were many and varied, from Hiawatha to kings from ancient Mercia. It was even rumoured that they would be called *Agamemnon* and *Achilles*, with other engines in the class taking similar

names from Greek mythology. But the need for relevance to contemporary British society and the strength inherent in a dignified title meant the engines became Princesses: 6200 *Princess Royal*, named after King George V's third child, and 6201 *Princess Elizabeth*, the Duke of York's eldest daughter.

Within days of 6200's appearance, the editor of the *Railway Gazette*, who had been given access to the engine during its building, produced a short editorial announcing its arrival and a more detailed article inside. He found it hard to disguise his enthusiasm:

'Having been allowed by Mr Stanier to see his new express locomotive grow up, stage by stage, from the moment the frame plates were put on the machine to that at which the engine was ready for its steam trials, we are in a position to say something about it from a personal perspective. The engine, in our view, is a credit to everyone concerned in its design and construction. We are not prepared to go to the extent of saying it is above criticism, and, even though we thought it and said so, we should not presumably find everyone, among those competent to judge, agreeing with us. We do however assert – and here we believe the critics will be with us – that it scores very high marks indeed, and adds something of a definitely outstanding character to the status of modern locomotive practice.'

The new Pacific had arrived on a wave of optimism and good publicity, but only the weeks, months and years ahead would show if the design could meet expectations. It was a trying, but exciting time.

CHAPTER 5

TO TEST AND PROGRESS

Once 6200 returned to Crewe on 29 June the serious work of getting her ready for main-line service began. She was checked over to see how all the new metal had responded to such an early, albeit slow run to London and back. Having accompanied her on the three-day sojourn, Frederick Lemon had mixed feelings over her state of preparedness and her performance. In reply to a congratulatory letter from William Stanier he expressed his thoughts:

'*The breakdown south of Rugby was unfortunate, though not unforeseen. In other circumstances I would have had the engine brought back to Crewe for attention. However, by cannibalising 6201 for replacement parts, we achieved our goal and the repairs held up well during the return trip. It was unfortunate that we were unable to give the engine a few runs and adjustments before this trip. The problems we faced might have been significantly reduced if we had been given longer to prepare.*

'*I was not displeased with the engine, which seemed to possess many good characteristics. Testing can now begin in earnest and we shall see if my early good opinion is borne out by the work ahead. However, I did note a number of items for attention. Steaming, even when running light, was not all it should have been.*'

The trip to London had been a risk and one that might have rebounded on Stanier if Lemon had been unable to effect repairs and organise support so promptly. But the stakes were high and reputations could be made or broken by such a gamble. As it was, a suitably good impression had been made. Tacit approval by the Board for continued development was given, Stanier's star rose higher, shareholders in the Company saw a visual return on their investment and the PR people

A perfect photo showing off 6200's elegant lines and giving voice to those who thought she was a stretched GWR King. (AE/RH)

Euston. 6200 older and not drawing the same admiring glances as when new. (LMS PR/AE/RH)

had something they could sell. However, much remained to do to make sure this and the hundreds of other new locomotives due to be built were successful.

In the days and weeks that followed 6200's launch, the press continued to praise Stanier and his new engine. This only served to spur on the LMS' main rival, the LNER, which was already far ahead in its development programmes, in commercial and engineering terms. Large numbers of their Pacifics had

been thundering up and down the East Coast route for many years, and harvesting good publicity in the process. As Stanier's Pacifics slowly appeared they were taking even larger steps forward, continuing the one-sided race that had been at the core of Stanier's appointment. Ever ready to exploit new ideas, Nigel Gresley was designing two new express engines: a 2-8-2, designated the P2, created specifically to pull loads over the trying route from Edinburgh to Aberdeen, and a

streamlined Pacific, the A4. If successful, these locomotives would not only supplement the LNER's already impressive fleet, but also take them even further ahead in the contest for trade and headlines.

The LMS' response seems almost tardy in comparison, but Stanier and his Board realised that glamorous express services, though getting great publicity, did not earn the revenue created by freight or commuter traffic. Here the Company was catching and overtaking their main rivals, on rail and road. So, despite pressure for larger express locomotives, the need was really for other types of engine – fewer in number, stronger in capacity and more efficient in performance. And between 1933 and 1935 they appeared in huge numbers, allowing older, inefficient types to be phased out.

Josiah Stamp, as a leading economist of the day, recognised that success or failure was measured on a balance sheet and not by the esoteric vagaries of public relations. Standardisation, then rationalisation remained the sole course towards profitability, particularly as trade was slowly recovering from the great economic depression that had gripped Britain and the world for many years. The race to have the biggest and best express services was a distraction from the business of making money, which essentially called for an egalitarian, mass-market approach.

6200 needed few extra maintenance tasks at Crewe or repair after her London trip. Attention was directed at the remaining fitting-out tasks so that testing could take place and a controlled running-in programme begin. Over the next few weeks there were a number of runs gradually growing in length, with loads of increasing weight slowly added. If any significant problems were encountered, they were not severe enough to warrant a long period in the shops. She was painted red and finally named, permission to use Royal titles having been granted. In photographic registers kept at Derby there are references to pictures

of the event, but no negatives or prints seem to have survived in public hands. Many pictures of 6200, from July 1933, still exist and show this elegant locomotive in all of her glory, an image of suppressed power, unlike anything that had been built by the LMS up to that time, and a fine tribute to the work of Stanier and his team.

After nearly 5,000 miles of trouble-free trials, the signs were good that 6200 would soon be in service and managers felt sufficiently confident to arrange a very heavy run from Euston to Crewe and back. Whether the original intention was to make it a high or low-profile trip is uncertain, but planning soon took on the appearance of a publicity stunt when the press were invited to ride on board and witness this new engine in full flow. In early July, a month before this outing, Robert Riddles found himself selected by Stanier to replace Sandham Symes as his Technical Assistant at Euston. During his first few weeks in post, he became the centre of many activities, but the development of the two Pacific locomotives took precedence. One of his first duties was to plan and participate in the forthcoming 'trial'. The test load would be as heavy as possible to simulate what she might need to pull in service. There were fourteen carriages and a dynamometer car, totalling 505 tons. The scheduled time for the run was 165 minutes and no banking engine out of Euston was to be used. One crew, Driver Albert Parsons and Fireman Harry

Betley, both Crewe men, were in charge for the outward and return journeys. Riddles later recalled what happened:

'Following my move to London, and whilst Stanier was absent, a run to Crewe and back pulled by 6200 was arranged for the Press. Ernest Lemon, who was not long back from the USA having accompanied the Royal Scot on her tour and enjoyed footplate rides, rode on this new engine. To avoid overcrowding I leaned out of a carriage window to watch proceedings. All was going well until 10 miles from Stafford when the train came to a standstill. I jumped down on to the track and walked up to the engine, to find the left-hand driving box on fire. The driver had sensed it was running hot and had*

Ernest Lemon on the footplate awaiting 6200's departure from Euston for her press run in August 1933. (LMS/AE)

6201 enters service.
(LMS/AE)

decided to get forward to it by climbing through the cab window and creeping along to see if there was anything he could do. With few options he simply poured oil over the box hoping to cool it, but it was so hot that a fire broke out.

'Once I got forward we soon put this out and Lemon asked me what we should do. My first thought was that he should not have let the driver leave the cab. But with the Press on board it was a nasty problem and the driver felt he had to do something to keep the engine going. It would take at least an hour to call up a replacement engine and Lemon was insistent that we should carry on if at all possible. I decided to let the engine continue, but at a greatly reduced speed and gave the necessary instructions. I remained on the footplate for the

remainder of the journey. Luck was with us and we arrived at Crewe 45 minutes late. The axle was so badly scored that it had to be scrapped. We returned to London later that day, seven carriages shorter, pulled by a Royal Scot (No 6151) which was due to enter the Works for a heavy general repair, so was not in the best condition.'

It seems to be a measure of desperation to allow a locomotive to continue in such a state, but Lemon clearly felt this was a risk worth taking. It was remiss of him to stand by and allow a member of staff to do something so dangerous as leave the cab while the engine was moving. In 1933 the safety of railway workers was a significant issue. Victorian principles of worker exploitation still

held sway across much of industry, but the rise of trade unions in post-war Britain highlighted the carnage this cowboy attitude to health and safety was causing. Monthly statistics produced in response to a Government initiative had drawn attention to the scale of the problem, although only focused on the most severe accidents. In the three months before 6200's run to Crewe there had been thirteen deaths and twenty-eight very serious injuries across the four main railway companies. Of these the LMS was responsible for four fatalities and thirteen serious, life-changing injuries.

Despite the problem near Stafford on the northbound leg of the journey and the return with another engine, the Press response was positive. Good hospitality might have been partly responsible. The *Railway Gazette*, as a 'trade' journal, was more discriminating in its editorial and poured praise on the footplate crew who, 'deserved the congratulations offered to them on arrival at Euston, for the excellent handling of the two locomotives concerned.' But the engine was also singled out for praise as well and its partial breakdown was listed as being 'just one of those things'. In reality the problem was a common one that could happen at any time to any engine. Only if other failures occurred would the issue become significant, but over the following weeks the engine performed fairly well.

Riddles' next duty in his new post was to finalise a draft paper that had been circulating in the HQ for a while. It described in great detail all the features of 6200 and her sister engine. Having been Works Manager at Crewe, when they were being built, he was best positioned to do this. Although a technical treatise, it was suitably worded to allow staff in workshops and running sheds to understand the basic engineering. It also became a document read by staff working for railway periodicals and those with only a rudimentary knowledge of locomotive design. Early versions were circulated in July for comment, but they seem to have remained within a close circle of managers and were not given wider distribution. Understandably, Stanier might have felt the project was so sensitive that he did not wish competitors to get wind of these details. Few copies have survived and one version is reproduced in Appendix 2 of this book. It is, in reality, the most detailed specification of the class still in existence, most other papers having been destroyed as the steam age came to an end in the 1960s.

As 6200 continued her trials, 6201 rolled off the production line and was given a 'date built' on her record card of 3 November 1933. By Christmas she had covered more than 7,000 miles, and 6200's mileage had increased to nearly 27,000, much of it between Euston and Liverpool or Carlisle, but not yet regularly to Scotland. Both engines were allocated to Camden initially, with 6201 moving to Polmadie, Glasgow, early in 1934, so the LMS could begin simultaneous through workings of heavier trains between

6201 pulls out of Euston with the fireman taking a 'breather', although the fire will soon need to be built up again after the long drag up Camden Bank. (AE)

6200 undergoing maintenance, apparently at Camden Shed. (AE)

the two capitals in both directions. Up until then the Royal Scot class, the usual engines for this work, only had the capacity to reach Carlisle.

Generally, the engines were well received by footplate crew, although the cylinder arrangement made servicing more complex and time consuming. The cabs were spacious and well laid out, and the engines were noted for their excellent riding characteristics. The main reservation concerned their steaming capability, which seemed to be related to lack of superheat capacity, as an editorial in the *Railway Engineer* suggested:

'It may be said that an express locomotive working for a percentage of its time with steam at a high rate of expansion requires more superheat than goods engines, where the steam is not used at such a high expansion rate. It is questionable whether full consideration has been given to this point.'

Stanier, in designing the 'Princesses', followed GWR practice in many areas, but particularly on one key George Churchward dictate. He believed in a low degree of superheat, so fewer tubes were needed to achieve this, which allowed greater space between the tubes for upward circulation of water at the firebox tubeplate. A sound principle when practised on GWR engines, but falling short when extended to the more demanding role for which the 'Princesses' were designed. Success largely depended on near-perfect steaming, and often

this came down to the quality of the coal used and the way each crew fired an engine. The new Pacifics also had a grate area of 45 sq ft, much larger than firemen on the LMS were used to, and some spread their fire all around the firebox, which was usual practice on other express engines. If, as was often the case with the LMS, the coal was of poor quality, then the task of providing sufficient steam became even more difficult.

The role of superheaters in a locomotive is crucial. They take the saturated steam produced by the boiler and reheat it, greatly increasing thermal efficiency, and improving a locomotive's steaming qualities and performance. In the 'Princesses', which only had a 16-element unit, the degree of superheating was insufficient, and this resulted in heat being lost through the expansion and exhaust processes. By the time this happened the steam entering the cylinders had dropped back to pre-superheater temperature levels, so added nothing to performance.

As experience of the type grew, poor firing techniques and the quality of coal improved, but lack of superheated steam could only be corrected by more elements. Stanier might have been expected to remain a strong advocate of low levels of superheat, but he was a pragmatist by nature. When a problem continued and an effective solution was presented, which ran counter to his beliefs, he could change his mind. During 1934, a new boiler was designed at Derby that saw a 32-

element superheater installed. In the meantime, 6200 and 6201 ran with the old-style boilers, relying on the skill of the drivers and firemen to get the best out of them. However, for a while 6201 did run with an experimental double chimney and double-blastpipe nozzles to see if this improved performance, but this only made matters worse and was replaced with a single chimney.

Roland Bond, who replaced Riddles at Crewe, later recorded how the need to keep 6200 and 6201 running successfully was paramount, with no news slipping out about failures or problems:

'We were perhaps more caught up at Crewe than any other Works in the anxieties which arose from the troubles, small in themselves, but large in the context of departmental politics. Stanier had gained the wholehearted loyalty and respect of his own staff. But there were subversive influences elsewhere, unhelpful to the new engines, against which Riddles, as Stanier's principal assistant, waged implacable war.

'It was especially important that the two Pacifics should be universally acknowledged as doing well. They were for some time plagued by minor troubles. The smoke regulator, combined in one casting with the superheater header, was a perfect pest. Hot bogie boxes and outside slidebars were other troubles which brought the engines back to the Works more often than was good for

The highly-publicised arrival soon led to Bassett-Lowke producing an O gauge model, which sold extremely well among the more affluent. (THG)

Princess Louise, brand new with a long life ahead of her, passing through the Lune Valley near Lancaster. (AE)

their reputation, particularly after the unfortunate Press demonstration from Euston in August 1933.

'Riddles gave me verbal instructions that the Pacifics were not to be taken on the Works if any minor defect was within the competence of Crewe North Shed to put right. Whatever may have been the state of relationships in high places at Euston, we at Crewe, 158 miles away, worked in close and friendly contact with our opposite numbers in the Motive

Power and Operating Departments. Though I forget now what exactly the trouble was, I was asked one morning to take 6201 on the Works for some minor job which could have taken the Shed a couple of days, but which we could do and have the engine back in traffic the same day. As it seemed to my simple mind that the object of the exercise was to keep these two engines out of service for the shortest possible time, I readily agreed and the job was done by lunch

time. Somehow or other Riddles heard that 6201 was back in the Works. He was soon on the telephone demanding an explanation. He was no way mollified when I told him the engine was already back in traffic. I was sharply instructed to kindly obey orders in future.'

1934 saw both of these engines beginning work in earnest, teething problems having largely been solved. As Bond later recalled, day-to-day running problems were

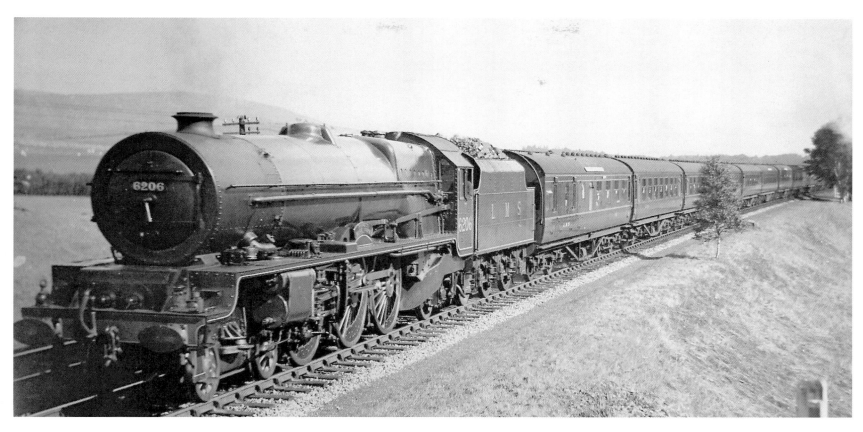

generally minor and no worse than other engines in service, but these first Pacifics had much to prove so as to expand the fleet. There was a fear that a major problem would set these plans back. Bond described one such event:

'There was the remarkable case of one of these engines, working the Up Merseyside Express non-stop from Crewe to Willesden, developing a hot inside big end near Rugby. The brass disintegrated. The resulting knock loosened the big end cotter and gudgeon pin, both of which fell on to the track. The rod, now free, was shot out on the ground through the narrow space

6206, seemingly without effort, pulls up one of the many steep inclines in the Lune Valley. (LMS/AE)

At speed with number partially obscured, although it appears to be 6200. (AE/RH)

Taking water, safety valves lifting, with a full load behind heading for Glasgow. (LMS/AE)

between the leading and trailing bogie wheels. This sounded such an extraordinary story when I heard it over the 'phone from the Motive Power people, that I went off to Rugby on the first available train to see for myself the extent of the damage to the engine, by that time safely in shed. Some new parts were obviously going to need putting in hand in the Shops forthwith. How the connecting rod got itself out on to the track without derailing the locomotive we *shall never know – it was one of the classic "might have beens" of which those outside the service seldom hear anything.'*

More by luck than judgement a major accident had been avoided. A locomotive running fast, with a long rake of fully-loaded coaches behind, leaving the track at speed would surely have resulted in many casualties and raised questions about safety. Development of these locomotives might have stopped

until the cause of the crash had been found. Confidence in the design and Stanier's own professional judgement and skills could also have been called into question. As it was, the project continued. In 1947, a high-speed derailment by engine 6244, *King George VI*, on a curve at Grendon, near Polesworth, resulted in five deaths and sixty-four injured. This crash graphically demonstrated what might have happened to the

Princess in 1934 if luck had been against her, although in this case the cause was thought to be faulty track and not a defective engine.

Meanwhile, after years of struggle, the LMS appeared to be making ground financially in a difficult market. In a presentation to shareholders in February 1934, the Chairman offered hope to anxious shareholders that business was improving and dividends would be paid:

'*Against the loss of earnings (in 1933) of £325,000, I am glad to say there has been a saving in working expenses of* £1,133,000, *so that there has been an increase in the net revenue of £808,000, a remarkable result in the worst year from the gross revenue standpoint which the Company has experienced, worse even than that of 1926 [the year of the General Strike]. For the second year in succession capital expenditure has been reduced by the withdrawal of rolling stock and the sales of land. While I do not say that we have reached the end of economies, there is a limit to the savings that can be achieved in this direction.*

'*A substantial contribution to our economies has been made by the increased technical and operating efficiency of our locomotive stock. During the 11 years since amalgamation the number of locomotives has been reduced from 10,316 to 8,226. Compared with 1925 we now get 5% more train miles per train hour per passenger locomotive and 17% for freight locomotives: we have 41% less assisting with a second locomotive for passenger trains and 63% less for freight trains.*

'*Tractive effort and design cannot be allowed to remain static, and many of you may have been interested in our latest product of construction – the new 4-6-2-type superheated 4-cylinder simple*

Princess Victoria, unobserved except by the photographer, passes through Tring Station. (AE)

6204 *Princess Louise* working hard. (AE)

A grimy 6204 pulls out of Carlisle Station. (LMS/AE)

engines, designed and built in the Company's works for the Anglo-Scottish services. You will realise the economic import of the new design by the fact that two engines, The Princess Royal and Princess Elizabeth, are hauling alternately throughout, without change or assistance en route, the 10.0am from Euston and the 10.0am from Glasgow, a distance in each direction of 401 miles, which when worked by the "Royal Scot" type required three locomotives (in each direction).'

In a long report Stamp emphasised the importance of these new developments and the need to continue the standardisation programme, confirming that orders had been

placed for a substantial number of new locomotives. With revenue likely to remain below outlay, and only savings and sales to balance the books, it was important to give a positive message about the benefits of new engines. The success of his two 'Princesses' was key to this upbeat statement, so it was little

wonder that his staff were keen to make sure nothing untoward slipped out and only a positive image was portrayed. In hindsight this is a fragile foundation on which to base the Company's future success, but in 1934 it appeared to be sufficient for shareholders and stakeholders alike. Two engines

seemed a meagre start to this programme and there was no haste in adding to this particular class, though other, more general-purpose locomotives multiplied quickly. This suggests the Pacifics were either more a luxury than a money spinner or were simply not ready to be mass produced. Whatever the cause, more

Princess Louise at Shrewsbury, with her driver taking a short rest quietly observing life in the Station. (LMS/AE)

6201 in her stride, with her fireman observing the photographer. (ET/RH)

than two engines would soon be needed if the LMS really wanted to compete with the LNER for long-haul, non-stop traffic to Scotland and the North.

1934 and 1935 saw the 'Princesses' undergo tests, some very public, that combined engineering and PR marketing needs. Development in both areas was crucial to the Company and the reputation of managers charged with guiding the business to success. And, if successful, orders for more engines would follow.

Between January and June, the mileage of both Pacifics increased and confidence in their reliability grew. Footplate crew understood their new mounts and coaxed good performances, but insufficient superheat remained to retard running power – not badly enough to make the locomotives inefficient or worse than the engines they were replacing. The first formal trials were set for October 1934 and saw 6200 running against Royal Scot No.6158 over the Euston to Carlisle route. These tests were seen as a simple comparison between types to prove the superiority of the Princess Class. Expecting a positive result, and with trust growing in their stability and performance, Board approval to build ten more was sought in June by Stanier. Not a huge number, in comparison to the substantial fleet of Pacifics operating on the LNER, but enough to keep momentum going. And ten would not put an excessive strain on workshops, already struggling with a huge construction programme, or the Company's

ROYAL SCOT
PASSING ROYAL SCOT
AT COMBINED SPEED
OF 140 M·P·H

SILVERTOWN RAILWAY OILS *and* SILVERTOWN MECHANICAL LUBRICATORS

SILVERTOWN LUBRICANTS L.TD

MINOCO WHARF
WEST SILVERTOWN
LONDON · E·16·

Locomotive suppliers were eager to have the latest engines in their adverts, a practice fully supported by the LMS' Publicity Department. (THG)

financiers who were ever conscious of their budgets. Authorisation was given to include these additional engines in the 1935 building programme, at an estimated cost of £107,000.

The draughtsmen at Derby reviewed the design of the first two engines, absorbing data from many sources and, from this, establishing lessons learnt and how the design might be improved. With little time to spare and many other tasks to manage, the comparison trials in October were scrutinised by Chambers and his team. It was a trying time for the Chief Draughtsman. He had laboured long and hard during the late 1920s to get the Royal Scots built in a very short timescale and now he was being asked to discard that work in favour of a concept that was not his. He was

highly professional and pursued the task as Stanier wished, but he must have found it difficult. This might even have contributed to the continuation of arguments and disagreements that punctuated his relationship with the CME and led to his transfer to Euston in 1935.

Although programmed for October to November 1934, the first set of comparison trials ran on until the following February and were listed as a means of 'determining the consumption, general character and relative value of coal from various pits'. This nicety of words clearly disguised another purpose. Both engines were chosen because they had a similar mileage since their last service, but the first-choice Royal Scot was substituted mid-trial by 6117 when defects in its smokebox were discovered. Even before the

Queen Maud was a popular engine among footplate crew and a loco rarely photographed in comparison to others of her class. (AE/RH)

final report appeared, word reached Stanier, via a memo from Ernest Lemon, that the gap in performance was not as great as expected. Fuel consumption and steaming were similar, across all types of coal, and pilot engines had to give support at different times to each locomotive, although 6200 only needed help when running low on coal; the others when the load was too great. Lemon added one more brief comment: 'A noticeable feature of

these trials is the number of occasions that time lost through signal checks and speed restrictions was regained by Engine No.6200.'

The Princess had performed moderately well, but the effect of the different types of coal used, from seven collieries, was more pronounced on her than on the two 'Royal Scots'. She had again displayed steaming problems because of insufficient superheating. When the report for these tests

(Number 52 in the sequence) was issued, in April, many of these problems were hidden in the text and only a broad precis of the quality of the different coals made the summary: Grimethorpe, Frickley and Barnboro' received good ratings across the board, but the rest were deemed much poorer.

There was then a three-month pause before the next trials, but by this time work on the next ten Pacifics (6203 to 6212) was well advanced and all would soon be completed; three in July, four in August, two in September and the last one in October. They incorporated many changes, as expected, to improve on the performance of the first two engines. The most obvious was to the boiler, and here work on the new turbine locomotive (6202) proved significant. A turbine needs a considerably higher steam temperature than conventional engines to operate effectively. To achieve this, a superheater was fitted to its boiler with a 32 double return element unit arranged in four rows, instead of the 16 contained in the boilers for 6200 and 6201. But before it could be fitted to 6202, which was being built alongside her ten new sisters at Crewe, 6200 needed a boiler change and received the new unit in April 1935, it being the only available spare. Her boiler was then modified to the same spec and was fitted to 6201 in November 1935. The impact on their performance was immediate and their steaming qualities improved significantly. By this convoluted route a solution to a major problem was suggested. However, it was felt that performance could be boosted in other ways and Stanier had ordered a broader rethink of boiler design.

One thing had become clear – the GWR concept of low-degree superheat did not translate well to LMS operating conditions. Long, arduous runs coupled with the lower calorific value coal used by the Company needed something more. Even though 6200 and 6201 soon had

boilers capable of achieving this, Stanier remained wedded to the GWR solution and only agreed to increase the number of flues from 16 to 24, and the boilers for the next four engines included this modification. However, due to the success of the remodelled boilers on 6200 and 6201,

he agreed that the remaining six new engines be fitted with 32-element superheaters as well.

Meanwhile Eric Langridge, at Derby, was addressing another concern about the boiler – its tube ratios seemed to be incorrect, producing an uneven performance.

6200 now well into her stride, but in need of a good clean. (AE/RH)

6209 *Princess Beatrice* nears completion at Crewe in July 1935. (LMS PR/RH)

6209, with 6203, were involved in comparative trials in late 1935 to determine the relative value of superheater elements: 24 in 6203 and 32 in 6209. 6209's front end is enclosed by a protective shield to allow engineers to monitor performance in 'safety'.
(LMS PR/RH)

By using a sloping throatplate the tube length had been reduced to 20ft 9in, but even allowing for this modification, the ratio of total surface area to the cross-section available for gas flow was too high. At the same time, the ratio of free gas area to grate area was low. Langridge looked to the design of the Fowler Pacific for a possible solution. On this proposed locomotive a combustion chamber would have been mounted in front of the firebox to create the shortest possible tube length. Langridge adapted this design and ended up with a boiler with tubes 19ft 3in long and an 18in long combustion chamber, which necessitated modifications to the rear ring of the barrel, the firebox, the grate, the frames and the cab. When the boilers were modified in this way, and the 32-element super-heaters

were installed, performance reached the levels expected from such a powerful class of engines. The new engines also looked different to 6200 and 6201 with their shorter barrels and lengthened fireboxes. Some felt this gave them a more balanced appearance.

When built, 6200 and 6201 were attached to straight-sided Midland-style tenders that held 4,000 gallons of water and 9 tons of coal. But in service these tenders proved unsuited to carry so much coal and were replaced by a new high-sided type in spring 1935. These became standard on the entire class, but they, in turn, were all replaced by tenders able to carry 10 tons of coal during 1936/37, with running experience driving this change. There were also alterations to the steam pipes that passed to the inside cylinders in the smokebox, the chimneys, the

slidebars, the mechanical lubricators and the reversing gear rod among other things.

When the locomotives emerged from the workshops they were studied closely for changes. The railway press quickly reported on the new engines, with the *Locomotive* magazine taking the lead:

'During 1935, the London, Midland and Scottish Railway expect to put into traffic a further ten 4-6-2 passenger locomotives of the "Princess Royal" class. Generally these engines are modelled on the lines of the two earlier locomotives, but certain modifications have been made as dictated by experience gained by the prototypes.

'The principal changes are in the increase in the firebox heating surfaces and, what is more noticeable, a very considerable increase in the superheater. The changes alluded to are effected in the case of the boiler by the adoption of the

forward portion of the firebox to form a combustion chamber and the increase of the superheater flues from 16 to 32. The superheater elements are of the bifurcated (split) type from single downcomers, which are provided with spherical ball joints to the superheater header.

'It is unnecessary to describe the details of the engine which are identical with the two earlier examples, but

mention should be made that the boiler feed is by a Davies and Metcalfe exhaust steam injector on the right-hand side and a live steam injector on the driver's side. Sliding trays are fitted underneath the water delivery nozzles inside the boiler to permit periodic cleaning.

'The four cylinders are each 16 ¼ in. in diameter by 28in stroke, with piston valves 8in. dia with a stroke of 7 ¼ in.

actuated by Walschaert motion. Roller bearings are applied to the motion pins of the valve gear, with the exception of the driving bearing of the outside eccentric rods, which are fitted with "Skefko" double row self-aligning radial ball bearings.

'The trailing two-wheeled Bissel trucks of five engines are fitted with roller bearings, the remaining five have

6200 at high speed, with her driver or fireman looking at something left in the wake. (LMS)

6209 back in service shortly after the trials had been completed. (AE)

plain bearings. The tenders are larger. The coal bunker has been designed so that coal will be self-trimming. On the left-hand side a cavity is arranged for the accommodation of the fire irons.'

And so on through a sea of minor details. The tone of the report, and others at the time, suggests the changes were so slight as to be unimportant, the original two engines having been great successes. In reality the problems had been greater than publicised, but had, for the most part, been kept within a small circle of managers and away from critical eyes. For a company struggling to make headway in its

locomotive-building programme, with partisan attitudes to be overcome and long-held beliefs to be changed, these Pacifics were a significant success. Although their evolution was convoluted, the end result was a worthy one, despite the variations in their form. As 1936 dawned, the LMS had a fine fleet of Pacifics to exploit.

Trials continued to prove the strength and suitability of the class. From May to December 1935 three sets of tests were completed: the first two solely with 6200, and the last involving the newly-built engines 6203 and 6209, to establish what

level of superheating was the most effective. 6203 was fitted with 24 elements, and 6209 had 32. Stanier's advocacy of low levels of superheat evidently still held sway and the trial was simply to prove which option was best for the class.

During March 1935, Chambers, Stanier's most constant and challenging sounding board, moved to Euston to be replaced by Tom Coleman. As Stanier's personal choice, following careful assessment of his work, the signs were good that this very talented designer would be a strong supporter, a worthy advisor and a very able manager. And he would still have Chambers' undoubted skills and knowledge to draw upon when needed in his new role as Personal Assistant. Coleman became the focal point for the trials and the analysis of the results.

The tests beginning in May had two objectives: to 'obtain the coal and water consumption of 6200 fitted with four rows of superheater elements, also to compare the superheat temperature obtained through Sinu-Flow elements with that of the standard elements'. The engine did a series of return trips from Euston to Glasgow, with loads varying from 252 tons up to 587 tons over different sections of track. Three trips were made with the blast-pipe cap as originally fitted, having a diameter orifice of 5 1/16in, and three trips with a cap having a 5 ½in orifice. Grimethorpe coal was used for good combustion.

Running conditions for all six tests were good and the engine

'maintained the booked times without difficulty, making up any time lost due to Permanent Way restrictions or signal checks'. The steaming qualities of the engine were enhanced by the 5 ½ inch blast-pipe cap, but the most important result was the difference in superheating achieved by the standard and Sinu-Flow elements.

Overall the standard system generated heat between 35F and 100F higher, although the average was nearer 60F, so no advantage was gained by using Sinu-Flow elements. Coal consumption averaged 40.27lbs per mile heading north and 38.2lbs per mile on the return, and no appreciable benefit seemed to have been gained from changing the

dimensions of the blast-pipe cap. Water consumption averaged 35 gallons per mile over all six runs. The report, number 56, appeared in July and did not comment on these figures or draw any conclusions. This would have been left to individuals with access to a broader range of data to consider. In a short note to Stanier, Coleman commented:

During 1935/36, 6209 became a well-photographed engine by the PR Department.
(LMS/AE)

PART 37— GIANT AMERICAN LOCOMOTIVES

RAILWAY WONDERS OF THE WORLD

7D WEEKLY

6200

'The engine performed well and seemed to take a load approaching 600 tons with ease. This bodes well for the future. The new boiler certainly makes a significant difference.'

The next set of tests, which began on 25 June and ran until 30 June, explored 6200 working an accelerated service from London to Glasgow with 500-ton loads. This was a key measure of success for the Company and now they hoped their Pacific could pull such a prestigious service at greater speed and offer real competition to the LNER. In this they were successful, as the report, number 57, recorded:

'The accelerated timings schedule a reduction in comparison with the normal of 17 minutes between Euston and Crewe, and 32 minutes between Crewe and Glasgow. It will be seen from the tables that in practically every case the scheduled accelerated sectional times were kept and, in several instances, time was gained, the engine being fully capable of working to the accelerated times.

'Particular attention might be drawn to the exceptionally fine run on the return trip between Crewe and Euston on Thursday, 27 June. In this case the train arrived at Euston 13 ½ minutes before time, and the average speed between Crewe and Euston was 70.7 mph, the maximum speed registered being 87 mph.'

Acceleration means burning fuel at a higher rate and on the Glasgow

Publicity in any form was encouraged and this 1930s series of magazines included many references to the Princess Class, including this cover painting. (RH)

run, coal consumption reached 52.6lbs per mile, 10lbs per mile greater than usual. Water consumption fell within the range usually applied to the route for an engine of this class.

The final tests, in November and December, had only one intention – to compare the effect of different configurations of superheater elements on performance. In the two newly-built 'Princesses' the lower and higher superheat camps had their champions. 6203 had a three-row, 24-superheater element, 6209 four rows and 32 elements. Some must have hoped these trials would end, once and for all, the long-running debate on this issue.

Running over the Euston to Glasgow line, 6209 completed four trips and 6203 only two, fog affecting her ability to run to any schedule. Grimethorpe coal was used throughout and a range of comparable loads were pulled over different sections of track. The engines were worked by crews from Camden, Carlisle and Polmadie.

The tests were conclusive: on each run 6209's performance was better. Her average coal consumption was 44.3lbs per mile and water 35.7 gallons per mile, whereas her sister only managed 46.4lbs and 38.1 gallons. This amounted to a saving of 4.9 per cent in coal and 5.7 per cent in water. 6209 also recorded steam chest temperatures 7 per cent higher than 6203. 6209 was also reported to have steamed better than her sister, although this can often be subjective. Stanier's reactions to the report

6203, now long established, eases northwards, with her driver or fireman enjoying the scenery and noticing the photographer ahead. (THG)

6211 enters traffic, with one of her earliest runs captured here in this classic photograph. (LMS PR/AE)

6012, with her distinctive, alternative smokebox door arrangement, pulls out of Euston in 1936.
(LMS PR/AE)

(number 59) when it appeared in early 1936 are not recorded, but it seems certain that any concerns he had about using a higher degree of superheat were calmed. The four Pacifics fitted with three-row, 24-element superheaters continued in service, but in time were modified. It is not clear if their marginally poorer performance meant they were deliberately rostered to duties of lesser importance or were not liked by the crews who operated them.

This enlarged fleet of Pacifics came into their own in 1936. With this number of locomotives, they were expected to significantly impact schedules and boost the image of the LMS. It had been a long, often difficult programme, but the result was a worthy one. The Pacific development also mirrored Stanier's gradual and measured approach to making his department more responsive to change, to think about the future, and be less concerned about the past and old allegiances.

CHAPTER 6

STANIER'S GREAT EXPERIMENT

In December 1926, Henry Guy, a leading research scientist working for Metropolitan Vickers in Manchester, presented a paper entitled *The Economic Value of Increased Steam Pressure* to the Western Branch of the Institution of Mechanical Engineers (IME) at a meeting in Bristol. He had for many years been leading the development of turbines, and the steam-pressure issue was one result of his work. In a glittering career, beginning with an apprenticeship on the Taff Vale Railway, followed by study at the University College of South Wales, he was promoted to be a Chief Engineer at Metrovicks while still in his twenties. Here he developed many groundbreaking areas of research. He was, by any standards, a man of exceptional talent, a scientist of significance and an innovator.

During 1926, he had been asked to address members of the IME by its soon-to-become President, Sir Henry Fowler, Chief Mechanical Engineer (CME) to the London, Midland and Scottish Railway (LMS), on a subject of his own choosing. Fowler felt Guy's pre-eminent role in developing advanced engineering solutions had wide appeal and so could be helpful in his own industry. He actively encouraged his colleagues to attend, as the presentation was repeated in London and several other locations around Britain. Many did, including such notable engineers as Nigel Gresley and Richard Maunsell, CME of the Southern Railway. As Chairman of the Western Branch of the Institution, William Stanier needed little encouragement to attend. In Guy he found a man after his own heart. Their professional relationship turned into friendship and led the GWR man, as he was then, into a world of scientific research and development quite unlike his own. For his part, Guy found in Stanier a man of keen intellect, whose endless sense of academic curiosity mirrored his own. This was a meeting of minds that benefited both men considerably.

In the dry tones of academia, Guy set out his thoughts on steam power and how its tractive qualities might be enhanced:

'The steam cycle itself has changed as a result of the general adoption of regenerative feed-heating by extraction of steam from the turbine at successive points in its expansion, and also in some cases by taking the steam from the turbines after partial expansion and re-superheating before returning it for the expansion to be completed. The advantage to be derived from both these operations is a function of the initial steam pressure. It is the purpose of this paper to

The Turbomotive in June 1935 at Crewe. (LMS/AE)

Henry Guy, with Stanier, the prime mover in 6202's development. (THG)

consider how far the increase of steam pressure affects the operation.

'Let us consider first the gains to be expected from the adoption of increased pressures in a simple condensing turbine installation.'

And so his presentation slowly unwound to reveal one small part of his work, which fed into a far larger area of experimentation. Guy was intrigued by the capabilities of turbines and had, with Richard Bailey, a fellow scientist at Metrovicks, sought to exploit their potential, over many years. By 1927 their work had resulted in sophisticated turbines being installed in power stations. At sea the Royal and Merchant Navies were

developing advanced steam-turbine technology to gain superiority over commercial and strategic rivals. Even in fledging aviation companies, the growth of this technology was attracting the interest of unconventional designers determined to push back the boundaries of their science. The possibilities seemed endless and, even in the more hidebound world of the railways, some engineers were taking note. And the railways had much to gain by harnessing turbine power. Experts believed it was more efficient and cost effective, could achieve substantial savings on fuel, water and maintenance of locomotives and track, and could also take steam-engine development to a new level. However, there was much to prove before the wholesale emergence of turbine locomotives became a reality.

Throughout their lives, Guy and Stanier devoured scientific journals and papers from learned societies and institutions. They saw the need to keep abreast of all technical developments, and knew that exciting innovations often resulted from this collective approach to discovery and invention. Many major advances had come about when apparently unrelated creations, sometimes spread over long periods of time, came together. But, by their nature, commercial concerns are generally risk averse. Profit and loss are often best served by taking a traditional, well-established path, and there were many failures to restrict the level of adventurous behaviour. Business

demanded certainty, not the elusive gamble of cost-escalating research and development. Yet some railway engineers did take the technology forward and experimented with new ideas. For the most part these evolved on steam locomotion, a dying science, and not new, more efficient forms of traction.

Stanier and Guy followed the development of turbines, and the efforts of engineers to adapt this technology to the railways. They read about Guiseppe Belluzzo's work in Italy and his production of an experimental engine in 1908. This was a converted 0-4-0 shunting engine that successfully kept running in the railway yards of Milan until the 1920s. Meanwhile, in Britain, Hugh Reid and D.M. Ramsey produced a condensing turbo-electric locomotive in 1910 with limited success, although further development stopped when war was declared in 1914. In the early post-war years a second turbo-electric model appeared, designed by Ramsey for Armstrong Whitworth. Testing began in 1922 and ran for a year, but once again its performance offered little promise and the engine was written off when trials ended.

Undaunted by this lack of success or acceptance, Ramsey, with James McLeod, developed a geared turbine steam locomotive for the North British Railway Company. *Challenger*, as she became known, was built in time to appear at the British Empire Exhibition at Wembley in 1924 and sat close to Nigel Gresley's latest design, the

The Beyer, Peacock and Ljungstrom experimental turbine engine under test. (RH)

Flying Scotsman. This scene provided an interesting juxtaposition of technologies -- one the product of generations of a fairly traditional science, the other leaping forward and crossing new boundaries, even though in this it proved lacking. Trials, begun in 1926, soon showed the engine's deficiencies and she was withdrawn in 1927.

Although McLeod's direct part in turbine development for locomotives came to an end with *Challenger*, his interest and influence did not. He was a close associate of both Guy and Bailey at Metrovicks, and his research influenced work in this field through them. They all agreed that projects so far had produced engines too large and inefficient to compete with traditional designs. What worked in static power stations or ships' engine rooms, where weight or space were not major considerations, did not translate easily to the highly-mobile world of steam locomotives. One significant problem revolved around the need for a condenser, a substantial and heavy piece of equipment deemed essential to successfully operate a turbine.

A condenser takes steam, after use, reconverts it to water and feeds it under high pressure back to the boiler. Water is easier to manage in this situation than steam, which is more difficult to pump under high pressure. So the condenser ensures more rapid recycling, and makes the turbine more effective and efficient. In addition, the difference between the inlet and exit of steam in the turbine is a critical measure of control. With a condenser the steam flow is fast and steady with no back flow, and this allows the turbine's RPM to be regulated.

Whereas designers in Britain were unable to make a major breakthrough in this field, the Ljungstrom Company in Sweden moved ahead. In 1926 Beyer, Peacock and Co Ltd, of Manchester, saw these advances and sought a partnership to help build a turbine locomotive. At a cost of £37,000 it was approximately five times more

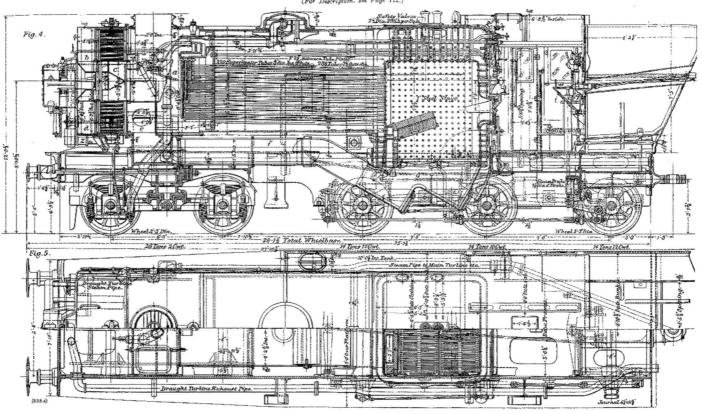

2,000-H.P. LJUNGSTRÖM TURBINE LOCOMOTIVE.

CONSTRUCTED BY MESSRS. BEYER, PEACOCK AND COMPANY, LIMITED, ENGINEERS, MANCHESTER.

(For Description, see Page 772.)

The ungainly and ultimately unsuccessful Beyer, Peacock and Ljungstrom condensing turbine locomotive. (RH)

expensive than one of Gresley's new Pacifics, so hardly represented good value for money unless it led to many orders and commercial success. From the first it struggled to make headway. Trials began in 1926 and ran until 1928, mostly on the lines between St Pancras in London to Manchester and Leeds. These prolonged tests showed that the turbo offered no appreciable advantages over existing locomotives used on these routes. It used less water, but coal consumption was greater by an average of 4 per cent. Some argued the addition of a condenser, although necessary, made the engine too heavy and so restricted its effectiveness. Either way this brave and expensive experiment underlined that turbines were best suited to more static uses. And there the matter might have rested except for Ljungstrom's desire to keep experimenting. They judged the main obstacle to development was the condenser and sought to remove this limitation by creating a non-condensing version. As the new decade approached they partnered with turbine and locomotive manufacturers Nydqist and Holm of Trollhattan to resolve the problem.

The Grangesberg-Oxelosund Railway needed freight locomotives to pull very heavy iron-ore trains, of 1,750 tons, over track from the mines of central Sweden to the Baltic coast. Inclines were long and could be as steep as 1 in 100. It was difficult work, needing engines of great power and stamina. A 2-8-0 design

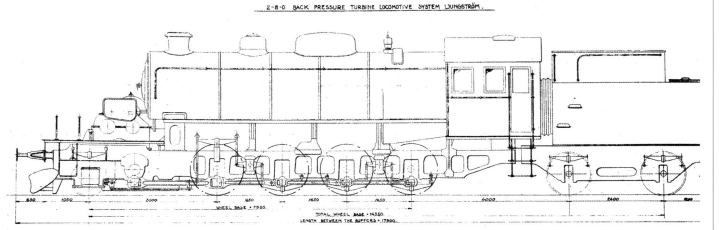

2-8-0. BACK PRESSURE TURBINE LOCOMOTIVE SYSTEM LJUNGSTRÖM.

650 · 1050 · 3000 · 1650 · 1650 · 1650 · 4000 · 2400 · R200

WHEEL BASE = 7950.

TOTAL WHEEL BASE = 14350.
LENGTH BETWEEN THE BUFFERS = 17900.

TRACTIVE EFFORT	20000 KG.	MAX. SPEED	70 KM/H.
DIAMETER OF DRIVERS	1350 m/m	OUTPUT AT RAIL	1270 HP AT 40 KM/H.
TOTAL WHEEL BASE	14350	HEATING SURFACE	149,2 m²
LENGTH BETWEEN THE BUFFERS	17900	GRATE SURFACE	3,0 "
ADHESIONS WEIGHT	72000 KG.	SUPERHEATER SURFACE	100 "
LIGHT WEIGHT OF THE LOCOMOTIVE	91500 KG.	STEAMPRESSURE	13 ATM. EFF.
WEIGHT IN WORKING ORDER	117500 "	STEAMPRESSURE BEFORE THE TURBINE	11,5 " "
WATER SUPPLY	15000 "	AFTER " "	0,3 " "
COAL SUPPLY	5000 "	STEAMTEMPERATURE	400°

Ljungstrom's successful non-condensing 2-8-0 turbine locomotive proved itself on the heavy ore trains running in Sweden. (HG/RH)

The Ljungstrom 2-8-0: continental in looks, but more traditional in shape than previous turbine-loco experiments. (HG/RH)

A dramatic interpretation of how the Turbomotive would look, a picture that Guy kept in his office at Metrovicks and which appeared in the Company's journal. (HG/RH)

had been devised and by the late 1920s a number were running. Although they managed this work fairly successfully, fuel consumption and other running costs were considered high, and an alternative design was sought. By this time, a development team, headed by Fredrik Ljungstrom himself, had produced a design for a non-condensing turbine and a working unit had been built. Static tests showed promise, but it needed to be attached to a working locomotive so its capabilities could be judged in operation. An existing 2-8-0 was then rebuilt with the new technology

married to its more conventional base. It appeared in 1932 and, when run in, proved itself in service. Remarkably, it achieved a 23.8 per cent fuel saving, proved very reliable, could pull weights up to 1,830 tons, and was liked by footplate crew and maintenance staff. It ran an average of 70,000 miles between general repairs, in comparison to the 36,000 miles of the reciprocating 2-8-0s. So successful was the first engine that two more were built and all three remained in service until the 1950s when replaced by diesel locomotives.

Guy and Bailey had been close associates of Fredrik Ljungstrom for

many years, and their great experience of turbines proved invaluable to the Swedish company when designing this non-condensing version. When word of its success reached them in late 1931 they would not have been surprised, even though the absence of a condenser, without any loss of performance, was a major step forward. Rather appealingly it looked like a conventional locomotive too, without all the oddities in shape characterising the turbine engines that had appeared so far. The absence of a condenser meant draughtsmen had more scope to

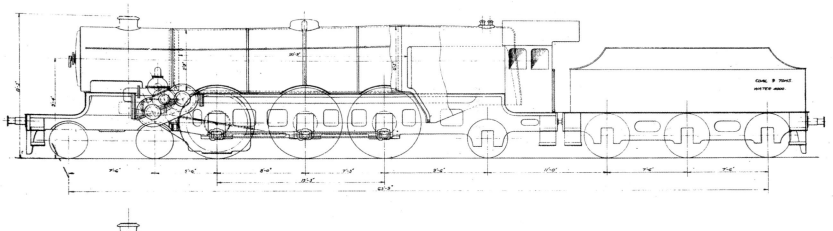

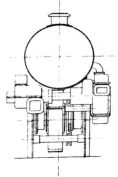

PROPOSED 2600 HP TURBINE LOCOMOTIVE SYSTEM LJUNGSTRÖM.

DIAMETER OF DRIVERS	6'-9"	GRATE AREA	45 SQF.	TRACTIVE EFFORT MAX.	20.4 MET. TONS
STEAM PRESSURE	250 LBS.	HEATING SURFACE TOTAL	2100 SQF.	MAX. SPEED	90 MILES P.H.
		WEIGHT ON. DRIVERS	68 MET. TONS		

match form and function. Freed of this restriction they could achieve a more balanced, aesthetic design that would appeal to traditionalists, as well as sell ideas and concepts.

The world of science is an international one, where specialisms can cross boundaries, allowing information to be shared. Guy read all Ljungstrom's research material, which confirmed in him the belief there was much to be exploited in this work, with other applications stretching beyond locomotive design. However, as an ex-railway apprentice, who had considered long and hard whether to make his career

in this field before moving into the bigger world of engineering, he was fascinated by its application to engine design. There was no suitable outlet to exploit within Metrovicks at that point, so any development had to be in partnership with a locomotive builder. The trouble was that experimentation was costly, and the recent experience of many railway companies made them loath to commit themselves to speculative research and development. In the late 1920s the LNER had failed with their new 4-6-4 engine, designed around a high-pressure maritime water tubed boiler, and the LMS had fared just as badly with a similar experiment. And, of course, the various turbine test engines had wasted time and resources. With industry still pulling itself out of

recession, the principle of safety first was reinforced by these failures.

It is difficult to identify when Guy and Stanier first discussed developing a British non-condensing locomotive. According to several sources they met frequently at Institution meetings during Stanier's time at Swindon and later when he became CME to the LMS. Each was a very strong advocate of the other's skills and achievements, and they clearly formed a strong bond. The strength of this can be judged by the fact that Stanier volunteered to write an obituary for Guy, for publication by the Royal Society, when he died in July 1956. Engine design and turbines were undoubtedly a common thread winding through their conversations, but such debates were theoretical while both men

When Stanier, Guy and Chambers returned from Sweden, the Chief Draughtsman produced this initial drawing for the LMS turbine locomotive based on the Princess Class. (HG/WS)

On a turn to Liverpool, one of her
regular haunts. (ET/RH)

lacked the position or backing to take ideas further. Stanier's promotion to CME, in a Company desperate to compete with a rival already far ahead, changed the dynamics of their relationship and their aspirations. In his obituary for Guy, Stanier recorded:

'I came in close contact with Guy during 1934 when he brought to my notice the work of the steam-turbine locomotives in Sweden and as a result of a visit to Sweden, and from data supplied by Guy, the LMS Railway Company decided to build a steam-turbine locomotive for which the Metropolitan-Vickers Company were responsible for the steam turbines and gear drive. The subsequent design for the power unit was a very sound engineering project and the engine worked very successfully on the main line service for the LMS Railway.'

Stanier was a modest man who invariably gave credit where it was due. He even played down his own part in many projects, allowing a team or an individual to be praised and receive a boost to their morale. He was a man with many noble instincts and wanted Guy to take credit, in death, for the turbine locomotive. However, Stanier's part in the development was pivotal and success was as much his achievement as anyone's. It was his skill that created the opportunity, drove the plans forward, achieved funding in the face of accountants playing for safety, and brought the project to fruition. The process was not a quick one, with progress largely depending on Stanier fulfilling the promise invested in him by the LMS Board and achieving

significant goals. This did not happen overnight, but by 1933 his progress was so substantial that he could use his burgeoning reputation to pursue the dream of a new age for locomotion. Such a man would not call this his 'Great Experiment', but he must have been aware that his credentials as a scientific innovator were limited. The turbine project became his nod to science and the future – a worthy goal to round off a career of great substance.

For Guy it was different; a passing idea to be explored to see if it could be cultivated and adapted for wider application. But without an industrial collaborator there was little chance of the concept being developed further. Stanier and the LMS provided this partnership, essentially one of equals, although not in terms of commercial risk. Any failure by the railway company would always gather more publicity, good and bad, with greater commercial consequences than their research and development partner, where risk-taking was a part of business life.

Before seeking Board approval for such a project, Stanier needed to gather information and reach basic decisions over costs, savings, potential and suitability. This was a joint exercise beginning in 1932 and not 1934, as Stanier suggested in Guy's obituary, and involved both Bailey and Herbert Chambers.

A key part of these deliberations centred on one question – build a completely new locomotive or adapt

6202 on duty at Euston in 1936. (LMS PR/AE)

Although suffering much downtime due to mechanical problems, 6202 was considered a good engine by the footplate crews. (AE/RH)

High speed at Hatch End. (AE)

an existing design. In this the Swedish choice (taking a standard 2-8-0 loco and modifying it) was crucial. Building on a tried and tested model could mean fewer problems in service. And in the LMS where so many new locomotives were being built, in such massive numbers, taking one and converting it had many attractions. But which one was best? The most obvious choice was to follow the Swedes and use a 2-8-0-configured engine, a new version of which was under design by the LMS in 1934. However, these only appeared in small numbers during 1935 and were quickly eaten up by heavy freight traffic demands. As an alternative the new Pacific came into focus, mainly because it was in an early stage of development, and its size created substantial amounts of space in which to fit the turbine and all of its associated equipment. Whether the publicity value of such a prestigious locomotive appearing in a new, experimental guise played a part in these deliberations is not recorded, but it would undoubtedly grab headlines.

When preparing the 1933 locomotive-building programme, Stanier included three Pacifics in his estimates. The first two appeared on schedule that year and parts were ordered for number three, although no construction work began. This caused much puzzlement and conjecture, particularly in the Drawing Office at Derby, where Chambers appears to have kept his involvement in Stanier's plans to himself. But they had both already taken a huge step towards converting the third engine into a turbine locomotive.

With Harold Hartley's full agreement and Josiah Stamp's backing, the LMS had decided to assess the value of this design, influenced in part by very persuasive arguments put forward by their CME and Henry Guy at two meetings at Euston. It was agreed that a small party should visit the Ljungstrom Works to see the work in progress. In late 1932 Stanier and Guy, plus Chambers and Bailey, sailed to Sweden and over a few days evaluated all the designs and performance reports, and rode on the engine's footplate. They were impressed and put

together a concept document and justification paper for the Boards of the LMS and Metrovicks to consider. At the same time Chambers prepared outline drawings based on the Princess design.

In a seventy-page document they set out their case, which is summarised best in three short paragraphs:

'The Ljungstrom non-condensing turbine locomotive provides a new prime mover for railways which has the promise of superior economy in fuel and maintenance together with such advantage that may arise from smoother running.

'The precise measure in which these advantages may be realised can be determined only by exhaustive trial and running experience.

'We recommend that such a trial be made by building a 2600 HP Pacific-Type locomotive and are of the opinion that to such an extensive user of locomotives as the LMS Rly such an experiment is justified.'

Approval followed swiftly, presumably because Stanier, Hartley and Stamp carried such weight, and Chambers set his team the design task. He also had to establish a good working relationship with Metrovicks, where the more complex elements of the task would be undertaken. Although the Ljungstrom turbine was a working

At speed and pulling her heavy load with apparent ease, allowing the driver or fireman a rest. (AE/RH)

6202 at Crewe during one of her many visits for repair and maintenance. (LMS/AE)

unit, it was not simply a matter of buying and installing one of their models. The concept would remain the same, but the final product had to be tailored to a completely different engine and a different purpose – hard-running, high-speed passenger services, not slow and steady freight traffic. The need to design, build and then test the turbine would determine if and when the locomotive would appear. Delivery of a successful unit would not be a quick process.

This suited the LMS because it gave their engineers time to assess the two new Pacifics just entering service. Teething problems were expected and soon revealed themselves. The hope was that the turbine locomotive, numbered 6202, would benefit from this analysis and any modifications made. And so it did. Noting the poor steaming qualities of her sisters, the draughtsmen designed a new boiler with a firebox of greater volume and a 32-element superheater. A double blast pipe and chimney were also fitted, as were Timken roller bearings to all wheels. One other significant change saw a feed water heater, in series with the exhaust steam injector, provided. This was a Metrovick recommendation, its engineers having identified the benefits of bled steam feed heating to turbine drive.

While these lessons were being learnt and the locomotive modified,

6202 was a great favourite among lineside photographers, here captured by the ever-present camera of Bishop Treacy. (ET/RB/RH)

Euston, and her safety valves shrieking.
(AE/RB/RH)

Guy and his team looked at controlling the engine. They believed 6202 should have a single turbine capable of forward and reverse movement. This was something of an innovation, because the established norm was that a single turbine was most effective working in one direction only. Guy thought a single two-way function could be built into a single unit, but was not certain how long this would take to design. Not wanting to delay the project or move away from a principle that worked to an expensive and unproven alternative, Stanier advocated two turbines. Guy and Bailey revisited this debate in the years ahead as problems befell the reverse turbine.

Gradually all of these issues were ironed out and serious building

work began in early 1935 on the production line at Crewe. Word soon spread that something special was emerging from the workshops, influenced in part by the publicity departments in Metrovicks and the LMS. The media were embraced and some railway journalists were even given an *entrée* to the locomotive as building proceeded. The *Railway Gazette* made full use of this access and produced a detailed article that was later turned into a fully-illustrated booklet. The author was effusive in his praise:

'We congratulate Mr Stanier on his latest achievement, and it is with a feeling of confidence, that we predict a measure of success which will justify the enterprising step he has taken in introducing this type of locomotive, which incidentally marks a new stage in

the locomotive history of this country by the construction of a turbine locomotive in a railway company's works.'

While around her many other new locomotives were taking shape, including ten new Pacifics, 6202 drew the attention. There was something special about her, but no great effort was made to manage expectations. With such an innovative design this could prove foolhardy, and after the near debacle of 6200's early days, when many risks were taken, a repeat seemed unnecessary. However, this time the engine was, at least, painted, and had undergone some basic tests and running in before venturing out for public scrutiny.

When in service she was based at Camden for most of her life. As she arrived there the District Locomotive Superintendent, Alfred Ewer, looked over this new, experimental engine and later recalled:

'She was a splendid looking locomotive. Very graceful lines, though these were somewhat spoilt by the cut-off casing on her right side (the casing on the other side ran the full length). Everyone who saw her – and we had many visitors from Lord Stamp to engine cleaners – was impressed. Sir William even took the opportunity of taking the Chairman on the footplate and rode up and down the yard. I well remember how animated he became in describing this new engine. His enthusiasm was infectious.

'My main job was to see the engine running successfully, to report failures or defects to Euston and make sure the crews knew what they were doing. I was surprised that a more scientific approach

On her launch the LMS PR Department worked hard to get 6202 into the public eye through national newspapers and the railway press. Journals and newspapers were happy to oblige. (LMS PR/RH)

wasn't adopted to testing. It seemed that we were supposed to treat her just like any other engine, except 6202 would always carry a fitter to make sure the turbines ran smoothly or corrected any problems. For most of the time the engine worked very well, but occasionally, and not surprisingly, the turbines played up. We could have corrected many of these problems on shed, but we lacked spares and Ernest

Lemon directed that the engine be returned to Crewe when problems appeared. 6202 lost a lot of time in service because of this.'

As 1935 drew to a close, 6202 began her working life alongside her twelve sisters. The years ahead proved very challenging, but with modifications they were performing as Stanier hoped they would and the future held great promise.

A photo used widely by the LMS for publicity purposes. (LMS/AE)

6202 always drew attention, but particularly at Euston. Here the driver is more interested in the photographer. (LMS/AE)

CHAPTER 7

EVOLUTION AND ECLIPSE

With all thirteen 'Princesses' now available, the London, Midland and Scottish Railway (LMS) could begin their revolution in high-speed passenger services and crown their efforts to modernise the Company. It had taken four long years to achieve this goal, but with so many other competing claims on workshops and designers, the length of time was hardly surprising. As the class made its appearance, William Stanier was asked to write an article for the 'in-house' *LMS Magazine* describing these engines and why they were needed. It is unclear, so many years later, whether this was an attempt at internal propaganda, to win over a less than enthusiastic workforce, or a means of raising their awareness of these exciting developments. But the fact that Stanier, who generally let others exercise their literary skills on his behalf, wrote the article is revealing. His input might have been influenced by the need to justify the change. In his draft he wrote:

'The LMS since 1927 has had a well-known class of 70 express engines which were built to work the heavy and fast trains to Scotland. The first engine of this class was called the "Royal Scot", and made history by making an extended tour in the USA and Canada.

The class, as a whole, also made history on its appearance by making the run of 300 miles from Euston to Carlisle without a stop during the summer months, and even when not engaged on non-stop working, nevertheless inaugurated and made possible the policy of extended locomotive runs on the LMS, which had not been possible with the design of engines previously available.

'Excellent as is the performance given by the "Royal Scot" class, it has, however, certain limitations. The adhesive weight available on the coupled wheels will only allow sufficient tractive effort built in to the engine to allow it to take 420 tons unaided through to Scotland.

'With an engine of this class it is difficult to arrange for a larger grate area than about 31 sq ft, and this handicaps the engine when required to make a continuous run of 300 miles. It also limits the power output of the boiler to meet the demands of the cylinders, and

Possibly engine 6206. (RH)

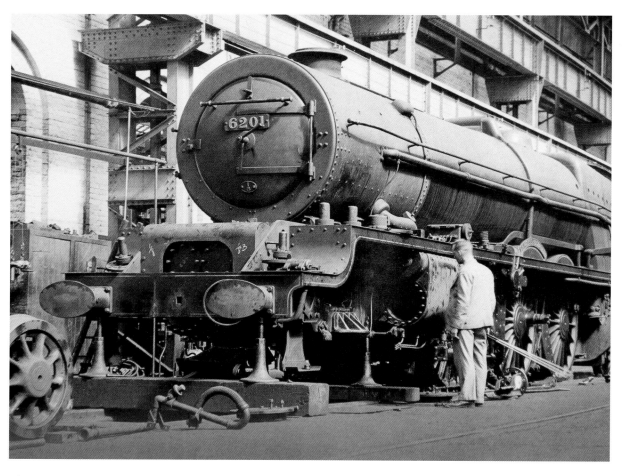

6201 at Crewe, with her outside cylinder stripped for inspection. (LMS/AE)

blow", which is affected by the number of cylinders. A two-cylinder engine is the worst in this respect. A three-cylinder engine is much better, but a four-cylinder engine is best, because, if the cranks of adjacent inside and outside cylinders are fixed at 180 degrees, and the reciprocating parts are the same weight in each case, these parts will balance themselves completely. In consequence, no additional balance weights are required in the wheels and there is no appreciable hammer blow.

'So an engine having four cylinders and no appreciable hammer blow may be permitted to have the weights on the coupled wheels increased by the amount of the hammer blow for the three-cylinder engine, without putting any additional weight on the bridge or on the track.

'It was therefore decided that the new engine should have four cylinders, and the Chief Civil Engineer agreed, in consequence that the weight on the coupled wheels could be raised to 67 ½ tons, allowing a tractive effort of 40,000lbs to be provided.

'To provide sufficient boiler power and allow longer runs to be made, it was necessary to increase the grate area and have a wide firebox carried on top of the frames behind the coupled wheels, and an additional pair of carrying wheels to take the overhang. The "Princess Royal" was thus evolved as a four-cylinder 4-6-2 engine with 45 sq ft of grate area.

'These engines are now working, and they have well justified the confidence of their designers and builders. Many new problems in design and construction were set up by the introduction of a type of engine previously unknown on the LMS, and the Drawing Office at Derby and the Works at Crewe had many

the period in which the fire can remain clean and free from the accumulations of clinker.

'Consequently, it was decided, in 1932, that something more powerful was required, and that a new design should be prepared.

'Reference has been made to the adhesive weight available on the coupled wheels, and this has a very intimate bearing on the problem. If more power is required at the drawbar, more weight has to be carried by the coupled wheels, otherwise the engine will slip.

Now the weight of 62 ½ tons on the six coupled wheels of the "Royal Scot" represented about the maximum which the Civil Engineer could allow with safety to pass over the existing bridges. How then could this be increased without going to eight coupled wheels, an undesirable arrangement for express passenger engines?

'When an engine is travelling at speed over bridges, there is, of course, the weight of the engine itself which the bridge has to withstand, but added to this is another effect known as "hammer *moments when they thought no other engine existed.*

'The duties of a CME are easy when everyone in his department is enthusiastic, and anxious to carry out and develop ideas; without this support he fails. The success of the "Princess Royals" is a measure of the loyalty of the staff of the CME Department.'

With so many projects in hand this praise had been hard-earned. Any shortcomings Stanier had perceived when taking over the post had been resolved. He had instigated change at senior level, but had not taken a wholesale approach to restructuring in his department, preferring to be selective and minimalist. And most had responded in a positive way. Opposition still existed, but this is normal, even in the best-run organisations. What had not completely steadied, though, was the relationship between the Chief Mechanical Engineer (CME) and the Running Department under Ernest Lemon. After teething problems had been ironed out and a fine fleet of new standard engines began working effectively, Lemon's team could have few grumbles, but all was not well. Alfred Ewer, District Locomotive Superintendent for Camden and Willesden, later recorded his views:

'It seems that Sir Ernest (Lemon) and some of his managers at Euston were unhappy about the way locomotive policy and design was dictated by Derby and Crewe. They felt that they should have been managing these deliberations and not Sir William, and constantly questioned what he was doing or placed

difficulties in his path. This came to a head with the Turbine locomotive, when all Sir William's requirements for testing and running were largely ignored. Footplate crew and workshop staff were happy to help, seeing, I'm sure, how good all the new engines were, but it wasn't always possible for them to do as they wished, operating under restrictions put in place by some managers at Euston. It was a tough old business and we did our best, but more was possible.'

The Great Western Railway model, which saw the CME responsible for the running side of the business as well as workshops and design, seemed to eradicate this problem. The LMS solution, which separated these functions, appeared less successful. It is difficult to say, even with the benefit of hindsight, which method was better. However, the success or failure of any organisation is largely dependent on good working relationships and a wish to co-operate, not simply which methodology is used.

The LMS struggled on both counts, despite relations between Lemon and Stanier appearing strong, but at lower levels in the management chain, friction was more apparent.

One thing is certain – Lemon was eager to prove the strength of all the new engines coming under his control, in particular he needed to exploit the 'Princesses' very quickly, for publicity purposes if nothing else. And the Company had to make a significant impact as soon as possible, the London and North Eastern Railway (LNER) having again made a giant leap forward, in

Alfred Ewer, District Locomotive Superintendent covering Willesden and Camden between 1934 and 1948. (AE)

late 1935, with the appearance of its first four new, streamlined locomotives, the 'A4s'. These engines pulled specially-built, luxurious coach formations, which the Company hoped would be the last word in speed and comfort. Their domination of the lines from London to the North would be total unless the LMS could respond, and only the 'Princesses' were capable of doing this. Inevitably the LMS Board considered how they might compete with their rivals, and discussions on 2 November 1936, at their Executive Committee meeting, focused on one of Lemon's proposals:

'Mr Lemon stated that he has been considering the matter, and was of the opinion that the LMS Company should

6201 making light of a fourteen-carriage load. (THG)

run a high-speed train. The line capacity had been examined, and a train could be scheduled to leave Euston at 4.0 pm, arriving at Glasgow at 10.0 to 10.30, performing the journey in 6 to 6 ½ hours, at an average speed of over 61 miles per hour. This would cause little interference with the evening freight express goods service to the North. The train should be streamlined and be worked by an engine of the "Princess" class, and with a load of about 250 tons, a substantial time saving could be secured over the rising gradients, thus avoiding uncomfortable speeds elsewhere.'

Lemon then suggested a high-speed run could be arranged for 16 November, which the committee agreed to. With little time left to set

up this test, some must have thought the plan was seriously flawed. However, the idea was not a last-minute affair. It dated back at least three years to the arrival of the first 'Princesses' in 1933. Two things held up development: the experimental nature of these engines and the state of the track, which in many places did not lend itself to high-speed running. It would take time and considerable investment to make sure the locomotives and the infrastructure were fit for purpose, and by late 1936 the track work was far from complete. Lemon undoubtedly remembered the risks taken with 6200 to gain publicity, when she had not been tested fully,

and did not wish to repeat that mistake, especially on an even more high-profile run. A measured approach was needed and November was the earliest date on which he felt confident enough to commit to this course of action. On 9 November he reported progress to the Executive Committee:

'Mr Lemon referred to the arrangements which he had made in connection with the trial run of a high-speed train leaving Euston at 9.50 am on Monday, the 16th November, arriving at Glasgow at 3.50 pm. The train will be drawn by a "Princess Royal" class engine and the weight limited to 202 tons; a speed of 81 miles per hour is expected to be reached in the

Lancaster District, 70 miles per hour being maintained over most of the journey, although, of course, this will be considerably reduced at certain places. He said he intends to supply the President with a "passing" schedule, and will arrange for him to be advised of progress during the trip.

'On the general question of high-speed travel, Mr Lemon said that while the aim of this Company was for a uniform speed-up of all trains with comfort, it was necessary to make one or two trips in order to judge what alterations and improvements to the stock could be made to give comfort at the speed reached.'

The tests went ahead as planned – outward on 16 November and back the following day – and with such a public event and so many witnesses the possibility of failure must have lain heavily on many minds. Several accounts describing these two days have survived and each varies according to the author's respective position, on the train and in the LMS's hierarchy. The old adage that ten people will see the same event in ten different ways could not be more true, but here there was another difference. Dictated by the need for confidentiality, so good publicity was not put at risk by unguarded words, some of the more controversial accounts remained hidden for years.

The key to the whole enterprise lay in Ernest Lemon and Robert Riddles' hands. One bore ultimate responsibility for the enterprise, and the other made it work. It was the same partnership when 6200 took part in the risky press run during August 1933, but now Riddles rode on the footplate and Lemon in a carriage. Although both were engineers of great skill, Riddles' greater knowledge of engines and extensive footplate experience made this a far more sensible solution.

The first detailed account came in a thoughtful article written by the editor of *Locomotive Magazine* in December. Descriptions from such a knowledgeable source carried added weight, and were leapt upon by railway professionals as a

6203 on a run north, with her safely valves blowing. (LMS/RH)

16 November 1936 and 6201 heads north on her record run. (LMS/AE)

meaningful assessment. Of less interest were newspaper headlines that appeared in the immediate aftermath of the two runs, although the PR department, non-technical directors and shareholders were delighted by the coverage. Even *Locomotive Magazine* found it difficult to keep excitement in check:

'A World's record for sustained high-speed performance over long distances with steam traction was achieved by the London, Midland and Scottish Railway in the course of an experimental high-speed test journey of a special train from London(Euston) to Glasgow(Central) and back on Monday and Tuesday, 16 and 17 November.

'During these trials, which were carried out to determine the potentialities of developing high-speed long-distance express services when using standard locomotives and coaching stock, a total distance of 802.8 miles was covered, with an average load of 240 tons tare, at a mean average speed of 69 mph. Apart from the World's record so involved, and the hitherto unprecedented standards of performance set over the West Coast Route to Scotland, the LMS are confident that extremely valuable technical data has been secured.

'For the purpose of the trials, an experimental schedule of six hours was laid down for the 401.4 miles from Euston to Glasgow and vice versa, non-stop in each direction and involving a booked average speed of 66.87 mph. In actual performance, notwithstanding the severe character of the gradients between Carnforth and Glasgow, the fact that a total of some 50 speed restrictions were imposed in each direction, the test train considerably improved upon this schedule.

'On the down run on Monday, 16 November, the train reached Glasgow 6 ½ minutes ahead of time in 353 minutes 38 seconds for the 401.4 miles (68.1 mph), while the return journey the following day, despite the addition of an extra coach (making a tare tonnage of 255 instead of 225) and unfavourable weather conditions, the overall time from Glasgow (Central) to Euston was 344 minutes 15 seconds. Thus on the return journey the experimental schedule was improved upon by nearly 16 minutes and the previous day's performance by over 9 minutes, the overall average speed being 70 mph. Bearing in mind the nature of the route north of Carnforth, these standards of performance are claimed to be unprecedented with steam traction.

'The locomotive employed throughout the test was No. 6201 *Princess Elizabeth*, a standard 4-6-2 (Class 7) engine built at Crewe in 1933 to the designs of Mr W.A. Stanier, CME. Except for the addition of a speed recorder, no special fittings were made to the engine for the tests; Grimethorpe coal burned throughout. This type of engine, which has a working steam pressure of 250 lbs per sq inch, is designed to be driven with a fully-opened regulator in conjunction with an early cut-off; at no stage on the trial runs did the steam pressure fall below 220 lbs, and was repeatedly at blowing-off point. The maximum cut-off used in the ascent of Shap incline was 37 %, going north, and 35 % coming south; otherwise the locomotive was worked on an average cut-off of 15-18 %.

'The engine crew comprised Driver T. J. Clark and Fireman C. Fleet, of Crewe, with Passed Fireman A. Shaw, also of Crewe, as reserve engineman on the footplate. They were accompanied by Mr R.A. Riddles, principal assistant to the CME, who rode on the footplate throughout. Accompanying the train were Messrs. E.J.H. Lemon and W.V.Wood (Vice-Presidents), W.K.Wallace (Chief Civil Engineer), S.J.Symes (Chief Stores Superintendent and acting CME), S.H.Fisher (Assistant Chief Operating Manager), D.C Urie (Superintendent of Motive Power), J.Purves (Carriage and Wagon Assistant to the CME) and other officials [Stanier was in India at the time as a member of Sir Ralph Wedgwood's Committee of Enquiry into the state of railways there, but he was well represented by Sandham Symes and Riddles].

'The outstanding features of the performance of the train were, firstly, the high average speed and the exceptionally high speeds on the rising gradients, in

The phlegmatic Driver Tom Clark and Fireman Charles Fleet stare out at the crowd gathered to greet them when arriving at Glasgow Central Station. (LMS/AE)

conjunction with relatively low downhill maxima, and, secondly, the extremely rapid acceleration from the various speed restrictions.'

The article then gave a blow-by-blow account of both journeys, with a summary of speeds, restrictions, locations and performance over each stage. Although praising this great effort, rather tellingly the main editorial did not heap more acclaim on the LMS, but focused instead on the benefits of streamlining, neatly summing up the competition between the Company and the LNER:

'Experiments with model trains in wind tunnels at the National Physical Laboratory at Teddington should enable engineers to determine the exact advantages to be expected from various forms of streamlining. With ideal streamlining, the possible reduction in air resistance is one of 75%. The corresponding fuel economy is in the neighbourhood of £1 an hour at 100 mph. Alternatively the maximum attainable speed could be increased by 12-25% according to the degree of streamlining adopted. Air resistance could be reduced by 50% without drastic departure from conventional design. The ideal streamlined train was a continuous cylindrical body with well-rounded ends, having a polished surface free from external fittings.

'Whereas the "Silver Jubilee" train of the LNER is streamlined, the record-breaking train of the LMSR on the London to Glasgow run was one of conventional appearance.'

The debate over streamlining lasted for several years and was viewed by many as a 'form over function' issue, opinion being

influenced by the contrasting aesthetic values of the traditionalist when set against more 'radical' modernist values. The debate over aesthetics tended to cloud the central issue – whether streamlining significantly improved performance. In 1936 this was far from clear, but the LNER explored the concept, and the designs of the A4 and the 2-8-2 P2 were heavily influenced by this research. It also had a PR value.

The streamliners were modern and elegant, with a look that reflected a recession-weary population's aspirations for change and improvement. They became an advertiser's dream and conveyed a populist message that the LMS felt unable to ignore. But for the moment,

they still had to absorb the lessons learnt by the two high-speed runs.

The official performance report, when it appeared in late November, made interesting reading:

'When working the up train, and after the speed restriction at Lamington Viaduct, the speed of the train was increased from 60 to 70 mph at the summit. The maximum speed reached at any point during the test was 95 mph.

'It will be noted from the summarised results that the coal consumption on the drawbar horsepower hour basis is higher than in the case of the same type of engine working the normal "Royal Scot" train. This is due to the character of the loading, as in the case of the high-speed train, with its lighter load, a great proportion of the

The note on the back of this photo states 'returning to London on 17th November 1936'. If not 17 November or 6201, then the picture at least gives a good impression of the way Clark tackled this record-breaking journey in a locomotive of immense power and endurance. (RH)

6201 fully stressed taking a steep slope during 16/17 November. (LMS/AE)

total power of the engine is absorbed by the engine. It will be noticed that the consumption in lbs of coal per mile was very similar in each case.

'The evaporation rate is lower in the case of the high-speed train and this is attributable to the combustion rate of approximately 70 lbs per square foot of grate per hour as against a combustion rate of approximately 50 lbs per square foot of grate in the normal Royal Scot train.

'From all the data obtained from this test, it would appear that a 6-hour schedule with loads comparable with those of the test trains is quite practicable, and is within the capacity,

without undue stress, on the Class 7, 4-6-2 passenger engine.'

Such positive reports as these are often selective in their content and summary. Consciously or subconsciously, some elements might be suppressed in the desire for success and acceptance. In reality, problems were exposed and the nature of these trials should be seen in a different light.

For instance, there was an easier load than normal, the whole system was geared up to allow the fastest passage for this special train, other traffic was delayed to clear a path and there were mechanical problems

that could easily have ended the tests in embarrassment. There is also the cost to the men who crewed the engine. Although a tough breed, they were sorely pressed by the effort needed to bring this train safely home, in record times, and were justly proud of this achievement, but they should not have been asked to undertake such arduous duties. The official report mentions that the locomotive worked within its design limits, but no word on the capacity of men to meet such harsh challenges.

Thirty years later Riddles recorded his memories of these

operations, revealing the truth behind these headline-making events:

'In the morning at Willesden I watched the coaling up with nine tons of hand-picked coal. No 6201 was fitted with a speedometer specially for the occasion and was gone over with the proverbial tooth-comb. Similar treatment was given to No 6200 The Princess Royal, which was being prepared as a standby engine. Calculation was made of the best possible train loading consistent with the high average speed demanded. I was to ride on the footplate and had a continuous diagram made, on two small rollers, covering the whole of the journey.

'Before leaving Willesden I had impressed on the Mechanical Inspector that he must make sure that all steam pipe joints were tight in the smokebox. Judge my consternation when at 5.15 pm he telephoned me to say that the left-hand main steam pipe joint had failed. This was a special stainless steel coned joint and was not available locally. It was too late to transfer all the special

test fittings to No 6200. I telephoned R.C. Bond, Assistant Works Superintendent Crewe, at his home, and asked him to get a spare fitting from the Works and send it to me by the driver of the 6.46 pm, which was the last that day from Crewe. Bond was just in time to hand it to the driver and I met the train at Euston at about 10 pm, rushed the joint out to Willesden, and by 2-30 am the job was done and the fire lit.

'Our arrival at Glasgow 6 ½ minutes early was a great thrill, and to my relief the Inspector, on going round the engine, pronounced everything to be in order and cold.

'Later in the day we all sat down to dinner and all seemed set for a happy celebration. Halfway through dinner I was tapped on the shoulder and told I was wanted on the telephone. A voice the other end said, "I am sorry to tell you that my examining fitter has found all the metal out of the left-hand slide block." This was an awful blow; what on earth was I to do? We were due to leave

again next day at 1.15 pm and I was told that they had not even a Scot in good order. I said, "Get the engine to St Rollox; start stripping down; I will be there as soon as I can." An hour later, having been sitting without saying a word to the by-now happy company, Lemon looked at me and said, "You look tired; you had better get to bed; a big day tomorrow."

'"Yes Sir," I said, "I would like to," and made my escape. But what a job faced me at St Rollox! We had already experienced a lot of trouble with these crossheads, and I had arranged some months before for a centre line to be

LEFT: 6201 back in London to an even bigger welcome. Once again Driver Clark surveys the scene with great interest. (LMS/AE)

RIGHT: The record run and Driver Clark's enduring status as a top-link driver meant the LMS and Hornby could not let this moment pass. They combined their efforts to publicise, with Clark, a series of adverts for the new Princess model. (LMS/AE)

LEFT: The back of the photo simply records '6201 at rest following her record run'. The right engine, but the picture gives nothing away to confirm this. (RH)

RIGHT: 6209 *Princess Beatrice* pulling a relatively light load of seven carriages. Easy work for a Princess. (AE/RH)

marked right round them to avoid taking out the piston each time. This precaution saved the day; for even with this advantage it was not till 5.30 am that we were coupled up again, and then hauled off to the shed for firing up and preparation.

'I was wondering if we would ever reach Beattock with a newly metalled slide block! But just an hour later we swept over Beattock Summit at 66 mph and, despite bad weather, went on to reach Euston 16 minutes inside the six hours, an average speed of exactly 70 mph.'

Even allowing for dramatic licence in this account, written to appear in Riddles' biography, it seems certain that the trials could have gone badly wrong. Breakdowns are always part of any mechanical process and need rapid repair to maintain a service, but placing speculative trust in one engine for two such prestigious runs, without sufficient back-up, is foolhardy.

Alfred Ewer added an interesting footnote to these accounts:

'When the engine came on shed it was in pretty poor shape and should have been returned to Crewe for repairs. As it was these were managed by the fitters locally and with some difficulty. The footplate crew were extremely tired. Tom Clark was very long in the tooth and off work for a few days afterwards. His fireman was much younger, but even he succumbed. It was common knowledge that the LNER had corridor tenders so that the crew could be changed on long-distance, non-stop runs, allowing them to rest and reduce the strain. It was hoped that we would follow suit – the West Coast being a more arduous route north – but this was not to be. There was much grumbling as the high-speed, non-stop Glasgow run became commonplace.'

For Ernest Lemon it was a triumph. He had gambled and by the skin of his teeth won, gaining much knowledge in the process. The

engines were strong enough, the footplate crew were coping and, even with many infrastructure restrictions, the fast schedule set for the run could be achieved. But before becoming a regular service, it was crucial to complete improvements to track and platforms. At the Board meeting on 26 November, Lemon received his chairman's congratulations and thanks.

Perhaps the final words describing the two days should be left to the driver, Tom Clark, a man who earned the right to speak by showing great skill and fortitude. Born in Southport, Lancashire, in 1872, he joined the London and North Western Railway in 1888 and followed the traditional route from engine cleaner, via fireman, to become a driver. He spent most of his working life at Crewe, living with his wife, Mary, and four children in Maxwell Street. By the mid-1930s he had become one of the LMS' top-link drivers and was chosen to drive the most prestigious services. So it was no surprise when he was picked, with firemen Charles Fleet and Albert Shaw, to crew 6201 on these two test runs. With only a year or so to go before retirement, he must have welcomed this opportunity to demonstrate his skills.

When the train arrived at Glasgow it was greeted with great acclaim in the presence of a number of top-hatted dignitaries. In the photographs that have survived, Clark looks at the cameraman with a weary, but phlegmatic expression, and the two firemen just look exhausted after shovelling the best part of 9 tons of coal. Their arrival back at Euston the following day caused even more excitement among a large crowd, headed by Josiah

Stamp. Great celebrations followed, and later there were presentations and a radio broadcast by the BBC. But the press, ever eager for a story, had already gathered round the engine's cab in Glasgow seeking immediate 'sound bites'. Before the return run to London the *Daily Express* had already carried a report in its morning edition, with Clark their central focus:

'Engine Driver T.J. Clarke [the "e" in his surname added by the reporter] of Crewe, brought a train from London to Glasgow in 5 hours and 53 minutes yesterday, created a new world's record, and arrived at the end of the journey a disappointed man.

'It was the world's longest and fastest non-stop steam-locomotive journey. Officials of the railway company forgot their dignity and threw their top hats in

the air when the record-breaker steamed into Central Station, Glasgow.

'Driver Clarke shook a hundred hands gravely:

'"They made me put on the brakes every time we were doing more than 90 miles an hour", he told me, "I could have kept her at 100 miles an hour for a good part of the trip and she would have done 110 with ease. I managed to hold 95.75 miles an hour for more than a mile."'

The press coverage in Glasgow undoubtedly added to the excitement and the size of the crowd on their return to London the next day. Before retiring Clark got another chance to test his skills, when, on 29 June 1937, he was chosen to drive a new, streamlined Princess Coronation Class locomotive on an even more spectacular journey. During a press

A scene typical of the late 1930s as the 'Princesses' became an accepted presence on the LMS. (AE)

Duchess of Kent pulls away from Euston. (AE/RH)

outing to publicise the new engine, he coaxed her up to a record-breaking 114mph, running down the Madeley Bank to Crewe. The LNER put paid to this with *Mallard*'s record run on 3 July 1938, but Clark had reached the pinnacle of what was possible on the West Coast route and up to his death, in 1954, he remained important in the railway world, always happy to talk about locomotives and the LMS.

For the remainder of the class, except Turbomotive, the years before war came in 1939 were full of good performances and reliable service. Now certain of these engines' success, and with an ever-expanding number of Pacifics appearing on the

LNER to push competition even further, the LMS Board authorised the building of five more 'Princesses' in 1936. Orders were let and material gathered to begin construction. While this was happening, the Drawing Office at Derby reviewed the data collected during trials and the service life of the other members of the class to see if improvement was possible. Tom Coleman also wanted to make sure the modifications to 32-element superheaters were carried through, so ending the long-running debate on this issue. But, in Stanier's absence in India, the redesign work went much further than he might have expected, as his Chief

Draughtsman confirmed in a memo written in 1937:

'Some aspects of the design failed to live up to expectation and were proving unsatisfactory in service. We have slowly resolved the superheater question, but much remained to be modified, including the frames, position of the cylinders, rocking lever arrangement and the wheelbase. To start with we simply modified the Princess Royal design for 6213 to 6217 and believed that, in due course when major maintenance was being carried out, the older engines would be rebuilt to this pattern. But the CME was quite clear in his wish for us to undertake a more thorough review and, if necessary, change the design more radically. The Princess plans we had completed were stored and we put together a new design incorporating streamlining, on which Mr Johansen advised us. The CME approved the drawings when he returned from India, without significant changes despite the major differences.'

The evolution of the Princess design took a major diversion from its original concept. Undoubtedly the new locomotives owed much to the earlier Pacifics, but it represented a major advance and owed much to Stanier's selection of Coleman to lead the design team. It also demonstrated the CME's ability to delegate when trust had been earned and his openness to new or alternative ideas. Any leader must take credit for the success of a team, because they bear responsibility for what is produced and have most to lose when taking risks. But by nature Stanier gave credit where it was due and in Coleman he had an exceptional engineer and instinctive designer, who he trusted implicitly. In return his Chief Draughtsman was his faithful and dedicated associate. The result of their efforts was the Princess Coronation Class, arguably the greatest steam locomotives built in this or any other country and a worthy successor to their older sisters.

Streamlining was then in vogue and Nigel Gresley had exploited its possibilities with three designs of express engine. Many argued the benefits were mostly gathered by the publicists eager to sell a modern, sleek design, but this is a blinkered, uneducated view of serious research work that forever underpinned so many aspects of engineering and technology. It was form, but the function became more significant as knowledge increased and sophistication of thought grew. In this country steam-locomotive designers tended to be traditionalists, seeking to improve on existing, well-understood concepts, so acceptance of these 'radical' ideas was bound to prove difficult. Not so to Gresley, a man who was happy to experiment and prepared to make a leap of the imagination. Stanier was less so, and there is little evidence to suggest he willingly grasped the concept. He was probably persuaded by his Board, eager to match the look and performance of the LNER's A4 Pacifics.

At first, it was proposed to streamline the 'Princesses', then Turbomotive. Designs were prepared, wooden models built and wind-tunnel tests undertaken at a

newly-constructed facility built at Derby. Frederick Johansen, a scientist employed by the National Physical Laboratory, where he had undertaken pioneering research on aerodynamics, advising both the LNER and LMS as a consultant in the process, took this work further when Harold Hartley recruited him for his Research Department. He and Coleman worked closely to produce many workable designs, but their efforts only resulted in the new Pacifics being built in this way, modifications to the 'Princesses' remaining on the drawing board.

For the experimental Turbomotive, the pre-war years were difficult. A busy testing regime was put in place and she drew great interest from the press, public and industry itself. Innovation, especially

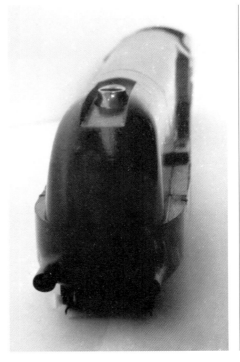

By 1935 wind-tunnel tests on locomotive designs was becoming commonplace. To demonstrate how the test models resembled the engine built, the LMS issued a series of photographs showing 6207 in both forms. (LMS)

Frederick Johansen, having been employed by the LNER to help design their streamliners, was recruited by Hartley and repeated this work for the LMS. Streamlined models of Turbomotive, the 'Princesses' and the 'Coronations' were built and tested. This photo shows how the 'Princesses' might have looked. (LMS)

The Turbomotive evolves, with extended casing and smoke deflectors being the most obvious changes. (AE/RH)

when the product is elegant, unique and offers many possibilities, draws interest, with laymen and professionals finding elements to hold their attention. Launched at Euston in June 1935, by 1936 she had become a familiar sight operating from Camden Shed. When not being trialled she was put into service on the Euston to Liverpool run, where conditions best suited the dynamics of turbine drive – continuous, steady, high-speed work. Formal testing began in April 1936, after engineers had allowed a long period to settle in and footplate crew became skilled in her operation. Inevitably there were teething problems. Oil leaked

from the turbine bearings, there was water ingress in the roller bearings and the reversing turbine failed three times in 1936. Correcting these defects kept the engine out of service for 150 days, during her first thirteen months of operations. Ernest Lemon decreed that a fitter be carried on the footplate at all times to monitor and correct any problems, making the engine's operation even more costly.

With Stanier and Henry Guy's predicted savings still fresh in their minds, Board members, particularly Hartley and Lemon, sought evidence to show the investment they had approved was showing benefits. As 1936 rolled into 1937 the signs were

not good. When operating, the engine proved very effective in terms of power and output, but final evidence of savings was elusive. Each test run during 1936, spread over three separate sets of trials, compared Turbomotive with a conventional Princess running over the same routes, but the results were inconclusive. The weather conditions each engine experienced varied considerably, so there could be no real like-for-like comparison, and the crew did not manage their engine effectively. Sufficient data was collected from these trials to suggest the turbine engine used marginally less coal than her sister engines – between 4 and 6 per cent. But Stanier knew that evidence of success was very limited and the engine had yet to justify expenditure or development, so he continued to advocate the turbine's benefits, and sought time to prove his and Guy's theories correct.

Engine testing in the 1930s was a developing art that Stanier and Gresley wished to refine and improve. They both felt that 'on the road' dynamometer trials did not bring out all elements of performance sufficiently and should be supplemented with static tests, using a rolling road, which would allow greater scientific analysis. George Churchward, on the GWR, had pioneered this concept and a facility was built at Swindon in 1905, but this was not copied by other railway companies in this country at the time. In France a large testing station had been designed by the Office d'Etudes de Matriel de

Chemin de Fer and built at Vitry-sur-Seine, opening in July 1933. This meant the two CMEs had working examples to use when trying to build a large facility in Britain that their companies could jointly use. In fact, Gresley strengthened this case by sending his newly-built P2 2-8-2 engine, *Cock of the North*, to Vitry in 1934 for evaluation, gathering significant publicity in the process. It was some years before their arguments succeeded and approval was given for a site at Rugby. Sadly, the coming of war brought the project to a standstill and it was only completed in October 1948, long after Stanier and Gresley had left the scene.

There is little doubt that Stanier would have used such a facility to test the Turbomotive and gradually iron out any faults. The benefits to his other designs would also have been great. As it was, the Company relied upon dynamometer testing only, which, by common consent, only told part of the story and suffered from the vagaries inherent in such a process. And the way trials were conducted became an issue between the CME and Ernest Lemon's department. Stanier felt the engine should only be crewed by a select few, who would then develop a thorough understanding of the technology and how to make best use of it. This was not to be: either Lemon or David Urie made it just another engine to be allocated as such. There was also the issue of maintenance. Stanier and Riddles both felt that some repairs could and should have been carried out at the running sheds.

Instead, local managers returned the engine to Crewe, even when the problems were minor.

Despite this slow progress and an ever-increasing bill, the LMS Board allowed the experiment to continue, although some sage voices suggested she should be rebuilt as a conventional Pacific. So great was Stanier's influence that these voices became a murmur and work continued with varying degrees of until war was declared. Perhaps it was a knee-jerk reaction to a crisis or, possibly, a reflection of contempt for the CME's experimental engine and past disagreements, but in September 1939 6202 was pulled out of service and placed in mothballs in the Paint Shop at Crewe for 'the duration'. It was an unwise decision since she had worked effectively

following a 147-day repair programme, and at a time when every engine would be needed. Nevertheless, she remained out of service until July 1941, when the need for motive power was so urgent that the argument for resurrecting any engine, let alone one as new and strong as 6202, became compelling.

While 6202 struggled to make headway, her twelve sisters saw their high-profile role gradually eroded by the streamliners. They still performed well and some drivers preferred them to the new Pacifics, but the expanding stable of 'Coronations' dominated the rosters. By 1939 there were twenty of them in service: five built without streamlined casing, with five more added in 1940, a further eight during

Barely a whisper of smoke as 6207 works hard. (THG)

6203, wreathed in steam, moves off. (AE/RH)

the remainder of the war and five afterwards. They had also benefited from the development work that went hand in hand with the Princess Class design and building programme, which had taken so long to reach fruition. Learning these lessons was invaluable to the new class and in Coleman, the CME had a very capable designer who took Stanier's outline and produced classic locomotives. When they appeared in 1937 they suffered fewer teething problems, were readily accepted by staff and performed well above expectations.

Even though the 'Coronations' were entering service and eclipsing all other express engines on the

LMS, they could not manage all needs by themselves and work on improving the other classes continued. During 1937, Stanier, instructed in part by his Board, instituted a study into ways of improving coal consumption. Every year expenditure on fuel equated to nearly 35 per cent of the Company's consumables budget, so any savings achieved would significantly improve profitability. The Turbomotive's development had suggested one solution, but the capital outlay needed to build a fleet of turbine engines was unlikely to be sanctioned. Introducing diesel and electric engines was another solution, but the technology was in

its infancy and cost was again a significant barrier. On these grounds alone the Company had to continue with steam locomotion for the foreseeable future.

The answer to a problem can be so obvious that it escapes attention and more complex remedies are sought instead, involving expensive modifications. Simplicity often brings about surprise results and an obvious, low-cost solution can pay substantial dividends. Although the debate on fire grate area and the level of superheating undoubtedly resulted in improved performances, greater economy was still needed. At Coleman's suggestion Stanier authorised trials with two

'Princesses', 6204 and 6210, in which the firing of each engine could be studied in detail and account taken of the variables affecting any running programme. Testing went on for some months, ending in spring 1937, but the findings were so detailed that it was not until 1938 that the report appeared. It made interesting reading:

'This report applies primarily to engines 6204 and 6210 of the 7P type, working between Crewe and Carlisle. Coal consumption is determined by two quantities – (1) the amount of coal evaporated, and (2) the efficiency of the combustion of the coal. The amount of water evaporated depends on the method of driving, weather conditions, the load and the general condition of the engine. The efficiency of combustion, which is expressed in terms of lbs of water per lbs of coal, is independent of the above factors under the conditions of the present series of tests. Nevertheless, with the same engine, this quantity has been found to vary considerably from test to test, and the opinion was formed that the variation was due to the method of firing used in normal practice. Realising this, it appeared probable that, with a suitably-devised firing technique, the efficiency of combustion could be considerably improved and maintained as constant as the boiler efficiency. In order to test this assumption, the method of firing on engine 6204 was left to the discretion of the fireman as in normal practice, but on engine 6210, some precautions were taken to avoid incomplete combustion by informing the fireman of the presence of excessive Carbon Monoxide in the smoking gas. The two methods of firing were thus rendered available for comparison.

'The results obtained on engine 6204 appear to indicate that the normal method of firing is based on false ideas of steam consumption. The rate of firing is increased on the chief gradients, Wigan to Coppull, Carnforth to Grayrigg, and Tebay to Shap Summit, presumably on the assumption that over these sections, the rate of steam consumption is greatest. The

Her number and name obscured, but a scene typical of the LMS in the last few years before war came. (AE/RH)

The coming of war brought huge challenges to the LMS. This staged PR photo, taken early in the war, featured in two publications the Company produced describing the LMS' contribution. (LMS PR/AE/RH)

value of this method of firing is reflected in the coal and water figures for both.

'The resulting figures (from both engines based on 35 different runs) are of great significance:

Average	Engine 6204	Engine 6210
Loads (Tons)	490	494
Coal Used (lbs)	7032	6166
Water evaporated (Galls)	5431	5172
lbs of water per lb of coal	7.72	8.39

'The average amount of coal used on the tests has decreased by 870 lbs from engine 6204 to engine 6210, although the average load was practically unchanged. This change is part due to a decrease in water consumption, but the average figures for lbs of water to lbs of coal show that the efficiency of combustion has also increased. It is quite fair to take this increase in lbs per water per lbs per coal as

due only to the increase in the efficiency of combustion, since a detailed analysis of both engines has shown them to be practically identical in all other respects.'

The report went into great detail to confirm these findings and all the evidence confirmed that the firing technique was more crucial to efficiency and economy than previously realised. The report concluded that this work has:

'... led to the evolution of a new and simple firing technique, which appears capable of saving 11% of coal normally used. With improved driving, it is possible that this saving might be increased to 16%.

'The relations between smokebox char, combustion and fire grate area has also been considered. It was found that the grate area of 45 sq ft is very suitable for the 7P class of engine, and reasons are stated for the suggestion that the

efficiency of combustion on the 5XP class would also be increased 6% by enlarging the grate from 29.5 to 39 sq ft.'

This research and the practical solution it recommended appealed to Stanier. It smacked of common sense, a keen understanding of processes and how to attain further efficiencies, a simple but effective solution, savings that were attainable without investment and results that could be easily verified. And for added value it touched on design with a sound engineering proposal that could improve the performance of other engines.

As the war approached, and the days of experimentation and expansion were restrained, Stanier's task was virtually complete. He had met and exceeded all the targets set for him, and you have to wonder whether he considered where he might have been if Hartley had not taken him to Euston in 1932. He would not have achieved so much, that is certain, but the influence of Churchward and the GWR clearly affected so much of what he did. But he was much more than a disciple of Swindon. People with his range of personal, management and engineering skills are few and far between. He was his own man and would have succeeded wherever life had taken him. It was the LMS' good fortune that they persuaded him to leave the West Country. It was also to the nation's benefit as the exceptional performance of all his engines and their sturdiness played such a major part in supporting the war effort. And the 'Princesses' played their part to the full.

CHAPTER 8

LIFE ON THE FOOTPLATE

In the 1930s many considered working on the railways an honour, prized for its status and security. This was despite the trying conditions for many of its employees on the footplate, in the sheds and across the many workshops. In such a heavily industrialised post-Victorian society, where poverty was still endemic, staff had few rights, and the working environment had advanced little from the stygian gloom and exploitation often portrayed by Charles Dickens. Yet employment was deemed a privilege to be earnt and those in work, no matter how terrible the conditions, felt lucky.

The world was changing. As the economic and social recession that followed the First World War slowly lifted, many workers felt limited improvements in their lives. Some employers, influenced by the commendable actions of nineteenth-century social reformers, had sought to improve the lives of their workers and families. The Cadbury family, and their Bournville development south of Birmingham, was just one model some companies tried to emulate. A secure and healthy workforce became their mantra because these factors increased and sustained production.

Some railways had followed suit, with housing around works and sheds, educational incentives for a few and limited employee rights. But working conditions remained extremely tough, which is hardly surprising when you consider the nature of the work. Heavy industry was dirty, brutal and subjected its operatives to harmful pollution. And the work was hard in the extreme and mostly deregulated, despite legislation to make employers improve conditions. There had been a number of factory acts, but by the 1930s these still had a long way to go before industry could be classed as reformed. The 1926 General Strike, and the reaction of employers, underlined the gap that still existed.

Life on the footplate of steam locomotives at this time was a microcosm of industrial society, its ills and its benefits: a secure job of great responsibility and status, and a career structure where advancement was possible and with a freedom of action few others enjoyed. On the other hand the work was demanding, dangerous and dirty, in conditions that taxed even the fittest man. Pay was poor, as was healthcare and welfare. Even allowing for these disadvantages, enginemen felt blessed and most gave their service unstintingly, no matter what the cost, for their entire working lives.

Between the wars, the London, Midland and Scottish Railway (LMS)

A steam train at night is at its most dramatic and here an unidentified Princess is caught in flashlight; blurring only heightens the drama. (LMS/AE)

An everyday scene familiar to all who worked in a busy engine shed. Two 'Princesses' are being prepared at Camden: 6209 and possibly 6203. (LMS/AE)

was no better or worse than any other railway company when managing staff and industrial safety. They operated within governance and regulation, no matter how archaic these practices now seem. So many aspects of this world have slipped from view, with most drivers or firemen being unable or unwilling to record their memories or thoughts of life on the footplate. The majority did not believe their endeavours were important anyway; it was just their job. It might have stayed this way, but for two things: an intensive PR campaign to boost reputations and sales, and the emergence of a younger generation eager to discover all they could about locomotives and their crew. These events created a wide audience and an information void that journalists and writers soon filled with books and articles.

The LMS, with its highly proactive Public Relations Department, led the way in allowing journalists onto their engines and for selected drivers to write of their deeds. Thanks to this we have a number of accounts, written by crew and their footplate visitors, to enjoy and illustrate their lives. The 'Princesses' and Turbomotive became some of the first engines to receive this extensive publicity. Through them we see some aspects of the lives of the enginemen, although the harsher aspects remain hidden and a wider presentation of the gritty realism that surrounded them has to come from our enlightened imagination.

Alfred Ewer, as a District Locomotive Superintendent, observed and managed the work of the

footplate crew. Not long before his death in 1963, in Rochford, he recalled aspects of their lives at two of the LMS's most important sheds, Camden and Willesden, in the mid-twentieth century:

'Most of the footplate crew lived within a short distance of the sheds, and many had been born and brought up in those parts of London. When they talked about their lives they often mentioned how they came to work on the railways. It was a respectable profession and offered a route away from poverty. Today we think of adverts for jobs and applications, but they, often as not, just attended the sheds, possibly encouraged by a family member or friend who worked there,

and asked for work, being taken on as cleaners of which there were many. Over time, if they were any good, they'd gradually progress up the ladder to become drivers. Labour was cheap and plentiful, and they knew that doing all that was asked of them was the only way of keeping their jobs. Were they exploited? Yes, but no more or less than any other workers at that time and by then the union movement was gaining in strength, so their rights were better understood and protected.

'Most men wanted to be drivers and worked hard to attain this goal. It was a greatly respected position, so was guarded jealously. Some drivers played on this and treated the fireman and cleaners as lesser mortals, whilst others

Cleaning and oiling were a dirty, but essential part of life in the steam world. Few mourned the passing of these grubby jobs. (RH)

How we tend to remember steam engines. A gloriously visceral and aesthetic vision. (THG)

were more appreciative of their efforts and would take a hand if things were quiet. Laurie Earl, for example, was a gentleman, and would let his fireman take the controls and shovel coal himself, giving his mate a breather, but also an opportunity to learn his trade. Another old boy was a stickler and rested solidly on his dignity, never allowing his firemen to get above themselves. Needless to say he wasn't liked, not that he seemed to care. He'd come to work each day in a clean shirt, collar and tie and neatly pressed overalls, so the others joked that he obviously treated his wife the same way as his firemen.

'Many of them had second jobs – watch repairing, working in pubs, carpentry and one even ran a tobacconist shop with his wife – which wasn't unusual in those days. Pay was never sufficient and the Company were often tardy or harsh in paying wages, and in the 1920s even had their cut pay. So second jobs became necessary to keep the "wolf from the door".

'Of all the duties available, from shunting to express trains, the Royal

Scot and the Princess Royal turns were favourites, and only went to certain, older drivers and their regular, trusted firemen.

'When they came into service, the big Pacifics quickly became the centre of attention. Not surprising really when the LNER had been grabbing the headlines for many years with theirs. All the drivers knew of the good work [Nigel] Gresley's locomotives were putting in and so welcomed the Princesses. But with only two, initially, competition was great, and all sorts of tricks pulled to get on the footplate and drive them. Strangely enough there were some who hated them from the start and much preferred the 4-6-0s, complaining bitterly about their performance if rostered to a Pacific. The turbine locomotive never suffered in this way. By 1935, when she appeared, the 4-6-2s were better understood so Turbomotive became a much sought after turn. It also helped that she was an experimental engine, so the opportunity to drive her was greatly valued, even when she experienced problems.'

From the first the 'Princesses' attracted attention and the PR

Department, with William Stanier and Ernest Lemon's agreement, allowed the press access. In July 1934 *Meccano Magazine* ran an article, written by 'A Railway Engineer', which described life in the cab of 6200 under the title *Impressions of a South-Bound Trip:*

'The regular daily duty of the two LMSR 4-6-2 locomotives, that of hauling the "The Royal Scot" express throughout between London and Glasgow, is without doubt the hardest continuous run that has yet been attempted in this country. These remarkable engines are doing the job with the greatest ease, however, as the trip described here shows.

'Coming south from Scotland recently, I was privileged to ride on the footplate of No 6200 for nearly the whole distance, and a finer performance it would be hard to imagine. It was at Symington, where the Glasgow and Edinburgh portions are combined, that I joined the train. The Edinburgh part arrived, in charge of a Caledonian 4-4-0 of the Pickersgill type. Not so many years

A typical view from the fireman's side of the cab in 6200. One hopes the cameraman has his arm stretched out and is not that far outside the cab. (LMS/AE)

ago this type were hauling the principal expresses on the Caledonian, and yet what small engines they seem now!

'A few minutes later came "The Princess Royal" with the Glasgow portion, and I joined Driver W. Harrison and Fireman David Hill on the footplate. The cab is beautifully laid out. When the engine was being designed, a wooden model was made and all the various fittings tried out beforehand so as to get the very best arrangement. In common with the practice of the old L&NW and Caledonian Railways, the engine is driven from the left-hand side, so I was given the right-hand seat in the cab, from which there is a splendid look out ahead, in spite of the gigantic boiler and firebox.

'By now the Edinburgh portion was coupled on in rear and our total load was one of 15 coaches, 465 tons empty, and 500 tons with passengers and luggage. On the stroke of time, 1055 am, we got the "right-way", and the great engine was soon into her stride. Two miles from the start the driver had "notched up" to such a degree that steam was being cut off in the cylinders as early as 15% of the stroke. In full forward gear these engines cut off at 75%, so that she was being run very easily indeed.

'Speed rose rapidly. At Lamington Viaduct, four miles from the start, we were doing nearly 62 mph. Now came the assent to Beattock. On this steady rise past Abington and Crawford, where the gradient is 1 in 240, some really marvellous climbing was done. With the regulator open, and only 20% cut off, the engine sustained 55 mph. She was developing 2,650 hp, and yet it was done so easily that I could hardly hear the exhaust even from the footplate. There was absolutely no sense of effort in spite of the work being done.

'By now, amidst the wildest mountains and moorland scenery, we were approaching Beattock Summit. The last 2 ½ miles are really steep, at 1 in 99; yet still going on at 20% cut off we came over the summit at 36 mph. The whole assent of 13 ½ miles from Lamington had been climbed at an average speed of 52 ½ mph, and we passed the Summit, 17 ¼ miles from the start, in exactly 21 minutes – a minute already ahead.

'The remaining 49 ¾ miles down to Carlisle were run under very easy steam. The highest speed reached was 70 mph, and in spite of a check for permanent-way repairs through Ecclefechan, we arrived half a minute early, having run the 67 miles from Symington in 70 ½ minutes.

'At Carlisle, drivers and firemen are changed, and on this occasion the Glasgow men were relieved by Driver Laurie Earl and Fireman J. Lubnow of Camden Shed. In the five minutes that we stood at Carlisle a great crowd gathered on the platform end to watch "The Princess Royal" start away. The engine was indeed the object of deep interest all along the route. Railwaymen of all grades paused in their duties to watch her pass, and we were "snapped" at a dozen different places by enthusiastic amateur photographers.

'Now we set off on what is the longest non-stop run in the world, made all the year round, from Carlisle to Euston, 299 ¼ miles. The booked time of 334 minutes demands an average speed of nearly 54 mph. Hard climbing begins at once, and continues almost without a break to Shap Summit, 915 feet above sea level. Once the train was well on the move, the cut off was brought back to 25%, and remained so unchanged right up to Shap. Starting steeply with nearly 5 miles at 1 in 131, the gradients gradually become easier until there is a welcome "breathing space", a level stretch of nearly three miles past Penrith. Here we go up to no less than 65 mph.

'As we swept round the S curve, through Penrith and over Eamont Junction, there was just time for a delightful glimpse of the mountains grouped round the head of Ullswater, and then we came on to the worst part of

More publicity and an unforgettable photograph of *Princess Louise* by the PR Department. (LMS/AE)

6211 powers past, but the few witnesses to this drama are looking in the other direction. (AE/RH)

6208's crew focusing on something ahead while picking up water at Whitmore Troughs. (AE/RH)

Laurie Earl, small in height, but huge in stature as a driver of Stanier's Pacifics. (LE/RH)

the assent. From the Lowther Viaduct there are nearly nine miles, continuously, up at 1 in 125, and on this length speed fell to a minimum of 30 mph, a notable figure under such easy working conditions. We had taken 28 ¼ minutes to pass Penrith, 17 ¾ miles from Carlisle, and we passed Shap Summit, 31 ½ miles, in a shade under 49 minutes – exactly on time.

'No exceptionally high speeds were run on the long descent to Carnforth. Most of the way we were running at about 70 mph, and the absolute maximum was 74 mph. At this speed it is remarkable how smoothly the engine rode. There was no vibration, and even when passing round the numerous reverse curves that abound on this part of the route, there was only the merest suggestion of a roll. One is always accustomed to a certain amount of bumping and hard riding on the footplate, but this engine rode almost as smoothly and as comfortably as a carriage.

'A bad slack to 28 mph for permanent way repairs just below Milnthorpe caused some loss of time, but Carnforth, 63 miles, was passed in 81 ¼ minutes, and we got through Lancaster, 69 miles, in 87 ¾ minutes. Then after mounting the steep mile at 1 in 98 beyond the last-named station at a minimum of 40 mph, there came a magnificent speed exhibition on the level stretch to Preston. With the regulator full open and on 20% cut off, the engine worked up to a sustained 73 ½ mph. The horse power being developed was nearly 3000, and yet the impression on the footplate was one of effortless ease. It was perhaps the most striking part of the journey.

'Approaching Preston we sighted signals at danger, but we were not seriously delayed, and passed that station, 90 miles from Carlisle, in 109 ¼ minutes.

'Up the steep rise out of the Ribble Valley, 25 % cut off was used at first, but at Euxton Junction, Earl went back to 20 again. This easy working took us up the three miles to Coppull Summit, where the gradient averages 1 in 125, at the fine minimum speed of 43 mph. Adverse signals checked us again on the descent to Wigan, but the engine recovered very quickly to make a lively sprint at 72 past the Vulcan Foundry Works at Newton-le-Willows. A careful slowing through Warrington followed, and then, up the gently-rising grades across the Cheshire Plain, a steady average of a mile a minute was maintained.

'By now we were approaching Crewe and nearly halfway to London. Earl eased up well before reaching the station, and we all took the opportunity of some "half time" refreshment. With speed reduced to 25 mph, we passed Crewe. Up to now our average speed was 50 ½ mph, but the worst part of the run was over. On the remainder of the journey we had to average nearly 57 mph, but we were well on time and the engine was going splendidly. In readiness for Madeley Bank, cut off was advanced to 25%, and the engine went up in great style. On the 1 in 177 gradient we steadily maintained 44 mph, but listening to her quiet purposeful beat, I was conscious not so much of the great

power being developed, but of the vastly greater power in reserve. What might she have done if given 30 or 35 %?

'At the top of the bank, back was brought the cut off to 20%, and so it remained for the rest of the journey. We kept a fine average through the Midlands, covering the 75 ½ miles from Crewe to Rugby in 80 ½ minutes, inclusive of the usual severe slowing round the curve at Stafford, and a slack to 40 through the colliery district at Polesworth. The highest speed on this section was 74 mph at Hademore Water Troughs.

'The engine had now been hard at work for over six hours and running non-stop for the last four hours; and yet, after Rugby, came the longest stretch of sustained high-speed running on the whole journey. The 73 miles from Welton to South Hampstead were covered in 65 ½ minutes, an average of 67 mph. On this flying stretch, speed rose twice to 77 ½ mph, and the minimum rate on the

six-mile climb at 1 in 333 over the Chilterns was 48 mph at Tring.

'We came triumphantly through Willesden Junction five minutes early, and stopped in Euston 4 ½ minutes early at 329 ¾ minutes from Carlisle. It was a fitting end to a magnificent run. Delays cost a total of 7 ½ minutes, so that the net time was only 322 ¼ minutes – nearly 12 minutes less than the schedule. The net average speed was 55.7 mph, whilst for 262 miles, from Shap Summit to South Hampstead, the average was 60 mph

'At the journey's end the engine was in first-rate order with all bearings beautifully cool. A word of congratulations to the enginemen, for throughout this long run she was driven and fired in most excellent fashion.

'It was altogether a most impressive demonstration of the capabilities of Mr Stanier's great engine. If she could make a superb run like this under such easy

A rather unkempt 46205 Princess Victoria with her crew closely studying something that is now long forgotten. (RH)

A driver's lot. An open road, glorious view, engine (possibly 6203) working well within its capacity and Shap Summit ahead. (RH)

working conditions, the question naturally arises as to what electrifying feats she might perform if really "opened out"! An indication of the possibilities in this direction was given recently by the performance of the engine on the "Liverpool Flyer", when, with a load of 380 tons, an average speed of 68 mph was maintained between Crewe and Willesden, a distance of 152.7, as recorded in the May MM.'

The schoolboy delight in being allowed on the footplate is so clear and makes the account sparkle with a barely-concealed juvenile excitement. This exhilaration also affected the 'Top Link' drivers and firemen, who were allowed to drive these powerful, elegant engines and, each day, test their mettle and their skills. Not for them the conditioned restrictions and oversight imposed by office or workshop life, but the open road and a high degree of freedom. This made up for the hard graft involved in being locomen,

although 'A Railway Engineer' barely describes these aspects of their lives. In many other accounts these elements are suggested, but remain in the background.

The working conditions on a locomotive were very trying. There were extremes of temperature, noise and movement, excessive dirt and dust, heavy chemical and biological pollution, hard labour for the fireman and little or no safety equipment to make the engine or its operation safer. The cab was a dangerous, uncomfortable place. Add to this a high level of personal responsibility few others would experience in their working lives and the constant threat of disciplinary action or the sack, even for minor misdemeanours. This was only part of the story, because their work did not begin or end when the locomotives picked up or dropped their loads. While shed staff cleaned and performed basic preparations, the engines were brought to full readiness by the driver and fireman.

Clocking on before dawn, having confirmed their rostered duties the day before, they collected the tools of their trade and worked hard for a few hours to get their engine ready for duty. The fire was brought up 'to scratch', the engine checked and oiled outside and underneath, more often than not, coal in the tender needed to be topped up and shovelled to make it safe, and then the water tank filled. Troughs built into the track existed, with water collected through a scoop, but most drivers liked to leave the shed with a full load, especially on the high-speed, long-distance runs. Finally, and after a great deal of effort, the engine was ready to transit from the shed to a station or yard to collect its load. At the end of the day the process was repeated before they gave up their mount to shed staff again.

In this tough, uncompromising, dirty world they existed and throughout it all they hoped their health would hold up, because being unable to work often meant no pay.

Not the usual rolling stock for high-speed passenger work. 6203 is pulling the Royal train instead.

46204 arrives at Euston and attracts barely a glance from her passengers. (RH)

Illness and incapacity were rife. Chest complaints, including emphysema, were common, as was tuberculosis, although poor living conditions probably also played a part here. They also spent their days surrounded by carcinogenic products that caused different types of cancer to form and spread, helped, no doubt, by heavy smoking. Skin complaints such as seborrheic and contact dermatitis affected many, brought on by constantly handling coal and oils of different types. Muscle and back problems were caused by the sheer physical effort imposed by life on the footplate. It was an arduous and trying life, without the benefit of good pay or a welfare system to support them. Then there were accidents, minor and major, to contend with. Steam locomotive operation, and the railways generally, were inherently unsafe working environments. There was little or no automation and the whole system relied, for the most part, on labour-controlled, manual systems to maintain safety; this, of course, came with the ever-present risk of human failure. It took many years and many accidents before the railways fully embraced emerging technology. As Stanier knew, only the Great Western Railway (GWR), of the 'Big Four', had made progress in improving safety systems, under George Churchward's guiding hand. For the most part, the footplate crew and signalmen still bore the brunt of responsibility for safety over the entire network, unaided by technology, and hugely reliant on individual skill and fitness.

The 'benefits' enjoyed by footplate crew came at a heavy price to their health and in the level of personal responsibility they took on, mostly without support. You can only admire their fortitude and great skills. Their generation might have grumbled among themselves, when having 'a blow with a wad and a wet', but in their recollections they invariably made light of the daily difficulties. Small wonder that when given the chance to drive a wonderful new engine, such as a Princess, they enjoyed the status such work could bring. George Bushell, in his book *LMS Locoman*, later recalled firing one of these

The moment footplate crew looked forward to – their engine ready to pick up her load and then off. (RH)

engines when based at Willesden, during the war, when operating conditions had been badly affected by the conflict:

'In July I was called on the Sunday evening for the 9.30 to Glasgow. This time my mate was Jack Williams, a Willesden driver well known for his dry humour. One of his comments which amused me concerned some buffer stops he had demolished – accidentally of course – and was due to go on the "carpet" to explain why. When I said, "I suppose it was in the blackout?" Jack said, "No, any idiot can do it in the dark. It takes a good bloke to do it in broad daylight!"

'At Camden we found 6206 Princess Marie Louise, one of the original Princess 4-6-2s, waiting for us. Several of the Camden men pulled a face, and generally gave the impression that it was a bad steamer and we were in for a bad trip. It was well known that most of the Camden firemen used to fire too heavily, but I stuck to my usual tactics, confident that if I could succeed with a Garratt with a light fire hauling 1400 tons of

46204 Princess Marie Louise leaves Rugby Station with the *Mid-Day Scot*, her driver adopting a classic pose – firmly in his seat, arm resting on the window ledge. (RH)

Laurie Earl apparently driving and an LMS publicity shot to grace his book *Speeding North with the Royal Scot.* (LMS PR/LE)

coal, I could manage this one in the same way on 15 coaches weighing say 450 tons. With a medium fire, I found 6206 responded very well to my methods, and I can still remember the way the Pacific seemed to stroll along in the late evening sunlight on the straight section from Harrow onwards with the track flying under our wheels. The whole trip was a pleasure; I fired regularly, most times nine shovels full each round and I couldn't understand why Camden men should be so diffident about this engine. We were relieved smartly on arrival and had booked off by 1.15 at Crewe North Shed. What a contrast between this quick 3 ½ hour trip and some of the long wearisome hauls with much heavier goods trains – bad coal, indifferent engines and sometimes a succession of delays over the same distance.'

When lay people or professional railwaymen recall the LMS and its footplate crew, a few names always come to the fore. Tom Clark, for his

stirring deeds with 'Princesses' and 'Coronations'; Bill Starvis, who, for a short time, became a household name when, on 5 September 1957, he probably recorded the fastest-ever

run between Carlisle and Euston, and several others. But it is Laurence (Laurie) Alfred Earl of Camden who most remember. Born in 1882, in a house on Mile End Road, he went from cleaner to fireman in traditional style, before becoming a driver as he later recalled in a letter:

'I started work on the railways in 1901. Not that I drove engines then. A great deal of climbing up the ladder of promotion has to be accomplished before a man is allowed to take charge of a locomotive. Like everyone else who aspires to be an engine driver, I started as a cleaner. Was I thrilled? I was indeed. You see, ever since I was a boy I had made up my mind to be an engine driver. In those days I lived in East London, and as I watched the trains go by I said to myself, "One day you will drive a railway engine." My boyish ambition has been realised, and what is more, my trains are bigger and faster

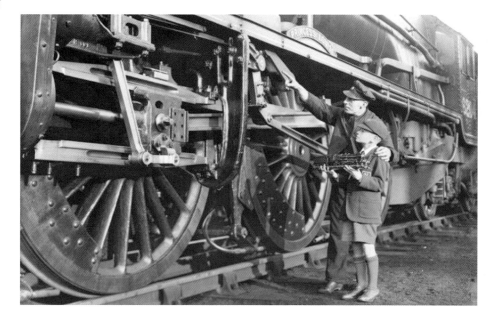

More publicity with the full participation of the driver and a small boy, and Hornby. (LMS/AE)

and better in every way than those I gazed at so eagerly as a youngster.

'It was a fine, bright morning in summer that I presented myself at the Camden Depot, and I told the gentleman in charge that I would like to enter the service of the railway company. I was half afraid of being rejected, because I am not quite as tall as the average person and I had a silly idea that the officials would reject me on that account.

'I spent three years as an engine cleaner, before being promoted to fireman. As the title implies he cleans engines. He goes over the whole of the exterior, including the wheels and the tender, and he cleans all moving parts inside. He also acts as a "call boy", which means he has to call the enginemen who have to be on duty very early in the morning, and those who are wanted for extra trains or to take the places of men taken ill. In addition to this we also had to clean the hostels where drivers and firemen stayed when away from home. We scrubbed sheets, blankets and floors. When we finished we would sweep out the locomotive sheds and perhaps lend a hand elsewhere if necessary.

'Promotion to fireman (in 1904) was quicker than it is today, because the engines were smaller and bigger in number, and it often happened that two locomotives were required to haul a train. It then took me 11 years to become a driver. This was probably earlier than normal because the war was drawing so many men into the Army, making the recruitment of locomen difficult at a time when the locomotives had much more to do.

'At first I drove goods trains and local passenger services, and my experiences on these were mostly repetitions of my early firing days, except that I now stood on the left-hand side of the engine footplate, which is the driver's position. But in 1924 I obtained what I really wanted. This was main-line expresses. Somehow or other I soon managed to create a few records. Rugby is 82 ½ miles from Euston; I have covered that distance in 75 minutes.

LEFT: Tom Clark and his fireman gathering more publicity for the LMS as they pose before their record run to Glasgow on 16 November 1936. (LMS PR/AE)

RIGHT: A pause to look around as the track drops away down a slope, allowing the crew a brief respite. (RH)

LEFT: Although basic, the facilties provided for locomotive crew and other workers at the big sheds did offer the warmth of friendship, and a place to enjoy a "wad and a wet". (LMS PR/AE)

RIGHT: Ernest Lemon lifts his glass to congratulate Tom Clark on his record run - Euston 17th November 1936. (LMS PR/AE)

Then, with the "Mancunian", which is one of the best known Manchester expresses, I have reached London from Polesworth in 92 minutes, a distance of 106 miles. With the "Royal Scots" I have been able to maintain a speed of 84 mph for 18 miles, and 77 mph for 48 miles.' In railway circles Earl became a celebrity, helped, in part, by his easy-going manner, his toughness, his great skill with engines of any size, his eternal optimism and his sense of fun. All the photographs that have survived capture the spirit of this ebullient and determined man. He enjoyed this attention and was encouraged by the Publicity Department to write a book, which appeared in 1939, entitled *Speeding North with the Royal Scot – A day in the life of a locomotive man*, with H.N. Greenleaf as co-author. The book's structure and tone is that of a travel brochure, and you can feel the influence of the Company, ever eager to exploit any opportunity to sell its services. But behind that you can see and experience his true feelings about life as a driver.

Such was his impact that he became friends with racing-car driver Mike Couper, who achieved fame in the 1930s racing Bentleys and Talbots at Brooklands. He was fascinated by speed and was invited to ride on the footplate of the *Royal Scot*, where he met Earl. He, in turn, was invited by Couper to join him at Brooklands to race at high speed around the high-banked circuit. This was followed by flights in the open cockpit of biplanes. Despite being offered a flying suit, he wore his driver's uniform and cap instead.

It is hard to ignore such a man. His reminiscences tell us so much about the men who rode on the footplate and served their company so well, no matter how difficult their duties and the personal cost. Earl saw everything around him with a poet's eye:

'I glance down the list until I see the time of my own train. Against it is written 6206. So we are having the Princess Marie Louise today. Well it will give us a good run. We cross the tracks to the pit where 6206 is waiting. Faint wisps of smoke are floating away from its chimney, and the powerful body glistens in the morning sunshine. The cleaners have been busy, but other men besides them have been at work on it, for the fire is roaring away and the engine is making that gentle sizzling sound which indicates a good head of steam. It takes six hours to get up steam on one of these big locomotives, so it was in the early hours of the morning that a man kindled the fire in 6206.

'Without loss of time my fireman and I "prepare" the engine for the day's run. First, I call at the Store and obtain oil. With this I lubricate all the exposed moving parts. Whilst I am doing this the

fireman obtains his shovel, the tools we may want on the journey, a case containing detonators and flags (for use in emergency), a hand lamp, a bucket and some sponge cloths. He also gets oils and fills the lamps which form the head-code in front of the engine; sees that the smoke-box door is screwed up tightly; and makes sure there are proper quantities of coal and water in the tender, and sand in the sand-boxes. After this he gives his attention to building up the fire. Over a ton of coal will be ablaze when we pull out of Euston with our train, so he has to get busy with his shovel.

'All this preparation takes time. I use 20 pints of oil, applying it judiciously through my long-necked can at 67 different points. After I have satisfied myself that all are full, I take a final look round to see that everything is in order, then climb up on the footplate to await the signal to "set back" into Euston.

There then follows a vivid description of the journey north, with many references to places of interest. It is virtually a travel guide, presumably inserted by the Company for publicity purposes, although no less valuable for that because it is a world that has changed significantly. Behind these scenes you still have Earl's undoubted pleasure in what he was doing. Many passages capture this so clearly and illuminate the lives of all footplate crew, who had the skill and desire to drive a Princess close to its limits:

'An express is coming up the line. It is past us. Colour-light signals again. Another station: Welton. I sound the whistle twice to remind the signalman that we are not stopping at Rugby, the next station. A black gap ahead. Kilsby Tunnel. I sound the whistle and Tom

opens the blower as we rush inside. The tunnel is 1 mile 666 yards long, and our path is pierced by rays of daylight that penetrate through two shafts which were built at the time the tunnel was constructed. I sound the whistle half-way

through, and again at the exit, when Tom closes the blower and rests awhile.

'I have my right hand on the brake handle now, for in a few minutes I shall have to apply the brake. We have entered Warwickshire and are approaching

46209 at speed passing through Lichfield Trent Valley with the *Mid-Day Scot.* (THG)

A typical day for a Princess Elizabeth crew (46201). (THG)

Rugby; this is a busy junction and we must not pass through the Station at more than 45 miles per hour. Tom has again operated the spray-pipe apparatus which has watered the coal in the tender, and is looking through his window, intent, like myself, on the signals.

'As we dash through Atherstone, Tom has for the moment finished his coal-breaking activities and is getting another well-earned breather on his side of the cab. Volumes of smoke ahead again; another express coming up. The number *of this engine too I see as it goes by. It is 6208,* Princess Helena Victoria. *With our* Princess Marie Louise *going in the opposite direction, it is a case of sister meeting sister. Another station. I sound the whistle. We flash through at 80 miles per hour. Tom is again firing.*

'Colour-light signals inform us our road is clear.'

Until his death, at home in Poplar in 1963, Earl remained a magnet for those interested in footplate life and the LMS. To the end he patiently recalled these exciting days for young and old alike, attending many meetings and answering many letters. His memories did not fade or become apocryphal in any way, and his biography still captures an optimistic view of life on the footplate. There was a darker side, but such a resourceful, resilient generation as theirs were loath to dwell on the dangers and the discomfort.

TO THE END OF STEAM

War, when it came in 1939, radically changed life in Britain. The obligation to fight irrevocably undid much that had been achieved by all the hard work and sacrifice underpinning the slow recovery from the last conflict. In 1914 war had been welcomed and celebrated by many, although this turned to horror when the realities of trench life and horrendous casualty figures hit home. 1939 was different. No longer was there a naive rush to battle because, for a number of years, there had been a growing understanding of what might lie ahead. There had been explicit warnings, conveyed through a stream of news reports, enhanced by disturbing images flashed across cinema screens, to reflect what was happening in Nazi Germany and in the states it was conquering. Most felt that Britain would be the next to succumb to bombing, then invasion, and the possibilities of survival seemed grim, especially after France fell and the British Army was forced into evacuation at Dunkirk. However, the harshness of life throughout the twentieth century had bred tough and resilient generations, whose efforts, when harnessed to profound injustice, created a daunting opponent for any aggressor. This spirit was captured by Rudyard Kipling in his poem '*The Beginnings*':

> '*It was not preached to the crowd,*
> *It was not taught by the state,*
> *No man spoke it aloud,*
> *When the English began to hate.*'

Dawning awareness was not a bad thing. It had, belatedly, brought reality to political leaders, and allowed rearmament and strategic preparation to go ahead before war was declared. The population would again fight and sacrifice, and industry would inevitably carry a heavy burden if war production were to keep pace with demand. Inescapably, many peacetime activities would be restricted or curtailed, nowhere more apparent than on the railways, where engineering strength existed and could be exploited. Add to this their power to transport vast quantities of war material and keep passengers, both military and civilian, moving in ever-increasing numbers. The changeover happened quickly, driven by the rapid deterioration of Britain's situation as retreat and loss became commonplace. It started

46212 just after nationalisation of the railways, resplendent in lined-black livery and carrying interim British Rail (BR) insignia. (RH)

46208 just out of the works, freshly painted in BR blue. (RH)

with the mass evacuation of civilians from cities, and rapidly moved on to troop movements and then support to industry.

For the London, Midland and Scottish Railway (LMS), thanks mainly to its ambitious development policy and massive locomotive building programme, the position was critical, but not impossible. Even so there were 'knee jerk reactions' in their transition to war, which spoke of lack of thought and clarity. Turbomotive was mothballed, a decision presumably justified by her experimental state, followed by a proposal to take all the Princess and Coronation Pacifics out of service as well. Someone must have thought them a peacetime luxury with no place in war, overlooking the fact

they were immensely powerful engines capable of pulling any loads, not just prestigious fast express services. Wiser minds prevailed and they did not share the Turbomotive's ignominious fate, instead serving effectively throughout the war in the most extreme conditions, with only minimal levels of care and maintenance.

Ultimately the Pacifics, although strong, were race horses in comparison to the bulk of the engines and probably suffered more than the others from wartime austerity – poorer-quality coal, lower standards of maintenance and lack of attention. Alfred Ewer, who remained the LMS' District Locomotive Superintendent throughout the war, recalled in a

letter written in 1953 how war affected the engines and crew under his control:

'All the locomotives were harshly treated during the war. There just was not the time or manpower to do more than just keep them running. We lost a lot of men to the Armed Forces, so a great deal fell on the shoulders of the older men and though they did sterling service the effort cost them dear, and made it difficult to keep the engines running effectively. They also had to cope with ever-increasing loads and the deprivations caused by war – bombing, longer shifts, less food and casualties.

'The Pacifics certainly earnt their keep, but the Princesses probably suffered more than the others because there were known weaknesses in their design, and they responded less well to the quality of coal available and reduced maintenance. They were prone to breakdowns, but were often kept running when, in normal circumstances, a trip to the Works was necessary. As the war progressed the condition of all the engines became so dilapidated that, at times, it bordered on the dangerous. There was no respite, though, and they remained in service because we couldn't do without them, so "patch them up and mark them duty", as the American expression went, became our byword too.

'I remember on one occasion 6207 had difficulties braking and could not bring its load to a halt safely even from moderate speeds, let alone something faster. More often than not, the train it was pulling would end up over-running the platform, and at Euston braking had to commence far earlier than usual to ensure it stopped at the buffers. The

crew knew this and adapted to the
reduced braking capacity, but were
greatly relieved when the engine was
finally withdrawn for attention. But
6207 was not alone in being kept in
service when it may have been unwise to
do so. It says a lot for these engines that
many crew still preferred them in this
poor condition to the other types we
operated, even when alternatives were
just out of the shops. They were strong
and capable of pulling huge loads,
whether it be freight or 20-coach
passenger trains.'

The 'Princesses' each ran an
average of 62,000 miles per year
during the war, and their younger
sisters clocked 76,000 miles and the
'Royal Scots' 71,000. Time lost to
maintenance for all three classes was
in the region of fifty weekdays per
engine per year. Of the three,
William Stanier's first Pacifics,
although running a substantial
number of miles, were significantly
less effective than the others. It is
only one measure of success, but
revealing nevertheless. The reasons
for the difference are difficult to
fathom so long after the event, but
Ewer probably touched on one cause
when suggesting some degree of
fragility caused by design
weaknesses. The frames and
cylinders were too often mentioned,
and the different levels of superheat
generated by the mixture of 24 or 32
elements seems to have played no
part in availability or mileage
achieved.

The war took a heavy toll on all
the rolling stock and the railway's
infrastructure, not only the
'Princesses', but also the men who

crewed the locomotives. Like the rest
of the population, they could not
escape the conflict's worst excesses
at work or at home. The rate of
attrition allowed little respite and
weariness increased exponentially.
George Bushell, who served
throughout the war with the LMS in
London, vividly captured the
disruption and violence faced by
railway workers when enemy action
was at its height, and the draining
effect this had:

'... the previous night's raid had
rendered Harlesden Station useless and
cut the Euston electric line. To keep
things going, we were running shuttle
passenger trains from Queen's Park
steam platform to Wembley steam
platforms. On one up run, we were
stopped at Willesden No 6 Signal Box.

At this stage of the night's raid the
adjacent factory estate in Park Royal
seemed to be one mass of fires. Nothing
moved anywhere; it was obvious that the
signalmen had abandoned their post.
Now and then our engine would
literally bounce on its springs as a bomb
whistled down and exploded somewhere
in our area.

'Towards the end of that September, a
land mine was lobbed down somewhere
in our area, luckily not exploding.
Everybody was turned out of their
homes whilst it was dealt with. My
fellow railway lodgers and I were given
permission to use the enginemen's
hostel, but the next day our little
community joined up again and shared a
room over a local shop where we all slept
fully dressed, expecting the worst. One
night I counted over 20 bombs that came

Again Eric Treacy
captures a classic
moment in a typical
steam day – sisters
pass by. (ET/RH)

The Turbomotive, soon to depart the scene and undergo conversion. (RO)

down around us, each generating the feeling that it was specifically aimed at the room we were in.

'With all the dislocation of traffic, hours on duty increased; one week 73 hours, another week 81 hours.'

Even when direct enemy action lessened, as the Nazis looked eastwards to the Soviet Union, the corrosive effects of war still mounted. To help with an ever-increasing workload, even engines destined for the scrapyard were recommissioned and pressed into service. Among them the Turbomotive reappeared in 1941, any argument about her fragility swept to one side. She had struggled to run consistently and effectively in

peacetime, and now, under more austere, wartime conditions, her weaknesses were quickly exposed. Within a month of reactivation her reverse turbine failed and she remained out of service until summer 1942, possibly due to a lack of spare parts and higher priorities at Metrovicks, where workshop time was fully committed to war tasks. Apart from a month of downtime to correct oil leaks from both turbines, she remained active until July 1943 when her coupled wheels locked without warning while shunting at Camden. A subsequent investigation at Crewe found the problem originated in the flexible drive between the slow-speed gear wheel

and the driving axle. A major repair was necessary, but as the forward turbine had not been opened for inspection since 1939 it was decided to give the engine a heavy general repair. The extent of the work kept 6202 out of service for nearly fourteen months and by war's end she experienced two more, fairly brief, periods under repair. Despite long periods in store or in the Works, between 1 July 1939 and May 1945, she still completed about 100,000 miles of service in those crucial years. A total nowhere near her sisters, but creditable nonetheless.

Inevitably, when the war ended and the railway companies assessed their assets, they were presented with a sorry picture. Britain had removed dictatorships, but it came at a heavy cost. The population was exhausted by the effort, a great deal of property had been destroyed, industry and the railways had been worked almost to the point of collapse, and the country was virtually bankrupt. Recovery and rebuilding took decades to complete, and while it did, Britain's infrastructure did not get the investment it needed to rebuild effectively or modernise. This was nowhere more apparent than on the railways, where survival was founded on the worn-down products of pre-war years. Even nationalisation in 1948, under the new Labour Government, failed to increase capital spending to an appropriate level.

Yet although most locomotives were in a sorry state, the strength of their design, particularly on the

LMS, was such that simply reinstating an effective maintenance regime and normal operating routines achieved significant improvements to the service. Wholesale redevelopment and modernisation had to wait. In the meantime steam power held sway, with restoration of their glamourous pre-war high-speed express services giving one sign that things were returning to normal. And the 'Princesses' and 'Coronations' were at the forefront of this programme, each type still capable of attracting great interest in an austere, post-war Britain.

Nationalisation changed many aspects of life on the railways, but it did so without the pre-war 'giants' who had dominated its development: Stanier and Nigel Gresley. The LMS man had retired in 1944, and his great and respected rival had died in 1941, just short of his 65th birthday. Their successors now had to work in an industry undergoing rapid change where old allegiances and old competitions had to be cast aside if possible. The freedom each Chief Mechanical Engineer (CME) had enjoyed and exploited for the good of their directors and shareholders no longer existed. Now they operated in a more unified environment, scrutinised by Parliament and their new owners, the public. After such a traumatic war, the returning servicemen and women demanded much more, emboldened by their sacrifices in another conflict. The railways had a significant part to

46210 on her regular run to Liverpool. (RH/THG)

The Princess Class had a perennial problem with the forward part of their frames. Movement allowed the outside cylinders to work loose. Eventually the front sections of the frames were cut away and replaced with strengthened units. These two photos show the work in progress at Crewe. (IE/THG)

play in recovery but also in meeting their customers' greater expectations.

Before this could begin in earnest, the locomotives, rolling stock and the railway's infrastructure had to be brought to an acceptable level, within the confines of affordability. By 1946 all railway workshops had abandoned their war work, releasing huge capacity to begin these essential tasks. With demobilisation rapidly disgorging men back into civilian life, the workforce was reinvigorated, although often the machine tools they returned to were as tired as the locomotives they hoped to restore to pre-war standards. Wherever you looked there were challenges.

When the 'Princesses' came to be surveyed, post-war before overhaul could begin, their condition was as poor as any other class. They had been kept running, but the law of diminishing returns meant that when the time came for major maintenance, the amount of work needed was excessive. Added to this was sorting out any perceived design

faults that hard service had revealed. Although Stanier had departed, Tom Coleman was still in post at Derby and oversaw this work, beginning with a careful assessment of their condition before recommending any extra tasks. He recalled the thought that went into this process:

'I remember pulling out all the drawings prepared in anticipation of five more, modified Princesses being built in 1936/37, before we went a step further and they became the first Coronations. I thought the time might be right to consider rebuilding the first 12 to this form and include elements from the later Pacifics in the design, for good measure. 6202, although proving that turbines could work, was not going to lead to more of the type being constructed, so rebuilding seemed unavoidable when the cost of keeping her going became too expensive. Nothing could be done whilst we were at war, but later when the workshops had more capacity, it became a possibility. Discussions followed, with the new CME, Henry Ivatt, but did not get very far because funds were strictly limited. All that would be approved were

heavy general repairs and some modifications to correct problems with the frames and cylinders, particularly. In some cases this was a continuation of work already started and would continue, on and off, for a number of years. 6202 would be tackled when a major problem arose with its turbines. This was not expected to be long in coming, based on past performance.'

Coleman was correct about a running programme of modifications, which was common practice in most manufacturing industries. With the 'Princesses' this focused on issues including the extension of the 32-element superheater philosophy to all the class, ending a long-running debate with a single solution. Work to convert the engines fitted with 24-element units to the higher spec began in 1943, but was not completed until 1952. Frame and motion plate flexing was also a long-running problem. It was thought this had contributed to distortion of fixing holes leading to slackening between the frames and outside cylinders, creating unsafe levels of movement as well as overheating of crossheads and fractures in the exhaust passages from the inside cylinders. Various solutions had been tried over the years: frame stay flanges were stiffened, steel gussets and extra plate stays added and cast steel inside-cylinder blocks fitted with varying degrees of success. But as the problems continued, the damaged front portion of the frames on all the engines were removed and replaced with new pre-shaped units, with shear strips welded to the frames to inhibit cylinder movement. This modification work began in 1951 and continued until 1956.

Despite Coleman's wish to undertake more modification work, the idea remained suspended until the class might need major rebuilding as needs changed or their condition deteriorated. Even without this work the engines performed well, but never reached the levels attained by the 'Coronations'. However, these proposals were eventually considered when the turbine units in 6202 were deemed beyond economic repair and conversion to a reciprocating engine was the only real solution, other than scrapping.

Through the 1940s into the 1950s the class still worked over the main express routes, but were now all based in northern sheds, although a few did find themselves back at Camden or Willesden towards the end of their working lives. Annual mileages were not excessive, with the average being about 50,000, although there were years when

46202 reappears at Crewe in August 1952, rebuilt as a reciprocating engine – part Princess and part Coronation.
(BR LM/RH)

individual totals went much higher: 75,729, 76,408 and 72,008 being three noteworthy examples. During the war, the 'Coronations' and 'Royal Scots' exceeded their regional partners' average annual mileage by nearly 14,000 and 9,000 miles respectively, and this gap increased in the years that followed. What was for a Princess an exceptionally heavy year, was more the norm for the later Pacifics, even the 'Royal Scots'. However, the early Pacifics' mileage did compare favourably to the main express locomotives in the other

regions: a lower average than the 'A4s', but better than the Southern's Merchant Navy Class, and the Western Region's 'Kings' and 'Castles'. In reality, the 'Coronations', and even the 'Scots', were a hard act to follow and, if they had been based in other regions, the 'Princesses' would have appeared well up or ahead of the competition.

With state ownership came a national renumbering scheme, and '4' was added to LMS designations. Although the appearance of unity was a clear aim, each of the old

46202 ready to depart. After seventeen years without a name she was finally christened *Princess Anne*, a title she only held for a short time. (BR LM/RB)

companies largely went their own way despite the best efforts of Robert Riddles, who had become the new Railway Executive's Member for Mechanical and Electrical Engineering, to rein them in. The changeover led to many leaving the service, including Coleman, in late 1949. It was a great loss because his work was so crucial to engine development on the LMS, particularly with the two Pacifics. He felt it was the right time to leave, doubting whether a nationalised future would provide a comparable challenge to his time with Stanier. Part of his department had already disappeared under a new head, and he saw only a future of reduced authority and tight bureaucracy stifling creativity. As Stanier was a disciple of George Churchward, so Riddles was of Stanier. He continued the inherited mantra of standardisation with British Rail (BR). So the future held promise, with much that Stanier and Coleman espoused continuing in a new form.

While these changes were taking place, the Turbomotive's future again came into focus, with concerns over the state of her turbines and the cost of replacement. There was little doubt the development programme would stop with 46202 and so she became something of an anachronism in a world embracing more reciprocating steam locomotives, diesels and electric motive power. Scrapping or rebuilding seemed the only options and this choice awaited only a cause, which came during 1950 when the engine was dismantled and surveyed at Crewe, with the turbines going to Metrovicks for assessment. The broad consensus was that the basic engine was sound, and the turbines were in decent condition. However, when asked by BR how much it would cost to replace or rebuild the turbine units, the Manchester company could not give an estimate. They felt the units might run on for some years so could not accurately predict the likely replacement costs. BR translated this reticence as meaning the cost would be high and, probably, uneconomic in comparison to rebuilding the engine to conventional form. From the existing documents, this decision was more a matter of politics than economic necessity. Someone felt the time was right to end the experiment, even though in its last year of service it performed as well or better than her twelve sisters.

The decision to rebuild was taken and planning her conversion began, using Coleman's pre-war plans for the next five 'Princesses' that were not built. She kept her 6'6" coupled wheels, but her main frames were modified with a Coronation Class front end. The inside cylinders were made of cast steel, the outside ones cast iron, with motion also drawn from the Coronation design. Progress was slow, with the Drawing Office at Derby struggling to produce plans when fully loaded with design work for the new classes of standard locomotives. Finally, by Easter 1952, planning was complete, allowing rebuilding work to begin at Crewe. On 13 August that year she was rolled out, painted in BR green, and named *Princess Anne*.

Two days later 46202 entered service running her usual route between London and Liverpool. Sadly, the engine did not have long to prove herself before being heavily damaged during the rail disaster at Harrow and Wealdstone Station on 8 October, which killed 112 people and injured many more. Although suffering a great deal of damage, many thought her repairable, but, after months of debate and conjecture she was finally written off and scrapped, anything reusable having been removed. So ended Stanier's worthwhile 'great experiment'. If the pre-First World War trials with turbine drive had been more successful or a non-condensing version had appeared much earlier, who is to say how far this concept might have been developed. It remains an intriguing possibility that the Turbomotive would have become one of many engines of this type operating around Great Britain. But she arrived too late and never truly became more than an interesting sideshow, supported and cultivated by two men of singular talents: Stanier and Henry Guy.

The crash at Harrow was not a solitary incident in post-war Britain. Whether the dilapidated state of the railways, lack of investment or simply human error were to blame is

46202 broken down into her constituent parts ready for transfer to Crewe where her fate will be decided. (BR LM/RR)

The scene at Weedon immediately after the crash and when 46207 was being righted, then slowly removed for assessment and repair. (BR LM)

unclear even now. The London Midland Region suffered more disasters than most as BR made sense of the myriad problems it inherited. If the carnage then seen was replicated today, the outcry would have led to public enquiries, heads rolling and privatised companies being stripped of their franchises. Perhaps, in the aftermath of two bloody wars, people had become inured to death and destruction.

In the four years between 1948 and 1952, Princess Class locomotives alone were involved in three fatal accidents. Harrow was the worst, but this was preceded by disasters at Winsford and Weedon.

17 April 1948

On a fine, clear, moonlit night, engine No.6207, *Princess Arthur of Connaught*, was pulling the 5.40pm express from Glasgow to Euston, when it was brought to a shuddering halt near Winsford Junction when the communication cord was pulled by a young soldier on board. It was thought he committed this foolhardy act because he was close to home

and believed the train would not stop at Winsford to let him off. He disappeared without trace shortly afterwards, so it was impossible to verify this story. His action, although criminal, was not held to be liable for what happened next.

Shortly after the express left Glasgow it was followed by the 6.25pm postal train to London, pulled by 6251 *City of Nottingham*. Normally it overtook the 5.40pm train near Lancaster, but was running late and 6207 was given precedence; now it was stopped in a dangerous and vulnerable position. It was imperative that warnings be set and any following traffic halted, while the cause of the emergency stop was found and corrected. The parcels express was only seventeen or so minutes behind, so these actions had to be carried out quickly. Even allowing for such a short time all should have been well, except a local signalman made a fatal

mistake, as the official report by Lieutenant Colonel G.R.S. Wilson made clear:

'… the collision resulted from the signalman at Winsford Station clearing the block instrument although he had not seen the train pass the box and subsequently accepted the Postal train. This train thus entered the occupied section under clear signals at Winsford Junction (1 ½ miles north of Winsford Station), but the driver braked when he saw a red light displayed by the guard of the passenger train about 400 yards in rear of it; detonators were also exploded, and the speed had been reduced to 40-45 mph when the collision took place.

'The impact demolished the rear coach of the passenger train and half of the coach ahead, and there was severe telescoping between the second, third and fourth vans of the postal train. There was a fairly full load of passengers in the former train, and I regret to report that 16 were killed and 8 subsequently died of their injuries in hospital; all were in the last two coaches. Fourteen passengers and four of the Post Office staff were detained in hospital. Serious damage to the engine of the postal train was confined to the front end, and the driver and fireman were uninjured.'

The concertina effect of crushing coaches protected the bulk of the train and its passengers from serious injuries, although 6207 was shunted some yards forward, even with its brakes on. Later that day its crew, Driver T.D. Jones and Fireman J.E. Pryce, took the loco, under its own power, to Crewe for detailed assessment. Nothing undue was found and she quickly returned to service. *City of Nottingham* appeared

46207 at Crewe awaiting repair. (BR LM)

badly damaged, but, when surveyed, was remarkably intact and back in service by late May.

21 September 1951

6207 was again the unlucky engine in 1951 when pulling the 8.20am express from Liverpool Lime Street to Euston. In conditions described as 'fine and dry though not particularly warm', a fault in the engine's wheels caused a derailment at Weedon, fourteen miles south of Rugby, with appalling consequences. Written in the dry tones of an official report, Wilson found it difficult to hide the obvious horror:

'The Up express-passenger train from Liverpool to Euston, comprising 15 bogie coaches hauled by a Pacific engine,

'Engine cold' waiting her next turn of duty. (RH)

was travelling at 60-65 mph on the leaving transition of a left-handed curve of about 50 chains radius, when the leading bogie wheels were derailed to the right. The derailment was not noticed by the enginemen at this stage and the train continued forward at a speed for more than ¾ mile on the straight without serious damage to the flat bottom track. No more wheels were derailed until the train reached the bull-head rails just beyond the short Stowe Hill Tunnel, when the leading bogie wheels began to smash the chairs and break up the track, with the result that the whole of the

train left the rails except for the last two vehicles.

'The engine went down the 12ft embankment to the left, and fell on its left-hand side, on soft ground. The wreckage of the coaches at the front of the train was severe, and I regret to state that seven passengers and one of the dining-car staff were killed outright and seven passengers died subsequently in hospital. In addition, 26 passengers, the engine driver, and nine members of the dining-car staff were admitted to hospital. The driver (Driver Tomlin, aged 52, from Camden Shed), who was

on the left-hand side of the footplate, had a fortunate escape from serious injury when he was buried in coal from the tender as the engine overturned: the fireman (A.S. Wallis, also from Camden Shed) clung to the right-hand side of the cab and was unhurt.

'At the time of the derailment, engine no 46207 had run 980,537 miles since it was put into service in 1935, and 139,395 since the last general repair in May 1949. It had run 81,405 since the tyres had last been turned to restore their profile at a "Heavy Intermediate" repair in May 1950 and 39,985 miles since all

the axle boxes were refitted in March 1951. On the 19 June 1951, the engine was stopped for piston and valve examination, and at the same time was lifted for renewal of the rear-truck bearing pads. The weight distribution was adjusted before it went into traffic again on 28 June. On 23 July the spring of the right-hand middle coupled wheel was found broken and was changed.

'At the routine examination a few days before the accident, it was found that the left leading bogie-wheel flange was wearing sharp, and the bogie axles (together with the axle boxes) were changed over, front to rear and vice versa, when the engine was stopped at Edge Hill Shed for the periodical "X" examination on 19 and 20 September. The train in question was the first which the engine had worked since the bogie axles were changed round, and subsequent examination, after stripping in Crewe Workshops, disclosed that the leading bogie axle boxes were too tight in the horn guides. As will be seen later this was the cause of the accident.

'There cannot be any suggestion that the Pacific-type engines of the former London and Midland Scottish Railway are, by their design of their wheel base and vertical lateral springing, unduly sensitive to inequalities in the track. They have been employed regularly on the fastest express trains since their introduction 17 years ago with no suspicions of this kind and, indeed, have a particularly good reputation for steadiness of running.'

It took more than a month for 46207 to be lifted from the bottom of the 14-foot embankment, down which she had rolled, and was only achieved when a wooden ramp was built for her to be rotated onto. A

Princess Elizabeth looking pristine despite staff shortages among engine cleaners. (RH)

46210's crew take a rest. (RH)

detailed evaluation of her condition was conducted at Crewe before repair work started, but in a little under three months after the crash she returned to traffic.

As the LMS Pacifics thundered up and down the West Coast Main Line, the debate about future motive power needs reached a critical point. Although BR had sanctioned a massive building programme of new, standard-class steam engines in the years following the war, many now argued this was a poor decision. Across the Western world steam locomotion was rapidly disappearing, replaced by diesel or electric engines, making BR's policy seem an anachronism. But things were changing rapidly. The Southern Region policy of electrification was advancing steadily and new classes of diesels appeared across all regions capable of matching steam's performance, once their teething problems receded. The changeover took many years to complete, but the technology was there, as was the will to invest, and so steam's death knell had been sounded. Its disappearance was now a matter of time, not debate.

In 1955 BR published its long-awaited Modernisation Plan, a key element of which was the electrification of the West Coast route. It was projected to take fifteen years to complete and involve huge capital investment. Maintaining a good service while the work was carried out was a primary consideration. It seemed likely that steam might be a stop gap until building was complete and gradually be phased out as

each stage opened. Accountants argued this policy might justify the massive building costs of the post-war steam locomotive programme and achieve value for money from this 'misplaced' investment. But if this happened there would be a problem of combining incompatible railway technologies – steam, smoke and other pollutants are not good bed fellows to overhead catenary and electric-power systems. Luckily diesel locomotives were coming on stream in sufficient quantities to give another alternative. It became a matter of

phasing – in and out – with steam clearly becoming obsolete.

The change was not simply a matter of technology. Steam locomotives were demanding beasts: of time in cleaning, running and maintaining; and absorbing large amounts of manpower and resources in comparison to other forms of motive power. In pre-war years, labour was cheap and a workforce was still largely beholden to an employer. Conditions of service were basic and favoured capital rather than labour, and poverty and lack of educational opportunities, for most,

An interesting comparison of three of Stanier's classic locomotives at Carlisle Station in 1960: a Princess, a Jubilee (*Warspite*) and a Coronation. (BR LM/RH)

46204 pulling the *Merseyside Express* near Rugby in 1958. Not yet 25-years-old, with a lot of life left in her, but soon to be cut up and scrapped. (RH)

produced a poorly schooled work pool happy to have any job.

This was nowhere more apparent than on the railways, where hard, uncompromising industrial processes dominated life and health. The end of the war brought greater democracy and greater aspiration into focus. Expectation grew and with it a desire for more education and better living standards. The railways, which were once employers of choice, were drifting on a downward spiral and BR, trying to reverse this trend, sought to improve conditions and terms of

employment, all the time pursued by unions growing in strength and opposition. Modernisation had to provide a significantly better working environment, not just improved trains and services, and for many this meant the grimy, labour-intensive world of steam engines no longer had a place. It was a view shared by those who travelled by train too.

There was also competition from the roads. In the 1930s, cars and lorries had started taking trade away from the railways, but the highways were a long way short of providing

an effective network, and for most people railways still dominated their lives, both socially and for work. The 1950s saw the beginning of the boom in road vehicles that has grown ever since. As incomes rose, roads improved and industry grew, so cars became a dream accessible to many, offering greater freedom and choice. The railways rapidly reduced in popularity and trade fell away.

Wherever they looked, BR managers and politicians saw decline and competition advancing rapidly, so modernisation was essential. The removal of steam locomotion and all it stood for became central to success, no matter if its elimination played badly on balance sheets. It was a policy underpinning Dr Beeching's study of the railway and the massive changes he recommended in the early 1960s.

On the West Coast routes the transformation began in 1960 with electrification of the Crewe to Manchester line. This was followed two years later by the Crewe to Liverpool section, then Crewe to London in 1965 and London to Birmingham in 1967. Complete electrification was not concluded until 1974, by which time steam engines were a distant memory. The cull began in the late 1950s and was all over by 1968, across the whole network. But in these last few years this aged technology performed effectively despite lack of interest and reduced maintenance. It was a decline well captured in photographs taken by lineside enthusiasts eager to record this passing age before it disappeared. Even though the engines mostly looked dirty and unkempt, they still drew the eye, none more so than Stanier's Pacifics. Up to the end they remained the epitome of power and elegance, easily surpassing anything that replaced them – diesel or electric.

By the late 1950s, all the old drivers who had worked 'Princesses' were long gone. They were replaced by a new generation brought up in a different world, although still remembering the stirring stories of their forebears' deeds. No longer was there the same level of national press attention, and their equally heroic efforts largely went unnoticed by all except a small band of devotees. The realm of steam shrank, slowly but irreversibly, footplate crew either retiring or being

An everyday scene, possibly at Polmadie Shed, in the 1950s or early 1960s, soon to be consigned to history. (RH)

46201 is turned ready for another duty.

retrained as drivers of the new engines. Few recorded their memories of these times and those who did, did so with sadness, marked with a sense of relief as they exchanged the hard life associated with steam to the less strenuous, cleaner and more efficient life on the footplate of diesel and electric motive power. George Dowler, who had survived the Harrow crash while fireman on 46202, described these last few years in a letter written in 1976:

'You asked me to describe those last few years at Edge Hill. It was certainly a difficult time. In days gone by, lads were happy to work as cleaners or apprentices and hoped they would become drivers or fitters later. Now they wanted other

things and found jobs in factories where the money was better especially on piece-time rates. Who can blame them? Most had been brought up in the war when everything had been rationed, and they'd had to live with all the bombing and hardships, so expected all the things they saw on TV to make up for it. But this left the railways short of men, and the old engines soon became tatty and poorly maintained. Even the few Lizzies and "Big Uns" we had suffered in the same way, though the drivers and firemen often took to cleaning the engines themselves.

'When I became a fireman during the war, the shortage of men meant that youngsters like me got to fire the big engines quite early, and worked with very old drivers who remembered working for the old LNW and the LMS

in its early days. Sitting in the canteen, they'd often talk about those days and chatted about the different engines. Some preferred the "Scots", but most thought the Pacifics much better, with the Lizzies fancied over the Coronations. When I came to fire and drive them I tended to agree. In the late 40s I read Laurie Earl's article in a trains annual called "Engines I Have Driven". I don't need it anymore and my copy comes with this letter. I was taken by his comments on the Princesses, with which I wholeheartedly agree.'

In the year he retired Laurie Earl wrote:

'Another time, when George Jack was firing for me on Pacific No 6212, Duchess of Kent, with a 466-ton train on the 11.45 pm Glasgow sleeper, he never

TO THE END OF STEAM • 167

needed to touch the fire from just beyond Lichfield into Crewe, a distance of 40 miles. Given good coal, there are few modern engines that will not run economically, provided that the firemen use their brains, and take an interest in what they are doing.

'One night, when I had No 6209, Princess Beatrice, and a 300-ton train, it was to be my last Liverpool trip for some time, and I wanted to celebrate the occasion. So I husbanded the steam in the boiler until we could let fly up the rise from Bletchley to Tring. My mate Tuffrey thought his watch had stopped when we passed Tring, because it showed something like 9 minutes from Bletchley. When we got to Euston, our guard, Robinson, a big six footer, came up to the engine. "Hullo, Robbie" I said, "How are you feeling? And what did you make the time from Bletchley to Tring?" Looking at me in an old-fashioned way, he said, "Why, nine minutes and I don't want any more of it either. I had to take my teeth out, you were shaking us up so much." Probably nine minutes was a bit on the fast side, but we certainly didn't take more than ten, and even that is 90 miles an hour for the whole of 15 uphill miles.

'One run on the "Royal Scot" I well remember was on a day when Mr Cecil J. Allen was on board, and I wanted to show him what could be done with one of the original "Princesses". Personally I have always thought we were better off with the 6 feet 6 inch drivers of these engines than with the 6 feet 9 inches of the later engines (the Coronations). This was No 6206, Princess Marie Louise, and we had 16 on,492 tons all told. It was after we had been held up by a bad permanent-way slowing at

Berkhamsted that I was able to get going. From Tring to Hillmorton, just outside Rugby, we averaged 77.2 miles an hour for very little short of 50 miles. Even up to Kilsby Tunnel we went at 70 an hour and we were twice up to 85 an hour with this big train. Later in the same trip we got our 492 tons up from Tebay to Shap Summit in 3 seconds under 8 minutes – not bad going for just over 5 ½ miles and most of it a 1 in 75 uphill grind. My fireman on this trip was G. Abey, and we were never short of steam anywhere.'

George Dowler provided a short postscript in a letter:

'My favourite Lizzie was 46211, Queen Maud, which came back to Edgehill towards the end of the 1950s and stayed with us until early '61, when she was taken into store at Carnforth, as no longer required. I'd fired and driven her many times over the years. She was, as far as I was concerned, the best of the class. She always steamed well and

never had any vices. All the engines were different, with a mixture of good and bad habits, but Maud was best all round. She also had a good turn of speed, and towards the end the drivers occasionally took liberties and pushed their engines as far as possible. I don't think it always made for the best journey for passengers, but we knew what was coming and wanted to see the old girls out in a bit of style. We had some fast stretches, and on one occasion we pushed 46211 to a 100 miles per hour and may have gone faster. I'm sure someone must have beaten the record set by Tom Clark before the war, but it was all done on the quiet, the powers that be discouraging any last-minute heroics. We were very proud to be drivers and wanted to have one last bash with Stanier's best.'

There can be no more fitting memorial to these engines, and the man who brought them into existence, than the words of those who crewed them in their prime

46211 at Euston. One last arrival, almost unnoticed in the twilight of steam. (RH)

A scene to be remembered – a Princess (46204) in all her glory. (THG)

and when their end was in sight. Whether Stanier ever realised the high regard in which he and his engines were held is difficult to verify, but in the last few years of his life he had to witness the demise of all he had created. With many years of good service still ahead of them they were withdrawn, as the need for steam engines gradually diminished thanks to electrification and the arrival of new diesels. And the 'Princesses' were some of the first to go, in 1961/62, their declining annual mileages symbolising that their end was near, coalescing the thought 'all things must pass'.

CHAPTER 10

MEMENTO MORI

I n his book *Disturbing the Universe*, renowned scientist Freeman Dyson concluded that: 'A good scientist is a person with original ideas. A good engineer is a person who makes a design work with as few original ideas as possible. There are no prima donnas in engineering.'

The British-born theoretical physicist and mathematician, whose wide range of advanced research covered such diverse areas as quantum electrodynamics, nuclear engineering and solid state physics, knew a thing or two about the role of specialists and their inter-relationships. I was struck by this assertion about scientists and engineers, and, having been raised by a design engineer of some standing in his field, I was loath to agree. It was the evocation of educational and professional snobbery that seemed unfair and untrue. 'I am a professor so I am better than someone with a BSc, who is better than someone who has an HNC' and so on. But I eventually saw the level of accolade his statement contained. The good engineer is at the centre of all development. They have to understand and modify often raw theories; turn them into practical, working solutions; guide, direct and manage projects, and in-service

needs; then constantly re-evaluate and test performance to make an output even more effective. Basically, they might need many more skills than scientists.

I looked for examples to test Dyson's theory and found that William Stanier's life and work made him the perfect model; his work on the Princess Class was a key part of this philosophy. All he knew, all he had been taught and all his instincts, as an engineer, leader and businessman, came together in this project for the first time. He had ultimate responsibility for the work, forged a team from disparate and often conflicting groups, fought for what he thought was right, and united all in a common cause and towards a worthwhile goal. And then there was the Turbomotive, the clearest possible demonstration of his scientific curiosity and ambition. If he had been given the chance of a more advanced education, rather than an apprenticeship, how far would he have travelled in the world of science? I believe he would have excelled here too, being a man of considerable intelligence, intellect, determination and drive, with the added benefit of an open, questioning mind. It was not to be and so the railways benefited hugely from his presence. It is no surprise that until the end of steam, in 1968,

his locomotives worked with great efficiency and were some of the last to go. Given a chance they would have kept running into the next decade or two.

The main difficulty when assessing Stanier's career is his own lack of words or writing on the subject. He preferred to let his actions speak for themselves or let others describe all that he had done, trusting their impartiality and perception to present a balanced view. He was the first to admit the written word was not his medium and any verbal presentation he gave

Princess Helena Victoria near Liverpool Lime Street Station in this classic Bishop Treacy photo. (ET/RH)

Princess Arthur of Connaught still immaculate, although approaching the end of her service, here awaits the next turn of duty. (RH)

reflected his dislike of that method too. But this modesty hid such great skills and achievements.

When President of the Institution of Locomotive Engineers, for the first time in 1936, he had to put his reticence in 'performing' to one side and presented his thoughts, in an address entitled 'Recent developments in locomotive design', to an expert audience eager to learn his secrets. Even here he presented a general analysis instead of describing his own evolutionary work on systems and techniques. In 1938 he again became President and this time, in his main address to members entitled 'Problems connected with locomotive design', he delved deeper into his working practices. His final contribution, in terms of academic papers, came when he became President of the Institution of Mechanical Engineers

in 1941. Staying with the steam-locomotive theme, he presented a paper entitled 'The position of the locomotive in mechanical engineering'. The sum total of these three papers fell short of the extensive assessment his great achievements deserved.

Even when he could, justifiably, have claimed much more, he deflected credit to friends and colleagues. In 1946 Roland Bond took all Stanier's work on the Turbomotive and, with his full agreement and assistance, produced the only detailed engineering assessment of that experimental engine. This was then presented to the Institution of Locomotive Engineers to great acclaim. And when Henry Guy, his collaborator in this project, died, in 1956, Stanier wrote a detailed obituary for the Royal Society, which gave most

credit to his great friend. He even changed dates and events to make sure this happened, claiming Guy came to him in 1934 with the proposal, when the collaboration went back as far as the late 1920s. A man who would do this was exceptional by any standards, and was worthy of an assessment by someone of equal status and ability. Such a man was Harold Hartley, his Vice President at Euston, whose research sat at the forefront of scientific achievement. They were both Fellows of the Royal Society, Stanier being only the second locomotive engineer awarded this honour; Robert Stephenson being the first. Hartley was asked to write a biographical memoir of Stanier, following his death in 1965.

He carefully reviewed all that Stanier had written and his own memories of their time together. He

then prepared a well-balanced and reflective biography, unsullied by cant or apocryphal elements. As a man of considerable scientific intellect and knowledge, Hartley structured his assessment around the way Stanier had developed as a man and as an engineer, before summarising his methods and achievements. Some of his thoughts, recorded in an early draft, are set out here:

'When he took the post of CME, with the LMS the effect he had was

Princess Louise running to Liverpool, passing Northchurch Box. (RH)

Lady Patricia being prepared for duty, possibly at either Edge Hill or Polmadie in 1959. (RH)

The name and number are partially or completely obscured, although the engine appears to be 46205 *Princess Victoria.* (RH)

immediate and profound. It was a promotion that finally allowed him scope to be the great engineer and leader he had aspired to become. For forty years he had been gaining experience in every aspect of the steam locomotive, in its design, fabrication and erection, and in its operation, and the day had now come when he could put that wealth of experience and judgement into independent action.

'During the years he was in charge of the Swindon Division, Stanier contributed a remarkable series of papers to the Swindon Engineering Society. These must have been so helpful and stimulating to the GWR staff, and they are of special value in showing the trend of his mind and interests during these formative years. They dealt with, "the equipment of a running shed", "lubrication and lubricating of locomotives", "feed pumps and injectors for locomotive purposes", and "engine working diagrams and arrangements". They show the subjects which he considered of importance to young engineers; they show his intimate knowledge of the details of each and his clear-cut view of the issues involved.

'His first presidential address to the Institution of Locomotive Engineers, in 1936, dealt with various types of exotic steam locomotives of the water-tube boiler type and others, including his own turbomotive. He dealt also with wind resistance to fast trains which became a significant factor over 60 mph. He also discussed some interesting measurements made by the Great Indian Peninsular Railway which showed the maximum resistance at a given wind speed occurred when the wind direction was at an angle of 45 degrees to the direction of the train.

'His second presidential address in 1939 was much more revealing as it described Stanier's own design philosophy. Starting with the locomotive as a vehicle, he described his design for the leading bogie or pony truck that

reduced flange forces exerted by the coupled wheels on curves and prevented oscillation on straight track. Then followed a description of his axle boxes and their lubrication that had done so much to reduce hot boxes on the LMS. He then emphasised the importance of streamlining the steam passages in order to reduce pressure losses to a minimum and to obtain the necessary draught from the blast pipe with the least loss of energy. This brought him to the front-end design and the need for a testing station in which various combinations of the variable elements in the design of boilers, grates and blast pipes could be tested on a stationary engine so as to determine the optimum combination for good steaming and fuel efficiency.

'His address to the IMech E in 1941 showed how his thought processes continued to develop even though nearing retirement. After summarising the development of the steam locomotive since 1900, Stanier described the great improvements that had been made in overall efficiency, and in costs of maintenance and in availability. When the boiler efficiency had risen from 60 to 70%, the thermodynamic efficiency had risen to 5.2 to 10.8% in the latest types of single-expansion engines and to 12.8% in Chapelon's 4-8-0 with

Princess Arthur of Connaught leaving Euston Station. (THG)

Princess Royal, stripped of some of her motion, awaits the cutter's torch. (RH)

compound expansion. Stanier then showed that the loading gauge of British railways made compound expansion of the Chapelon design impossible and explained why compound engines had gradually been abandoned here. After describing the results of testing the new LMS designs with a dynamometer car, he showed the need for a stationary testing plant in which all the inputs and outputs of fuel, water and energy could be accurately measured. At the same time, he emphasised the need for accurate testing on the road in order to determine the operating conditions for maximum efficiency of an engine by trials at different loads and speeds. Finally, he reviewed the great increase in

operating efficiency with corresponding financial savings as a result of improved designs leading to lower maintenance cost and greater availability.

'Retirement for Stanier only meant changes in his busy life. Until 1948 he continued to act as scientific advisor to the Ministry of Production. In this capacity he had always been a supporter of Whittle's jet engine and in 1944 he became a director of Power Jets (Research and Development), of which he was chairman from 1949 to 1963, remaining an active member of the Board until his death.'

It is common in obituaries that platitudes or the need to hide past differences hinder true assessments.

In this case Hartley and Stanier had not always enjoyed the smoothest of relationships. A dynamic working environment dominated by strong personalities, especially when success is elusive, invariably generates strong feelings and antagonisms. But it says much for Hartley and Stanier's supreme skills and sense of diplomacy that they achieved so much together. Someone of Stanier's strength of mind and clear engineering ideas was loath to change until wholly convinced his chosen solution could be bettered. The long-running debate over the level of superheat provided for his 'Princesses' is just one example of his tenacious self-belief. It was a slow struggle to convince him that 18 elements were insufficient and it took Tom Coleman until 1943 to get all their boilers uprated to 32 elements. A man prepared to turn hoses on striking workers at Swindon in 1926 would hold his ground, especially when convinced his position was correct. And it is here we find the true Stanier, a man with the determination, skill and ambition to take a jaded, hidebound organisation and produce the Company's first Pacific locomotive. By any standards it was a masterpiece of form and function to sit beside the other classic designs that appeared with the London, Midland and Scottish Railway (LMS) under his leadership. Even if it had not led to the Coronation Class, this engine would still have played a significant part in placing his reputation as high as his greatly respected friend and mentor George Churchward.

In ending his obituary, Hartley astutely observed that despite his many gifts and achievements: 'Stanier was a devoted intuitive engineer whose strength lay in his lifelong study of production techniques rather than outstanding originality or scientific approach.'

And here we have the nub of the issue. Did Stanier simply create the environment in which very clever design engineers could work and be sustained while they produced some of the best steam locomotives ever created, or was his creative input far greater? Hartley's view was that he was a hugely influential engineer whose greatest strengths were his

understanding of the workshop and production techniques, supplemented by extraordinary management and business skills. He might not have had the capacity to become a designer or scientist, but the posts he occupied, within the Great Western Railway (GWR) or LMS, did not need him to be so and others fulfilled this function, nurtured by his untiring support and leadership.

If this is true, his work on the 'Princesses' and the Turbomotive are occasions when he tried to move beyond Hartley's assessment of his skills and show himself to be a design engineer. Despite a measured and considered approach to projects, and all the success he achieved, I believe he judged himself by higher scientific principles and aspired to

much more than his work on the railways. He was limited in this field by the narrow boundaries imposed by the ageing technology and science of steam locomotion. The engines might get bigger, stronger and more refined, but by the early twentieth century their basic science had been fully explored and better systems awaited exploitation by less hidebound individuals. Turbine development was the exception, because it delved into a science still in its infancy in the 1930s, which had potential to go much further and across many fields of engineering. It was his close association with Frank Whittle, and his support for turbines and turbojet engines, that revealed Stanier's wider views and aspirations.

There is also the matter of luck; of being in the right place at the right

Princess Helena Victoria possibly at Edge Hill. (THG)

Although partially stripped and looking forlorn following withdrawal, *Princess Margaret Rose* would be sold to the Butlins empire for display at a holiday camp and was eventually restored to full working order. (RH)

time. The brightest and the best can not always achieve greatness if opportunity does not fall in their favour. If Stanier had been content to stay a deputy at Swindon, he would not now be feted as a great engineer. He would also have been a deputy in a Company that had modernised and achieved all it would from steam traction before his gifts lifted him to a position of influence. It

was bad luck to be stripped of an opportunity to lead the GWR, but it was his great good fortune to be available when the LMS came calling. His luck also held in the team he inherited, once the less able or less compliant staff departed. And Tom Coleman stands out. He was central to the success of Stanier's revolution. He was not only an instinctive engineer, but also incisive enough to

understand his chief and turn his broad proposals into locomotives of outstanding quality. He was in many ways a perfect assistant for the Chief Mechanical Engineer (CME): modest, unfailingly supportive, able to read other people, a talented engineer and draughtsman with an artistic eye, and a character with the strength and power of reasoning to push through ideas and justify diplomatically any proposals he put forward. His part in the initial design of the 'Princesses' was slight, but he analysed the concept in detail and improved performance. More importantly, he took an outstanding design and created an even better one – the 'Coronations'.

It would be easy to assume from this that Stanier simply took all he had been taught by Churchward and the GWR, then, through Coleman's capable hands, developed these ideas into the LMS's standardisation programme. This would do him a great disservice, because he was much more than a filter for other people's ideas or an organiser and guide for other engineers' expertise. Here we touch on the role of a leader, especially in such a specialist, industrial field. The leader takes the risks and the brickbats when ideas fail; develops a team to take on challenges; inspires and cajoles in equal measures; and sits in the precarious position between demand and delivery, pressured by all and supported by few if things go wrong. The leader has to give explanations and live with the reality that success has many parents, whereas failure is an unloved orphan. With the problems Stanier faced when taking the CME role at Euston, few gave him any chance of success in meeting the challenging targets set by the dynamic Lord Stamp and his Board.

Neither Churchward or Coleman or any of the other CMEs faced such daunting tasks. It is here where Stanier's true greatness rests.

He not only turned the Company round through his work, but also helped produce truly sublime locomotives that served his Company and country superbly in peace and war. The Princess Class was his greatest achievement because everything he did or aspired to, at a time of great challenge, met their apex in this design. They might have been seen as a stretched GWR King or an older, less efficient big sister to the 'Coronations', but they were more than just a stepping stone. They stand alone as a truer monument to Stanier's worth as an engineer and his exceptional qualities as a man than any other locomotive he produced.

I was lucky enough to see 46208 in the last year of her operational life. During a holiday in North Wales, my family and I were visiting Conway Castle, to find the railway line that passed through the building's portals busy with Saturday holiday traffic. We just caught a green Coronation thundering by, heading east to Llandudno, its sound masking the arrival of 46208, which was barely moving in the opposite direction towards Holyhead. Looking very

Princess Louise and *Princess Marie Louise* very late in their lives and soon to be scrapped at Crewe Works. (THG)

Princess Louise being cut up at Crewe Works early in 1962.
(BR LM)

Stanier nears the end of his very distinguished life.
(RR)

shabby in her badly-marked and grime-laden red paint, she was halted for a few minutes awaiting a signal to release her on to the next section of her journey. She drew many gazes from castle visitors, but there were no obvious signs of life on the footplate or waves to children, its crew attending to business inside the cab. In a minute she was gone in a swirl of smoke and steam, leaving barely a trace of her presence except receding sound. Although aged only 9, I was aware of these soon to depart scenes and was glad I had seen one of these

magnificent engines before they disappeared for good. Fifty years later I enjoyed the experience again, albeit in a heavily idealised form, with 6201, now preserved and running for a different reason. Although congratulating those with the foresight, dedication and money to make this possible, I still longed for a less-sanitised version to turn my head. Once more I wanted to stand in the presence of a locomotive in its glorious and grimy prime, to fill an everyday scene that conjured up a vision of a time now long departed.

PRINCESS CLASS – KEY BIOGRAPHIES

James Anderson: Born 3 April 1871 and died 15 January 1945. After serving an apprenticeship with the Great North Railway of Scotland, Anderson rose to become Assistant Chief Draughtsman for Robert Stephenson Ltd of Darlington. A move to Derby followed in 1903, where he was later promoted to Chief Draughtsman. Between 1915 and 1919, during Sir Henry Fowler's absence on war service, he was acting Chief Mechanical Engineer. Post-war he reverted to the position of deputy and was awarded a CBE for his work during the conflict.

When the London, Midland and Scottish Railway (LMS) was created in 1923, Anderson was appointed Motive Power Superintendent and in this role advocated a small-engine policy, although he was flexible enough to agree that the Lickey Banker should be of an 0-10-0 design, and the needs of the Somerset and Dorset Railway were best served by a 2-8-0 class of engine. But he virtually vetoed the building of two Pacific designs for the LMS put forward by Fowler and George Hughes, when they were each CME. Realising Anderson's influence did not suit the changing climate, and with William Stanier's arrival, Ernest Lemon eased Anderson out by enforced retirement in 1932. It is debatable whether he would have carried on his opposition to the Pacific Class if he had not been removed. If so, there would probably have been no Princesses.

Roland Curling Bond: Born 5 May 1903 in Ipswich and died in 1980. Bond was educated at Tonbridge School, and became an Engineering Apprentice at Derby Locomotive Works and then a pupil under Fowler, the LMS's CME. Once qualified, he oversaw locomotives built by contractors for his parent Company. He so impressed managers at Vulcan Foundry Locomotive Works that he was headhunted and became their Assistant Works Manager in 1928. A return to the LMS followed in 1931 with a posting to Horwich Works, then to Crewe as Assistant Works Manager. Despite his comparatively young age he was rapidly promoted and by 1946 had become Deputy Chief Mechanical Engineer for the LMS. Nationalisation of the railways did not hinder his progress and he succeeded Robert Riddles as British Rail's CME Central Staff in 1953. Before retiring in 1968, he held the post of Technical Adviser to the British Transport Commission before becoming General Manager of BR's Workshops Division in 1965. In recognition of his great contribution to engineering he became President of the Institution of Locomotive Engineers (1953/54) and the Institution of Mechanical Engineers (IME) (1963/65).

Throughout Bond's career with the LMS he strongly advocated the science explored by the building of the Turbomotive. Sadly, he was CME, BR, when the locomotive, in her modified form, was condemned and scrapped. His 1946 paper to the IME remains the primary source of information and analysis of the turbine experiment.

George Jackson Churchward: Born in Stoke Gabriel, Devon, on 31 January 1857 and died in Swindon in December 1933. In 1873 his childhood engineering skills were developed when he became a pupil of John Wright, Superintendent of the South Devon Railway's Locomotive, Carriage and Wagon

Works at Newton Abbot, a short distance from his home. When the Great Western Railway (GWR) absorbed this company three years later, Churchward transferred to Swindon to complete the final year of his education. He remained in Wiltshire for the rest of his life, progressing through the ranks to become the GWR's CME in 1902 (retiring in 1922).

Like his disciple Stanier, Churchward was considered an outstanding engineer, but not a great innovator. He understood that all variations on steam locomotive design had probably been discovered and tested by others, and that this could inform his own design work. He aimed to establish best practice and absorb this into engine design, and take steam development as far as possible. He also understood the need for standardisation, the complexities of engine testing and the streamlining of workshop facilities. He was ahead of his time and gave the GWR a huge advantage that other companies struggled to match. Some have said that after his retirement the GWR stood still, resting on its laurels. Churchward's impact on railways is undeniable, as was his influence on the great engineers who followed him. Stanier, in particular, benefited hugely from his leadership and patronage. Clearly his work for the LMS was informed by all he had learnt from Churchward, as was the need to develop all established engineering principles to their absolute limits. The turbine

experiment was a natural progression of this design principle.

Herbert Chambers: Born in Derby in 1885 and died September 1937. On leaving school, Chambers became an apprentice at the Midland Railway Works in Derby. Once qualified he found employment in the Locomotive Drawing Office, before being recruited by Beyer, Peacock in Manchester in 1911, returning two years later to Derby. In 1923 he was promoted to Chief Locomotive Draughtsman and four years later to Chief Draughtsman of the LMS. In 1935 he became Stanier's Personal Assistant at Euston, a post he held until his death. As Chief Draughtsman, and then Stanier's assistant, he played a leading role in the planning and building of the Princess Class, the Turbomotive and the standard locomotive designs introduced by the LMS.

Thomas James Clark: Born in Southport, Lancashire, in 1872 and died at his home in Crewe in February 1954. Clark joined the London and North Western Railway in December 1888 as an engine cleaner. Near the end of his working life, having risen to the 'top link' as a driver, he was chosen to take charge of Royal Trains, but also drive Stanier's new Pacifics. This culminated in the high-speed test with 6201 *Princess Elizabeth*, between Euston and Glasgow on 16/17 November 1936, to prove the validity of the big-engine policy. A year later, on 29 June 1937, he pushed a brand-new Coronation

Class locomotive, 6220, up to 114mph, then a record in Britain. Very late in his life he was able to enjoy the status this work conferred on him and was awarded the OBE shortly after his record run by King George VI.

Tom Francis Coleman: Born in 1885 and died in 1958. After serving his apprenticeship with Kerr, Stuart and Co in Stoke-on-Trent, Coleman was, during 1905, employed by the North Staffordshire Railway Co, rising to become their Chief Draughtsman following amalgamation. Another move to Horwich Works as Chief Draughtsman followed in 1926, where he remained until 1933 working on a 2F 0-6-0 Dock Tank, followed by a taper-boilered 2-6-0 engine and then the new Stanier Class 5 4-6-0 locomotive. Work on the Class 5 had barely begun when he was transferred to Crewe as Chief Draughtsman, without relinquishing responsibility for Horwich, and so began the most prolific period of his career. When Herbert Chambers became Stanier's Personal Assistant in 1935, Coleman replaced him – a post he held until retirement in 1949. For the work he did in supporting Stanier, many consider him one of the finest locomotive designers of the twentieth century.

When Stanier wished to develop the Princess Pacifics, it was Coleman who led the design. He wanted to improve their performance and ease of maintenance. Preliminary work was completed, but when construction of additional, streamlined engines was authorised, Coleman created a completely new class of engine – the Coronations. However, the design work for an improved Princess was not lost and eventually formed the basis of the Turbomotive's hybrid conversion in 1952.

Charles Benjamin Collett: Born in Worcestershire on 10 September 1871, the son of a journalist. Collett moved to London where he attended Merchant Taylors' School, then studied at London University before joining the marine engineering company Maudsley, Sons and Field, at their Lambeth Works. Seeking advancement, he applied for a post within the Drawing Office of the GWR at Swindon, beginning work there in 1893. Rapid promotion followed and by 1912 George Churchward, who had become his mentor, promoted him to Works Manager and then, in 1919, his deputy.

Three years later, on Churchward's recommendation, Collett became CME when his tutor retired. Until his retirement in 1941, he took all that Churchward had achieved and produced locomotives of exceptional performance, particularly the Castle and King Classes. He was lucky in having two particularly talented deputies in Stanier and Frederick Hawkesworth. Their support was markedly effective following the death of Collett's wife. Deep mental anguish drove him to a long period of solitude and self-reflection, which

meant his deputies carried a much heavier burden in running the Works. They successfully filled the void and assisted considerably in keeping the business functioning, and producing and running the new locomotives.

It was Collett's desire to carry on as CME, and the closeness of he and Stanier in age, that led to the latter's departure to the LMS in 1932 and his great achievements there. It is clear that Stanier and Collett had, in many ways, a significant impact on each other's lives.

Ernest Cox: Born in Lanarkshire on 17 June 1900 and died 19 September 1992 at home in Berkhamstead. Cox's father was a Principal Clerk with the Customs and Excise Department, and so the family often moved. His younger brother was born in Yorkshire and they both attended Merchant Taylors' School in Crosby, Lancashire. In 1917 Ernest began an apprenticeship at the Horwich Works of the Lancashire and Yorkshire Railway, under George Hughes. A gifted engineer, he was soon promoted and by 1934 was Assistant Works Superintendent at Derby, quickly becoming Personal and Technical Assistant to the CME at Euston. During the war, he was seconded to the Railway Executive and post-war his star kept rising until he became Assistant CME to British Rail. Cox held a number of unique positions within the LMS and BR, and was one of only a few chief officers to record his memories of those days. Many historians have questioned his veracity, but they still

contain many reliable eyewitness accounts of Stanier, his way of working and the Pacifics.

George Dowler: Born in Liverpool in 1925 and died at his home in Rainhill, on 24 July 1994. Dowler began his career as an engine cleaner, but staff shortages due to the war meant he quickly became a fireman. Having survived the Harrow Crash in 1952, he became a driver, moving over to diesel and electric traction when the steam era ended.

Laurence (Laurie) Earl: Born in 1882 in Mile End Road, London, and died in Poplar in 1963. Earl became an engine cleaner at Camden Depot in 1901, rising to fireman in 1904 and then driver in 1915. By the 1930s he was a 'top-link' driver and was something of a celebrity in railway circles, having worked so many prestigious trains. Encouraged by the LMS' Public Relations Department, he wrote a book with H.N. Greenleaf called *Speeding North with the 'Royal Scot'*. It was basically a travel guide with descriptions of life on the footplate. Earl was a man of some charisma and, following his retirement just after the war and until his death, was greatly sought after by railway 'buffs' as a source of information on the LMS and Stanier's Pacifics, of which he was a great advocate.

Alfred Ewer: Born in 1895 in Fulham, London, and died at his home in Rochford, Essex, in 1963. Ewer served an engineering apprenticeship with the London and

North Western Railway (LNWR) from 1911. In 1921 he was appointed Assistant Locomotive Superintendent at Holyhead. Three years later he transferred to Widnes as Running Shed Foreman, before moving to Swansea as Assistant District Locomotive Superintendent. In 1929 he transferred again to Kentish Town and five years later to Camden. From June to November 1938 he was seconded to Derby, then returned to Camden and Watford as Locomotive Superintendent, where he remained until 1948. In this post he came into close contact with all the LMS' senior managers as well as managing the day-to-day work of all Stanier's locomotives, but particularly his Pacifics. He was in a position of great responsibility and the records he left highlight in great detail many aspects of life on the LMS at that time.

On leaving Camden, Ewer moved to Llandudno Junction Depot, then under BR management, and ended his career at Doncaster.

Henry Fowler: Born 27 July 1870 at Evesham and died at his home, Sponden Hall, Derby, on 15 October 1938. Fowler was educated at Prince Henry's High School, Evesham, then Mason Science College where he studied metallurgy. He entered into an apprenticeship with the Lancashire and Yorkshire Railway, under John Aspinall, in 1887 at their Horwich Works. His growing reputation led to his appointment as Assistant Works Manager, now of the Midland Railway, then deputy to Richard Dealey in 1923, who he succeeded

two years later, now under the auspices of the LMS. The Company followed a 'small-engine policy' that many have argued held it back in its battle with its chief competitor, the LNER. In this role Fowler was responsible for the Royal Scot Class, but held an ambition to build a Pacific engine. He was thwarted in this by an Operating Department, over which he had no control, dictating need and types. Nevertheless, his work on a 4-6-2 design prepared the way for Stanier and highlighted the need to control any opposition to such a development.

In 1930 Fowler became assistant to the Vice President for Works, replaced by Ernest Lemon as CME, who in turn gave way to Stanier. For his services in peace and war, Fowler became a Knight in 1919.

Henry Lewis Guy: Born at Penarth, near Cardiff, on 15 June 1887, the second son of a local meat supplier. From an early age Guy demonstrated his engineering skills and, with his father's help, gained apprentice-based employment under T. Hurry Riches, the CME, on the Taff Vale Railway. Later he gained a scholarship to the University College of South Wales to study mechanical, civil and electrical engineering, being awarded diplomas in all three subjects in 1909, and winning the Bayliss Prize (awarded by the Institution of Civil Engineers) and a Whitworth Exhibition.

On leaving university, Guy became a lecturer at Crewe's Technical College, before finding employment with the British Westinghouse

Company in Manchester, where he specialised in the development of turbines. By 1918 he had risen to become Chief Engineer of the Mechanical Department of its successor company, Metropolitan-Vickers (Metrovick), a post he held until his retirement in 1941.

Guy had a glittering career marked by many prestigious awards and scientific advances. His influence spread to many spheres and he became the driving force behind the development of the Turbomotive, enlisting Stanier's support and help in creating and then sustaining this experimental locomotive. Behind the scenes at Metrovick he enlisted the help of Richard Bailey, another turbine specialist, in designing and then monitoring 6202's drive system. It is clear that the association between Stanier and Guy was of great importance to both men, and their subsequent work was affected by this meeting of scientific minds.

In recognition of his contribution to science, Guy was elected a Fellow of the Royal Society in 1936. In 1939 he was seconded to the Scientific Advisory Council of the Ministry of Supply. He later chaired many wartime committees dealing with the development of guns, ammunition, aircraft weapons and the technical organisation of the Army. In acknowledgement of his work he received a CBE in 1945 and was created a Knight Bachelor in 1949. Ill health forced his retirement in 1951 and he died at his home in Dorset in July 1956. Stanier, not someone who readily put pen to paper, felt so moved by Guy's death that he wrote a detailed obituary for the Royal Society, which appeared in Volume 4 of their Biographical Memoirs.

Harold Brewer Hartley: Born in London on 3 September 1878 and died 9 September 1972. Hartley was educated at Mortimer College and then Dulwich College. He graduated from Balliol College, Oxford, with first-class honours in natural sciences in 1900. He remained at the college as tutor and lecturer and married the Master of Balliol's eldest daughter. During the First World War, he rose from junior officer with the 7th Leicestershire Regiment to Brigadier General, Controller of the Chemical Warfare Department. He was awarded the Military Cross for gallantry and was Mentioned in Dispatches three times. He advised different governments on the development of chemical weapons until 1950.

Returning to the academic world on a part-time basis in 1919, Hartley combined this with work in different industries. In 1930 he resigned his tutorial fellowship at Oxford to become the LMS's Vice President for Works and Ancillary Undertakings and Director of Research – a move encouraged and sponsored by Josiah Stamp. His influence on many areas of railway work was immense, not least in the design of locomotives. But a man of his drive and ability was frustrated by the poor business sense and hidebound culture of the LMS in the early 1930s. He and Stamp saw in

Stanier a man who could move things forward, and they set out to recruit him. His arrival in 1932 provided the catalyst for change, and they gave 'their man' complete support and huge freedom to develop effective locomotives.

As a scientist Hartley was intrigued by new ideas, and the need for effective and novel research. Developing a turbine engine fell naturally into this field and he gave his wholehearted support to the project. There seems little doubt that this allowed 'trials' with the Turbomotive to continue far longer than would have been authorised by a hard-pressed Operating Department if left to their own devices – 6202's record of availability being poor in comparison to her sisters.

For the remainder of his life Hartley was involved in many industries and retained an interest in scientific discovery, chairing many eminent bodies that advised government. He was elected a Fellow of the Royal Society in 1926 and was knighted two years later. In 1944 he was awarded a KCVO and a GCVO in 1957.

Following Stanier's death in 1965, he wrote a detailed biography of his late CME that was published by the Royal Society. His assessment of Stanier was incisive and reflected the deep respect he felt.

Frederick William Hawksworth: Born in Swindon on 10 February 1898 and died there on 13 July 1976. After attending Sandford Street School, Hawksworth followed his father, a draughtsman with the GWR, into the

Company as an apprentice. After completion he was awarded the prestigious 'Whitworth Scholarship' and attended the Royal College of Science in South Kensington, London, achieving a first-class honours degree in machine design. Armed with this outstanding qualification he returned to Swindon in 1905 to work as a draughtsman. Rapid promotion did not follow, although he benefited, as did Stanier, from Churchward's sponsorship. In 1920 he became Chief Draughtsman, having worked closely on the design of most of Churchward's classic locomotives, including his Pacific, *The Great Bear*. When Stanier departed for the LMS in 1932, Hawksworth became Collett's assistant, but had to wait until 1941 to succeed him as CME. Since the war was at its height, railway companies had little freedom to develop new concepts or locomotives. Hawksworth must have found this restriction irksome and among the developments he advocated, and which were permanently shelved, was a new Pacific engine.

As close contemporaries, Stanier and Hawksworth gained extensive experience and great opportunities under Churchward and Collett, but the latter's desire to remain in post thwarted the ambitions of both men. Stanier moved on to greater glory, but Hawksworth remained and felt the frustration of a missed chance.

George Hughes: Born 9 October 1865 in Cambridgeshire and died in Stamford on 27 October 1945. Hughes began his apprenticeship at

Crewe in 1882 and became a fitter with the Lancashire and Yorkshire Railway at Horwich Works in 1887. By 1895 he had risen to become Chief Assistant in the Carriage and Wagon Department at Newton Heath, before returning to Horwich as Works Manager in 1899. 1904 saw him promoted to CME, having served for a short period as Chief Assistant. On the creation of the LMS, he became Horwich's first CME. Under his guiding hand locomotive development was dominated by a small-engine policy and his designs stayed within this framework, but he and his team did explore the potential of the Pacific configuration; planning reached an advanced stage before being dropped. It seems that James Anderson was again responsible for dictating and managing these development proposals.

Hughes retired in 1925 due, in part, to the intense pressures imposed upon him.

Nevertheless, he began the process of changing minds in the Company, which smoothed the path for Stanier's Pacifics.

Eric Arthur Langridge: Born 20 May 1896 in London and died in Polegate, East Sussex, on 18 May 1999. Langridge was educated at St Olave's School and began an engineering apprenticeship at Eastleigh Locomotive Works in 1912, with part of his training being undertaken at Hartley College, Southampton. Subsequently he worked in the Drawing Office at Eastleigh, but it seems that the London and South Western Railway could not offer him longer-term employment and he was recruited by the Midland Railway at Derby. He began work in 1920 and remained in the Drawing Office there for thirty-nine years.

In the years that followed, Langridge worked on the design of many locomotives, but eventually specialised in boilers, working on the Princesses. He also worked on proposals for an improved Princess Pacific – plans that were then shelved when the Coronation Class came into being. This work was resurrected in 1952 when the Turbomotive was converted to a conventional, reciprocating engine.

Langridge holds a unique place in railway history, having served for so long in one of the most important centres of locomotive development. In so doing, his work encompassed some of the major steam-engine developments of the twentieth century and embraced a future beyond steam traction. In retirement he wrote articles about his work, which were made into a two-volume book called *Under 10 CMEs*.

Ernest John Hutchings Lemon: Born in Okeford Fitzpaine, Dorset, on 10 December 1884, the youngest of six children, and died in Epsom, Surrey, on 15 December 1954. Lemon was apprenticed to the North British Railway Company in Glasgow, and completed his training in 1905, before spending two years at Heriot-Watt College developing his engineering skills. A brief period of employment with the Highland Railway at Inverness followed and then three years with Hurst, Nelson and Co, wagon builders, in Motherwell.

In 1911 Lemon became Chief Wagon Inspector for the Midland Railway, then, in 1917, Carriage Works Manager at Derby, followed, in 1923, by promotion to Divisional Carriage and Wagon Superintendent.

When Fowler retired in 1931, Lemon became the LMS's CME, despite the fact that he had little or no experience of locomotive engineering. But it proved to be a stop-gap measure only, the post being filled by Stanier in early 1932. Lemon became Vice President in charge of the Railway Traffic, Operating and Commercial Section. As CME he had not been idle, having completed a major review of locomotive stock, identifying and recommending future engine policy and needs. He also oversaw major changes in the way locomotives were maintained and repaired. In so doing, he laid valuable groundwork for Stanier to build the loco modernisation programme.

Lemon fully supported the development of the Princesses and made sure his department did the same when it came to the trials, including the permanent assignment of a fitter to the Turbomotive. However, his support waned when expected savings did not materialise. Stanier was critical of the way 6202 was run, believing that more could have been achieved if the number of engine crews had been kept to a minimum, allowing greater expertise to be fostered.

In 1938 Lemon was seconded to the Air Ministry, in recognition of his considerable skills of management and industrial manufacturing. He was appointed Director General of Aircraft Production, his primary responsibility being to solve the many problems that beset aircraft construction. He remained with the Air Ministry until April 1940, when his secondment ended. A knighthood was his reward.

Three more years of service with the LMS followed before retirement in August 1943, during which he and Hartley oversaw the reactivation of the Turbomotive in 1941.

Although retired, Lemon continued to be involved in various scientific and engineering studies, the last as Chairman of the Committee for the Standardisation of Engineering Products for the Ministry of Supply. Their report, published in 1949, was Lemon's final project. After this his health declined and he died five years later.

Frederick Arnold Lemon: Born near Castle Cary, Somerset, and died in a Watford nursing home on 23 October 1961. Lemon successfully completed an apprenticeship at Crewe and after several appointments entered Works management there in December 1920. His association with this department lasted until his retirement in 1941. By the time of Stanier's appointment, as the LMS's CME, Lemon had become Crewe's Works Superintendent, and so was responsible for the building and maintenance of Stanier's engines during the most dynamic and

pressured time of his tenure as CME. Without Lemon the level of success achieved might have been considerably less.

Frank William Marillier: Born in Bedminster, Bristol, on 29 November 1855 and died at his home in Westlecott Road, Swindon, on 14 June 1928. Marillier's father, who was the Vicar of St Pauls, encouraged him in his engineering studies, and after training as a civil engineer joined the Bristol and Exeter Railway Company, which became part of the GWR in 1876. He moved to Swindon and his work, much of it innovative leading to patents, saw him promoted, under Churchward, to Carriage and Wagon Works Superintendent. He remained in this post until retirement on 29 November 1920, shortly after being awarded a CBE for his work during the war, designing and building twelve hospital trains at Swindon. Due to his growing expertise in this essential field, he was selected to be Chairman of the Technical Committee for Ambulance Trains in England, France and North America. During this time, he developed adjustable casualty cots, which allowed a combination of walking wounded and bed-bound patients to be carried in greater safety and comfort. This quickened casualty clearance from the front to specialist hospitals and undoubtedly helped save many lives.

Marillier believed strongly in the apprenticeship schemes offered by the Company and made sure these young men got the best education

possible. Stanier, in particular, benefited greatly from his tutelage and support. Marillier was quick to spot the younger man's skills and promoted his cause whenever able, and encouraged him to be open in his studies and participate in the work of the Mechanics Institute and the Junior Engineering Society. He opened the door to science and encouraged Stanier's intellectual curiosity at an important stage in his development.

Robert Riddles: Born 23 May 1892 and died 18 June 1983. Riddles' engineering education began in 1909 when he was taken on as a premium apprentice by the London and North Western Railway at Crewe Works and then found employment as a fitter in the Erecting Shop at Rugby. When war came he volunteered for service and saw action on the Western Front with the Royal Engineers, becoming an officer in the process. Post-war he rose rapidly through the ranks, and specialised in streamlining and improving production processes. His first major success was as part of the team that reorganised Crewe Works between 1925 and 1928, now part of the recently-created LMS. He then moved to Derby where he undertook a similar exercise.

Such success did not escape Stanier and a year after his arrival, having carefully assessed his staff, promoted Riddles to be his Locomotive Assistant and then Principal Assistant in 1935. In this supporting role he played a significant part in the development and testing of new engine designs, including the Turbomotive. But as a 'rising star' he had to gain wider experience. In 1937 he transferred to St Rollox to become Mechanical and Electrical Engineer, Scotland, although for such an ambitious man this move felt more like demotion. He had hoped to be promoted to Deputy CME, a post that went to his rival, C.E. Fairburn. He need not have worried because shortly afterwards he was chosen to go on a high-profile visit to the USA, with a new Coronation Class engine and her rake of coaches.

The war changed the course of Riddles' life. His skills in production techniques were sorely needed and, under Harold Hartley's guidance, he found himself seconded to the recently-formed Ministry of Supply to become Director of Transportation Equipment. To meet wartime needs his principal responsibility was to produce new engines suited to military needs. As a result, the LMS's 8F 2-8-0 was selected and 240 were ordered. Later he led the design of two simplified austerity engines – a 2-8-0 and a 2-10-0 – and the building of 935 of them.

Riddles was awarded a CBE in 1943 and then returned to the LMS as Chief Stores Assistant, by which time Stanier had retired and been replaced by Fairburn. On his death in 1945, Henry Ivatt became CME and a year later Riddles was promoted to Vice President to replace Hartley, becoming Ivatt's boss.

With nationalisation of the railways in 1948, Riddles became BR's first CME, although initially this post went by other names. He took Roland Bond and Ernest Cox from the LMS with him as assistants. Before his retirement in 1953, he led the major programme of steam engine design and production, and attempted to bring together the diverse groups that had run the Big Four companies. It is said that his primary focus on producing more steam locomotives diverted attention from the development of diesel and electric alternatives, hindering BR's progress by many years.

In the years that followed he became a Director of Stothert and Pitt in Bath, finally retiring aged 75.

Josiah Charles Stamp: Born in London on 21 June 1880 and died 16 April 1941. Following education at Bethany House School at Goudhurst, Kent, Stamp joined the Inland Revenue in 1906 and, by 1916, had risen to Assistant Secretary. An avid scholar, he studied economics as an external student at London University, obtaining a first-class degree in 1911. His thesis on incomes and property became a standard work on the subject, and cemented his reputation as a leading economist.

In 1919 Stamp left the Civil Service to pursue a more ambitious career in industry, first with Nobel Industries, then as Chairman of the LMS in 1926. At the same time he served on many public bodies and became a Director of the Bank of England. His career was one of the highest office and immense achievement.

He was awarded a CBE in 1918, a KBE in 1920 and raised to the peerage in 1938, becoming Baron Stamp. He was also a prolific writer on many economic issues, and rose to become Colonel commanding the Royal Engineers Railway and Transport Corps.

A man of drive and huge talent, Stamp's role in the development of the LMS, and guiding it to success from a group of uncoordinated and conflicting companies, was immense. Although not an engineer, he understood the needs of business and recruited a team of specialists from many spheres who could take the Company forward. Stanier's appointment was key. Stamp backed his CME and gave him free rein to create some of the most potent steam locomotives ever built.

Sadly, Stamp, his wife and son, Wilfred, died when their bomb shelter took a direct hit during a night-time attack in April 1941. His passing was a significant loss for the LMS and his country.

William Arthur Stanier: Born 27 May 1876 at 10 Wellington Street, Swindon, and died at Newburn, Chorleywood Road, Rickmansworth, on 27 September 1965.

Stanier was the first child of William Henry Stanier, an employee of the GWR. He was educated at Wycliffe College, Stonehouse, Gloucestershire, before becoming an office boy at Swindon in 1892, then took up a five-year apprenticeship in the works there. On qualifying he spent two years in the Drawing Office before becoming Inspector of Materials. Under the guiding hand of Churchward, then Collett, rapid promotion followed from Acting

Divisional Locomotive, Carriage and Wagon Superintendent to Principal Assistant to the CME in 1923. In this role he led the way in the design and construction of two of the GWR's finest classes of locomotives: the Castles and Kings.

By 1931 it was apparent to Stanier that he was unlikely to become the GWR's CME. When an offer from the LMS was made by Stamp, later that year, to become their CME, he jumped at the chance and was appointed in January 1932. And so the greatest challenge of his career began.

The LMS was a colossal business (created at Grouping from many often-competing companies), greatly in need of modernisation if it was to meet the challenging business targets set by its Board. In the late 1920s great advances had been made, but when Stanier arrived its locomotives left much to be desired, reflecting the outdated and often limited requirements of the LMS's constituent companies. Stanier's target was to establish standardised design and construction methods, and provide a fleet of new, more powerful and efficient locomotives. And this he did, with the aid of very able assistants.

Such was Stanier's success that two of his designs – the Class 5 and Class 8F – were still in service when the last steam locomotives were withdrawn from traffic in 1968. His work also greatly influenced British Rail's standardisation work in the 1950s. But it is for his high-profile Pacific locomotives and the Turbomotive that he is best remembered.

The Second World War led to a great increase in Stanier's duties on the LMS, but also in the wider service of his country. In the early years he oversaw the building of weapons in LMS factories and in 1942 was seconded to the Ministry of Production, as one of three full-time Scientific Advisors. Later he became a member of the Aeronautical Research Council, then Chairman of Power Jets Limited, a Government-owned concern developing jet propulsion, principally gas turbines, and became a Director of several companies, including H.W. Kearns of Altrincham, and Courtaulds.

Stanier gathered many awards during his career, including a knighthood in 1943 and a Fellowship of the Royal Society in 1944 (only the second locomotive engineer to do so, the other being Robert Stephenson). Other forms of recognition included President of the Institution of Locomotive Engineers on two occasions, and President of the Institution of Mechanical Engineers, being awarded medals by both bodies.

LINEAGE OF THE PRINCESS CLASS (1903–35)

King's Cross in the early 1930s. Three of Gresley's many Pacifics on duty; 2795 *Call Boy*, 2579 *Dick Turpin* and 2549 *Persimmon*. This view sums up the level of competition faced by the London, Midland and Scottish Railway (LMS), and their pressing need for their own Pacific design. (RH)

Any invention or development is invariably the result of an accumulation of ideas and trends over a long period of time, each allowing potential for further advances. Very little that is new is truly original; inevitably it comes from assessments made of scientific knowledge as it then appeared. By the early part of the twentieth century, steam locomotion had probably reached the limit of its technical development, although refinements and improved performance were still achievable. But as a science, obsolescence beckoned. For this reason, any class of engine can easily be traced back to the earliest locomotives. The lineage of the Princess Class is an interesting

reflection of all that William Stanier had witnessed or experienced at Swindon, and by observing developments on other railways as they broke new ground with their own 4-6-2 Pacific designs. But principally the Princess Class came about because the LMS's most pressing need was for an engine of greater power and endurance.

Through George Churchward's work with the GWR, three models would have been of interest to Stanier: the Star Class, *The Great Bear* and the King Class. He had been involved in their development and operation in varying degrees, observing their design and construction, and assessing their performance. The Stars epitomised all that Churchward envisaged in

locomotive design and became the model for all the GWR's 4-6-0 engines that followed, with the Kings being easily the most powerful derivative. *The Great Bear* probably led Stanier towards another solution, but its application within the GWR, where needs were more than adequately met by 4-6-0s, was limited. In the three drawings produced here, the form and function of these influential designs is displayed. Their influence on Stanier, in his evolution of the Princesses, is part conceptual and part instructional.

Elsewhere in Britain and across the World, the Pacific concept was growing in importance, resulting in many new types appearing during the first thirty years of the 1900s. The most famous was probably the Great Northern Railway (GNR)/London and North Eastern Railway's (LNER) Nigel Gresley A1/A3 Class, showcased by 4472 *Flying Scotsman*'s appearance, in 1924, at the Wembley Exhibition. Other sturdy performers were also appearing, particularly in North and South America, and Australia. Argentina had its PS 11, the Victorian Railway in Australia ran their S Class successfully and in the USA the Pennsylvania Railroad operated its K series Pacifics.

The Star Class (as they appeared in the 1940s)

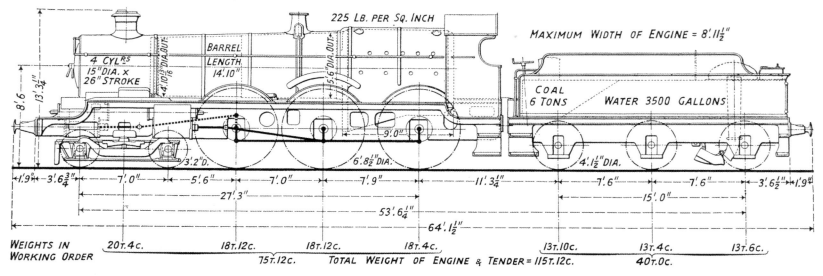

HEATING SURFACE, TUBES—							SUPERHEATER TUBES (TRIPLE ELEMENTS) ...	84–1 IN. DIA. OUTS.	
LARGE AND SMALL	...	...	...	...	1,686·60 SQ. FT.	LARGE TUBES ... ... 14–5⅛ IN. DIA. OUTS.	} 15 FT. 2 7/16 IN.
FIREBOX	...	...	...	154·78	,,	SMALL TUBES ... ... 176–2 IN. DIA. OUTS.	} BET. TUBEPLATES
TOTAL (EVAPORATIVE)	...	...	...	1,841·38	,,	GRATE AREA ... ... 27·07 SQ. FT.
SUPERHEATER	...	...	...	262·62	,,	TRACTIVE EFFORT (AT 85 PER CENT. B.P.) ... ... 27,800 LB.
COMBINED HEATING SURFACES	...	...	...	2,104·00	,,	

Recent change not shown on drawing : tender as for " King " Class

---

The Great Bear

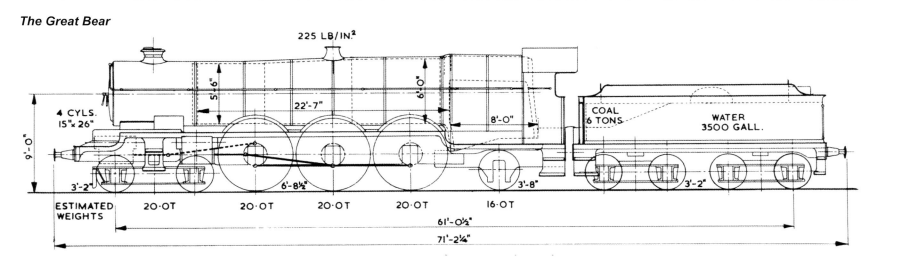

The King Class (as they appeared during the 1940s)

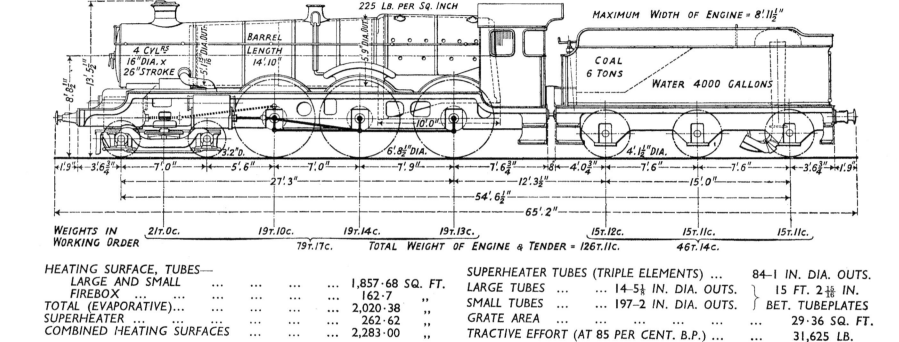

225 LB. PER SQ. INCH

MAXIMUM WIDTH OF ENGINE = 8'.11½"

4 CYL^RS 16" DIA. X 26" STROKE

BARREL LENGTH 14'.10"

5'.9" DIA. OUT.

COAL 6 TONS

WATER 4000 GALLONS

13'.5½"

8'.8½"

10'.0"

3'.2"D.

6'.8½" DIA.

4'.1½" DIA.

1'.9" | 3'.6¾" | 7'.0" | 5'.6" | 7'.0" | 7'.9" | 7'.6¾" | 8" | 4'.0¾" | 7'.6" | 7'.6" | 3'.6¾" | 1'.9"

27'.3"

12'.3½"

15'.0"

54'.6½"

65'.2"

WEIGHTS IN WORKING ORDER

| 21T.0C. | 19T.10C. | 19T.14C. | 19T.13C. | 15T.12C. | 15T.11C. | 15T.11C. |

79T.17C.   TOTAL WEIGHT OF ENGINE & TENDER = 126T.11C.   46T.14C.

HEATING SURFACE, TUBES—							SUPERHEATER TUBES (TRIPLE ELEMENTS) ...	84—1 IN. DIA. OUTS.	
LARGE AND SMALL	...	...	...	...	...	1,857·68 SQ. FT.	LARGE TUBES ... ... 14—5⅛ IN. DIA. OUTS.	15 FT. 2¹⁵⁄₁₆ IN.
FIREBOX ...	...	...	...	...		162·7 "	SMALL TUBES ... ... 197—2 IN. DIA. OUTS.	BET. TUBEPLATES
TOTAL (EVAPORATIVE)...	...	...	...			2,020·38 "	GRATE AREA	29·36 SQ. FT.
SUPERHEATER ...	...	...	...			262·62 "	TRACTIVE EFFORT (AT 85 PER CENT. B.P.) ...	31,625 LB.
COMBINED HEATING SURFACES	...	...	...			2,283·00 "		

Recent change not shown on drawing : height to top of chimney decreased by 3 in.

Australia's Victorian Railway's S Class, all four of which were built by Newport Works between 1928 and 1930. The design appears to have been heavily influenced by Gresley's early Pacifics. (RH)

Gresley's classic A3 Pacific

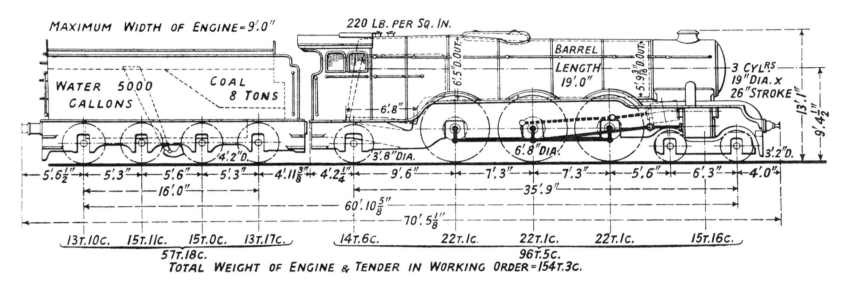

HEATING SURFACE, TUBES—
    LARGE AND SMALL ... ... 2,476·8 SQ. FT.
    FIREBOX ... ... 215·0 ,,
TOTAL (EVAPORATIVE) ... ... 2,691·8 ,,
SUPERHEATER ... ... 635·5 ,,
COMBINED HEATING SURFACES ... ... 3,327·3 ,,

SUPERHEATER ELEMENTS ... ... 43–1½ IN. DIA. OUTS. ⎫
LARGE TUBES ... ... 43–5¼ IN. DIA. OUTS. ⎬ 18 FT. 11¾ IN.
SMALL TUBES ... ... 121–2¼ IN. DIA. OUTS. ⎭ BET. TUBEPLATES
GRATE AREA ... ... 41·25 SQ. FT.
TRACTIVE EFFORT (AT 85 PER CENT. B.P.) ... 32,909 LB.

A3 Class (Super-Pacific)

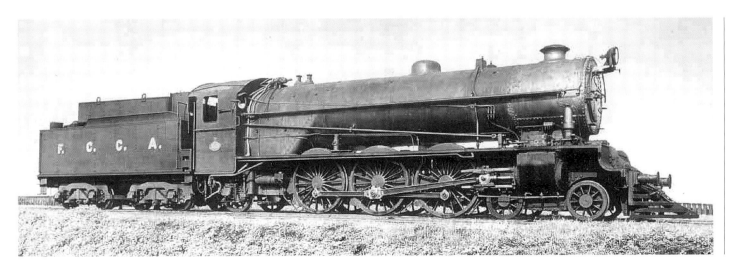

Gresley's classic A3 Pacific (derived from the A1 he designed for the GNR before amalgamation in 1923 and the creation of the LNER).

Argentina's PS 11. A class of twenty built by the Vulcan Foundry in 1930. (RH)

THE PENNSYLVANIA RAILROAD CLASS K4s PACIFIC — STANDARD PASSENGER LOCOMOTIVE OF THE WORLD

The Pennsylvania Railroad's K Class (in this case the K 4). The first Pacifics appeared in 1907, and by the time the K4s appeared in 1928, 697 had been built. (RH)

The LMS Princess Royal Class Development Programme (1924–52)

When Stanier arrived at Euston in 1932, he could draw on information from a great deal of design work completed by his predecessors, George Hughes and Henry Fowler, whose efforts to build their own Pacific types had been frustrated by bitter in-fighting. Stanier set this opposition very firmly aside, assisted by Ernest Lemon, and proceeded with his own Pacific design, drawing upon his own experience with the GWR, the combined knowledge of other engineers, plus Hughes and Fowler's efforts. The genealogy of the LMS' first operational Pacifics is clarified by the following drawings:

George Hughes' four-cylinder Pacific design for the LMS (1924)

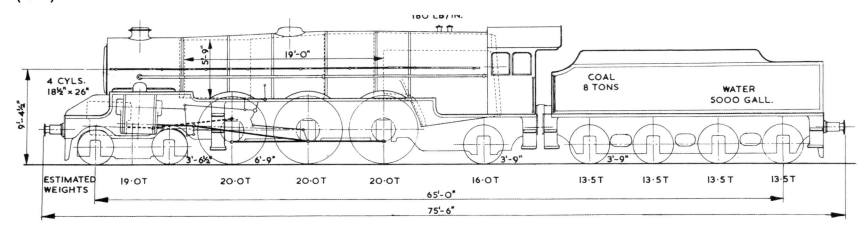

Henry Fowler's projected four-cylinder Compound Pacific for the LMS (1926)

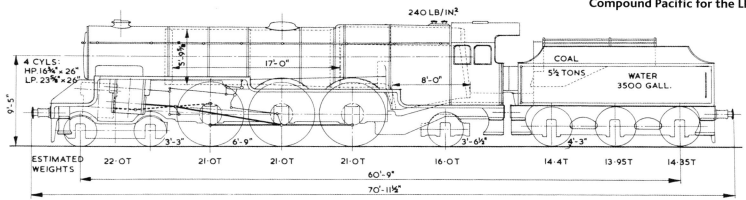

William Stanier's preliminary design for a Pacific (1932)

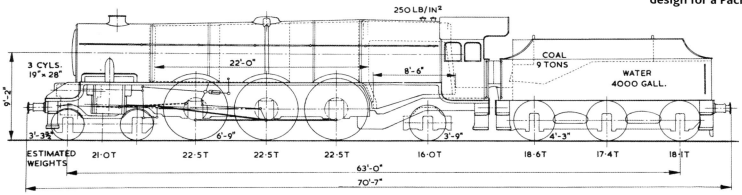

Princess Class Pacifics 6200/6201 (1933)

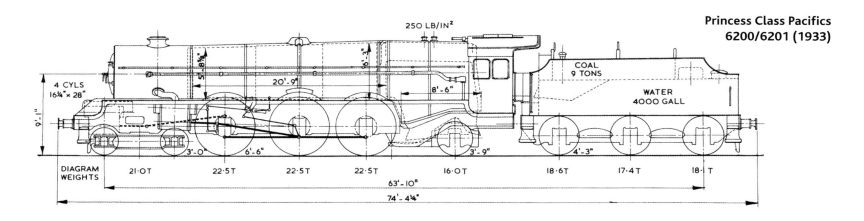

Princess Class Pacifics as they appeared in the 1940s

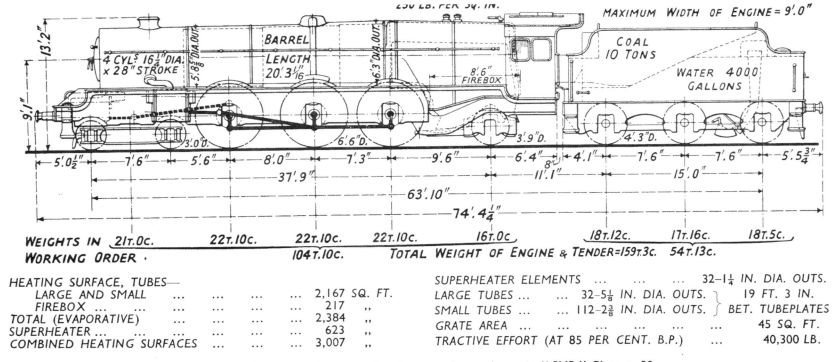

HEATING SURFACE, TUBES—

LARGE AND SMALL ... ... 2,167 SQ. FT.

FIREBOX ... ... 217 ,,

TOTAL (EVAPORATIVE) ... ... 2,384 ,,

SUPERHEATER ... ... 623 ,,

COMBINED HEATING SURFACES ... ... 3,007 ,,

SUPERHEATER ELEMENTS ... ... 32—1¼ IN. DIA. OUTS.

LARGE TUBES ... ... 32—5⅛ IN. DIA. OUTS. ⎫ 19 FT. 3 IN.

SMALL TUBES ... ... 112—2⅜ IN. DIA. OUTS. ⎰ BET. TUBEPLATES

GRATE AREA ... ... 45 SQ. FT.

TRACTIVE EFFORT (AT 85 PER CENT. B.P.) ... 40,300 LB.

Recent change not shown on drawing : tender as shown in " 5XP " Class, p. 30

Preliminary drawing of proposed Princesses 6213/6217 (eventually built as the first five Princess Coronations)

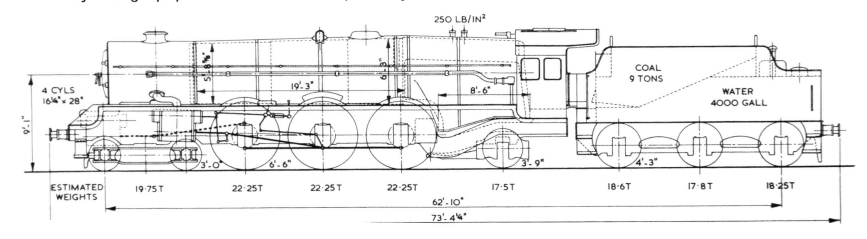

The Turbomotive as she appeared in 1938

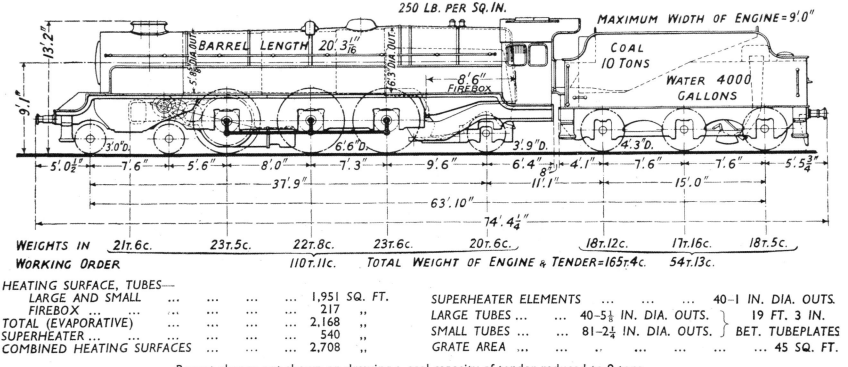

WEIGHTS IN WORKING ORDER	21T.6C.	23T.5C.	22T.8C.	23T.6C.	20T.6C.	18T.12C.	17T.16C.	18T.5C.
			110T.11C.	TOTAL WEIGHT OF ENGINE & TENDER = 165T.4C.		54T.13C.		

HEATING SURFACE, TUBES—
LARGE AND SMALL ... ... 1,951 SQ. FT.
FIREBOX ... ... 217 ,,
TOTAL (EVAPORATIVE) ... ... 2,168 ,,
SUPERHEATER ... ... 540 ,,
COMBINED HEATING SURFACES ... ... 2,708 ,,

SUPERHEATER ELEMENTS ... ... 40–1 IN. DIA. OUTS.
LARGE TUBES ... ... 40–5⅛ IN. DIA. OUTS. ⎱ 19 FT. 3 IN.
SMALL TUBES ... ... 81–2¼ IN. DIA. OUTS. ⎰ BET. TUBEPLATES
GRATE AREA ... ... 45 SQ. FT.

Recent change not shown on drawing : coal capacity of tender reduced to 9 tons

The Turbomotive rebuilt as 46202 *Princess Anne* (1952)

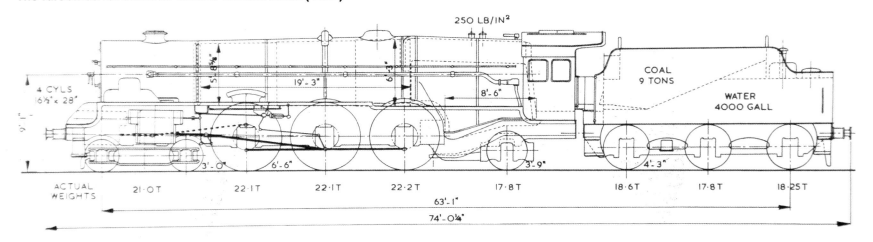

INITIAL SPECIFICATION FOR THE PRINCESS CLASS

How the first two 'Princesses' appeared in 1933. (LMS PR/RH)

It seems that the original specification for the first two Princesses was not preserved when records were being considered for retention or disposal. But in 1933 the Chief Mechanical Engineer published a document called *The new 4-6-2 Four-Cylinder Simple Superheater Passenger Tender Locomotive*, as a means of explaining the engine to the workforce and other interested parties. Although containing only a summary of the entire specification, it is all that now exists so is recorded here in its entirety, illustrated by a number of drawings and photographs.

Chief Mechanical Engineer's Office, Euston

10 July 1933 – *In view of the great interest that has been aroused in the technical press, and among the general public by the illustrations and brief descriptions of the first locomotive, No 6200, recently turned out of Crewe Works, it is felt that a more detailed description of the whole of the locomotive and tender would be welcomed, and the following particulars, which are given in general terms, so that they may be understood by all interested in modern locomotive design, will enable the general lines of this striking production of the LMS to be more fully appreciated.*

The leading dimensions are as follows:

4 cylinders: 16 ¼ " diameter x 28" stroke
Valve gear: Walschaert, travel 7 ¼"
Coupled Wheels: 6' 6" diameter
Boiler Pressure: 250lbs per sq inch
Firebox heating surface: 190 sq ft
Tubes: 2,523 sq ft
Superheater: 370 sq ft
Grate Area: 45 sq ft
Tractive Effort: 40,300 lbs at 85% boiler pressure
* Boiler barrel, tapered from throat plate to the smokebox

Boiler
Boiler and Firebox – *Drawings Nos D32-12666 and D32-12667 illustrate the design of the boiler and firebox respectively, and the following points may be noted as being of particular interest:*

The boiler barrel tapers from 6' 3" diameter at the throat plate to 5' 9"

diameter at the smokebox tubeplate.

The smokebox tubeplate is of the drumhead type. The distance between the tubeplate is 20' 9", and the following tubes are provided:

16 steel superheater tubes: 5 1/8" – outside diameter 7 SWG

170 steel boiler tubes: 2 ¼ " – outside diameter 11 SWG

It will be noted that the flue tubes are of steel, the ends of the firebox tubeplate being specially thickened up and screwed 11 threads per inch, and after expanding in position are beaded over. All the small boiler tubes are beaded over, and for both superheater and boiler tubes, six-roller expanders are used which provide a slight taper in the tube end, the larger diameter being on the water side of the tubeplate.

The pitching of the boiler tubes allows for a diagonal bridge of 7/8 " and a vertical bridge of 1 1/8", and between the tubes and the boiler barrel, ample water space has been allowed, this as a means of providing efficient water circulation.

Each of the longitudinal joints in the boiler rings is welded for a distance of 1' 0". The bottom corners at the foundation ring joints are also welded, and all the pads on the doorplate and boiler barrel for mountings are welded after riveting.

The smokebox tubeplate and firebox doorplate are suitably stayed with the standard type of longitudinal stays.

The firebox has a grate area of 45 sq ft, this with the object of a low rate of combustion, The safety valves clinkered, and so prevent satisfactory combustion, which in the past has been one of the failings experienced on long through runs on the 'Royal Scot' type of locomotive, which has a grate area of 31 ¼ sq ft.

The firebox at the front end is 7' 1" outside at the foundation ring, but at the doorplate 6' 1", this being specially arranged to facilitate satisfactory hand firing in the back corners. The provision of a large oval hole, which is 1' 7" long x 1' 2" deep, also helps in this direction.

The width of the foundation ring is 3' ¾ ", and the waterlegs gradually widen to 5 ½ " at the top of the firebox, this again to facilitate water circulation.

The dimensions between the copper crown plate is 2' 0", this to provide ample steam space above water level.

The provision and position of mud plugs and mud doors has received careful attention from the point of view of thoroughly washing out the boiler and firebox.

Firebox – It will be noted from the firebox drawing that copper stays 7/8" diameter, 11 threads per inch, are provided on the two outer side rows and on the top six rows, and the same applies on the doorplate, except that only the top three rows are copper. The other stays are of mild steel, 5/8" diameter, 11 threads per inch, to the following particulars:

Tensile strength: 28 to 32 tons per sq inch with an elongation of not less than 28% on 2" (British Standard test piece 'C').

The copper stays are riveted over, both on the outside of the steel plate and on the inside of the copper plate, but for steel stays, a nut is provided on the inside of the copper plate, the end of the stay finishing just inside the face of the nut. They are caulked only on the outside of the steel plate. Alloy stays of 80% copper and 20% nickel have been used at the throat plate. This material concerns the stays only in the curved portions of the throat plate and the two outside rows. The remaining stays on

Princess boiler awaiting completion. (LMS PR/RH)

Boiler, firebox and smokebox about to be installed in the frames.
(LMS PR/RH)

Regulator – The regulator is also a departure from LMS practice, this being incorporated inside the smokebox with the superheater header casting. The control of the regulator is of the usual type at the firebox doorplate, and a small sight feed lubricator is provided in the cab so that the driver can control the feed (about 1 drop of cylinder oil every five minutes) to the regulator to ensure easy operation, and as an additional means to this end, a balance weight is also provided on the regulator handle.

A distinct change from LMS practice has been the provision of a steam manifold on the top of the firebox doorplate. The main steam supply can be shut off as required.

Steam control valves are provided for the following:

Injectors. Ejectors. Steam brake for engine and tender. Carriage warming.

Pressure gauge. Ashpan flush injector. Sight feed lubricator to regulator.

Whistle – The whistle is placed in a horizontal position to be within the overall height above the rail, and is of the old Caledonian Railway type, which is well known for its melodious note.

Blower – The blower is fitted on the firebox doorplate on a separate pad below the main regulator, and is placed in a convenient position for the engineer.

Injectors – The injector on the fireman's side is a 'Davies and Metcalfe' exhaust steam injector with 12m/m cones, and on the driver's side a 'Gresham and Craven' live steam injector with 13m/m cones is fitted.

The injectors deliver through top feed clack valves. Sliding trays of the usual

the flat portion of the throat plate are of mild steel.

Boiler Mountings
The safety valves, water gauge frames and protectors, and other similar fittings, are of the Railway Company's standard type, but some of the details are of interest, as they are a distinct departure from LMS practice.

Safety Valves – Four pop type valves 2 ½ " diameter, set at 250 lbs pressure of the same type as used on the 'Royal Scot' engines, are fitted.

Superheater – As previously stated, 16 superheater flue tubes have been

provided. This, of course, results in a considerably increased ratio of evaporative heating surface compared with the standard type of LMS boiler, but, at the same time, the steam should be sufficiently superheated to meet all requirements. The superheater elements are provided with spherical ball joints, and the elements are 1 3/8" outside diameter and 11 SWG thick.

Main Steam Pipe – This is of the steam collector and drier type, the inlet being at the highest point of the firebox above the tubeplate, and then the steam is conveyed along the top of the boiler to the combination regulator and superheater header.

type are fitted underneath the water delivery nozzles inside the boiler to permit periodic cleaning.

Driver's Brake Valve and Ejector –
An outstanding feature on existing standard LMS locomotives is the 'Dreadnought' type of ejector which is carried at the front end of the boiler on the left-hand side. A departure is made on this 4-6-2 engine in that the ejector is fitted on the left-hand side of the firebox just immediately in front of the front cab plate. The 'Gresham and Craven' driver's brake valve is also of a modified design, this having three positions, viz: 'Running', 'Brake on' and 'Ejector off'.

The provision of the vacuum pump operated from the left-hand crosshead calls for use of the ejector only when standing or running at low speeds.

Clothing – The boiler, firebox and cylinders are covered with plastic magnesia, this being applied while the boiler is hot. The outer clothing plates are of sheet steel 14 WG and the usual belt fastenings are provided at the joints of the clothing sheets.

Grate – The fire grate is built up of two rows of cast-iron firebars of the standard pattern, the front firebars being slightly sloped and hind firebars level, the proportion of air space through the bars to the total grate area being 40.2%.

Ashpan – Owing to the position of the trailing 2-wheeled truck under the firebox, the ashpan had to be arranged to accommodate this, but by the provision of front, middle and hind damper doors, a percentage of 17.22 of air to grate is provided, and, in addition, side damper

doors between the bottom of the foundation ring and the top of the ashpan sides provide a further 9.43%, making in all a total of 26.65%.

It was considered very desirable to provide these top-side ashpan dampers, so that sufficient primary air would be available at the sides of the wide firebox where the bottom of the ashpan is very close to the firebars.

The three main ashpan dampers (front, middle and hind) have separate control handles provided in the cab, and an additional handle is provided to control the side ashpan dampers.

To facilitate cleaning out the ashpan, a flushing pipe is fitted on the inside, the water supply being taken from the injector feed pipe to the right-hand injector by means of a small 'Gresham and Craven' vertical pipe injector, controlled from the cab.

Smokebox – The diameter of the smokebox is 6' 1" inside and the wrapper plate ½ " thick (see drawing No D32-12678). This is carried at the front end on a saddle which is an extension on the inside cylinders. At about the centre of the smokebox, the exhaust branch pipe steel casting connects each of the outside cylinders and is also combined with a saddle to carry the smokebox.

The layout of the steam pipes on each side of the smokebox feeds to one inside cylinder and one outside cylinder, but the connection at the inside cylinders is in the form of a tee piece which combines the two feeds to one common supply for the inside cylinders.

The steel steam pipes are provided with cone joints.

The exhaust passages from the inside and outside cylinders to the blast pipe

have been arranged to avoid any abrupt change of direction, and also to provide a gradually diminishing area before arriving at the blast pipe cap.

The blast pipe cap is provided with a jumper ring, which, when the engine is working under heavy conditions, will lift due to the increased back pressure, and thus an enlarged blast pipe orifice will automatically reduce the back pressure and be a means of reduced coal consumption.

The departure will be noticed for the smokebox door fixing, this being of the

6200's smokebox.
(LMS PR/RH)

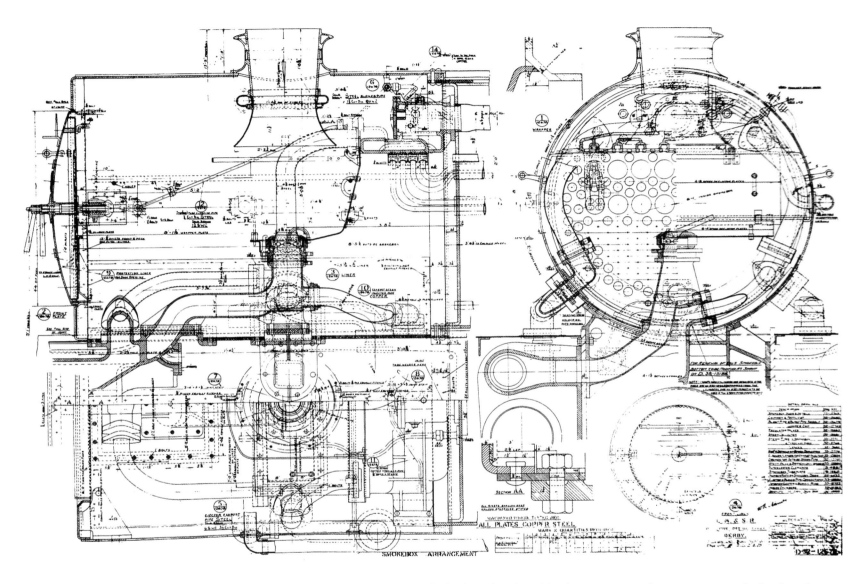

SMOKEBOX ARRANGEMENT.

Smokebox arrangement.

dart and centre bar type, the door joint being a bevelled face.

Chimney – *The chimney core is tapered from the throat to the top, the diameter at the throat being 1' 4 ¼ ". A baffle plate is provided across the smokebox, this is to equalise the draught over the boiler tubes, but this plate can be removed if necessary to facilitate cleaning the boiler tubes.*

The exhaust from the ejector is coupled up to a silencer which consists of a circular casting provided at the throat of the chimney and combined with this casting is a blower ring. The exhaust steam supply for the exhaust injector is taken from the base of the blast pipe in the usual way.

Motion

Cylinders – *The disposition of the four cylinders, which are 16 ¼ " diameter x 28" stroke, is as follows:*

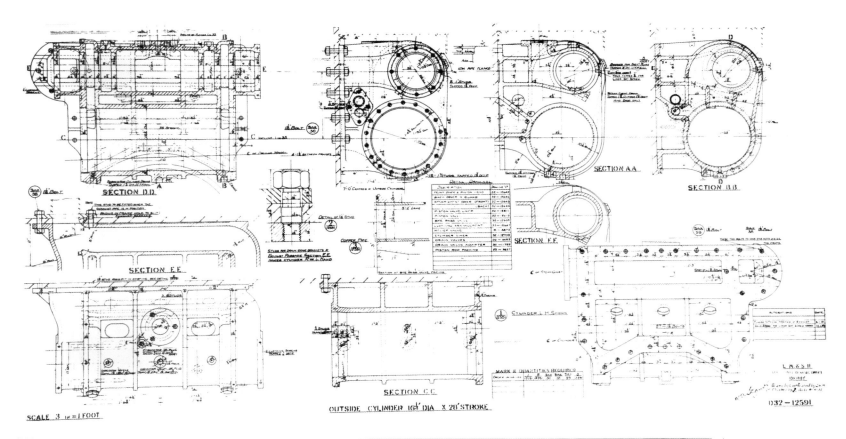

SCALE 3"=1 FOOT

OUTSIDE CYLINDER 16¼" DIA X 28" STROKE

D32-12591

The inside cylinders are practically central over the leading bogie wheels, and the outside cylinders are practically central over the trailing bogie wheels, these being arranged so that the weight of the cylinders is approximately equally distributed over the bogie wheelbase.

The piston valves are 8" diameter. The steam ports from the piston valves to the cylinders are straight, and as inside admission is provided, the two separate exhaust passages for the inside cylinders are carried over the top of the steam chest and merge together at the hind end where the cylinders form the

Outside cylinder arrangement.

The part-machined casting of an outside cylinder awaits completion. (LMS PR/RH)

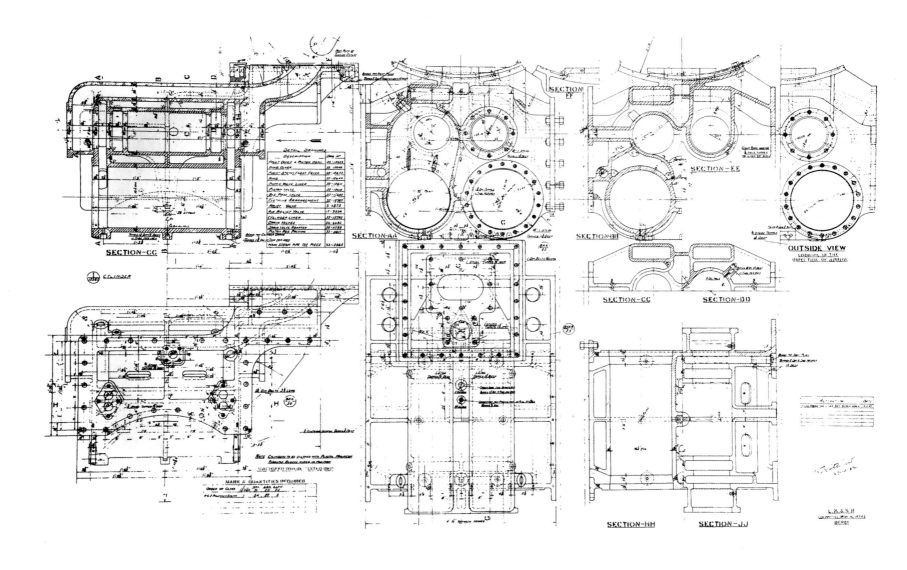

Inside cylinders' through section.

saddle casting for the front end of the smokebox.

The exhaust ports for the outside cylinders are taken through the main frames to a branch casting which also forms a saddle for the smokebox at about its centre. A further departure from standard practice is that bye-pass valves have not been provided, as, when coasting with the gear placed at about 45 per cent cut off, it is considered that, with the efficient valve gear fitted, excessive compression with its resultant troubles at the connecting rod big ends, is avoided. The standard type of cylinder drain cock is fitted, but the automatic spring loaded cylinder drain valves are of a smaller type than usual. The cylinder clearance volume is 9.4% of the swept volume of the cylinders.

Cylinder Lubrication – *A 16-feed standard-type mechanical lubricator is fitted on the left-hand side of the engine,* and supplies superheater cylinder oil to the following points:

- 8 piston valve heads
- 4 cylinder barrels
- 4 piston rod packings

In addition to these, 4 feeds are taken from the right-hand mechanical lubricator which supplies engine oil to the piston valve spindle guide bushes. This is in accordance with the usual practice, and as only exhaust steam is in contact with these bushes, no trouble has been experienced. These guide bushes are made of phosphor bronze lined with white metal, the inside diameter being 1 7/8 " and the length about 7 ¾ ". Water grooves are machined on the inside of the guide bushes.

Atomiser Lubrication – The 8 feeds to the piston heads and the 4 feeds to the 4-cylinder barrels are combined with a steam atomiser jet before the lubricant arrives at the point of delivery, and in the case of the piston valves the lubrication is carried into an annular space provided in the cylinder casting round the liners, and the atomised oil passes from this cavity through 6 small holes equally pitched round the liner, so that the whole surfaces of the piston valve liners are thoroughly lubricated.

Another interesting point is that the lubricant is introduced on the live steam side of the piston valve head, so that the natural flow of the steam carries it over the whole of the working surface of the liners and piston valves before passing on to the cylinders.

Frames – The main frames are shown in Drawing D32-12599. The distance between the frames is 4' 1 ¼ " and the

thickness of the frames 1 ¼ ", and advantage has been taken of this extra thickness to omit the usual type of horizontal frame cross stretchers which have been a feature on previous LMS standard stretchers, as it is considered that over-staying of the frames laterally is likely to interfere with the flexibility.

In addition to the vertical stretchers that are provided on the intermediate and trailing coupled wheels axlebox guides, cross stays have been provided to prevent the frames coming in at the bottom which is a common trouble when such large boilers are placed in position. Two separate hind and frame plates are provided at each side, and spliced to the main frame, the outer hind frames being splayed outwards and carried through to the hind buffer beam, these are 1" thick. The inner frames (1 ¼ " thick) are set slightly inwards to take the centre casting through to the hind buffer beam and the main centre drag box casting.

Inside cylinder being carefully guided into position before bolts are inserted. (LMS PR/RH)

LEFT: The frames are ready for the boiler to be installed. (LMS PR/RH)

RIGHT: The completed frames as seen from above. The way the inside and outside cylinders are staggered is very clear in this view. (LMS PR/RH)

Due to the limitations to the depth of frames below the throat plate of the firebox, it required careful scheming to provide the necessary strength to resist the heavy stress imposed when lifting the completed engine.

All the rivets at the main frame joints are a turned driving fit and riveted cold, and, in addition, the joint is welded at all outside edges.

The carrying of the boiler at the front end of the frames is just behind the smokebox tubeplate, and the second support is between the intermediate and trailing coupled wheels, and here a gunmetal bearing strip is provided between the bearer and frame support for the necessary movement due to expansion, and, in addition, clips are provided at the side.

At the front end of the firebox, the foundation ring is utilised as another sliding support, and on the bottom face of the foundation ring a gunmetal bearing strip is fixed.

At the hind end of the firebox, the foundation ring is carried below the plate joints, and a ½ " thick diaphragm plate in approximately a vertical plane is rigidly attached to this projection, and the bottom edge of the plate is fixed to the steel casting which forms the dragbox. This completes the carrying arrangement for the boiler.

Spring Gear – *The coupled wheels of the first and third engine will be fitted with laminated springs of a ribbed section, the material being silicon* manganese to the following analysis:

Carbon: 0.5% to 0.6%

Silicon: 1.8% to 2%

Sulphur: 0.04%

Phosphorus: 0.04%

Manganese: 0.7% to 1.0%

Treatment for ½ " and 5/8 " plates –

Plates heated to approximately 850 degrees, and bent to the required camber and cooled to below 600 degrees. Re-heated to 890-900 degrees and quenched in linseed oil.

Tempered in a furnace standing at 800 degrees for four minutes for 5/8 " plates, 3 1/3 minutes for ½ " plates or until on trial with a hazel stick, a heavy smoke and no sparks are produced or until the temperature of the surface of the plate measured with a pyrometer is 400-425 degrees

Screwed adjusting spring links will be provided, the material for the spring links being of a high manganese steel to the following analysis:

Spring Gear –

Carbon: 0.15 – 0.2

Silicon: Not more than 0.25

Sulphur and Phosphorus: Below 0.04

Manganese: 1.5 – 1.7

Nickel: 0.3 – 0.5

Molybdenum: 0.2 – 0.3

This material in bar form to be oil treated and tempered at 600-650 degrees and give the following tests:

Tensile: 40-45 tons per sq inch

Yield: 75% of breaking stress

Elongation: 20 - 25%

Izod: Not less than 70 ft lbs

The screwed ends of the spring links have a knuckle thread, and to provide for the necessary movement at the ends of the springs, the links pass through a shoe which is provided with gunmetal seating and a spherical washer of steel, the surfaces of which are ground.

The material specified above for the spring links is also used for the special bolts fitted through the leading crank pins for retaining the crank-pin washers.

Damper springs consisting of alternate layers of thin steel plate and rubber are also provided between the spring link head and the frame brackets.

The second engine will be provided with compensating beams between the leading and intermediate and trailing wheel springs, this is a means of ascertaining whether the compensating beams give a better riding engine.

Brake Gear –

The engine is provided with a steam brake which operates at the front of each of the coupled wheels. The total weight on the rails for all the coupled wheels is 67 ½ tons, and the brake percentage of this is 74% or, expressed as a percentage of the whole engine, is 47.8% .

Axleboxes, Coupled Wheels –

The coupled axlebox journals are as follows:

Leading: 10" diameter x 10" long

Intermediate & Trailing: 10" diameter x 10" long

No collars are provided on the intermediate and trailing axles.

The axleboxes are of robust design, being steel castings, and provided with pressed in brasses and the usual white metal crowns. Lubrication to the axleboxes is supplied from the 10-feed mechanical lubricator fitted on the right-hand side of the engine. The lubrication is fed to the crown of each axlebox where a back pressure valve is provided. A length of special rubber oil hose couples the back pressure valve to the pipe line bracket on the frame, this allows complete freedom to the axlebox movement. The oil supply is controlled by gear driven from the outside expansion links, which gives a constant travel for all positions of the valve motion, the minimum oil feed being 2 ozs per 10 miles per axlebox, this in the past having given quite satisfactory results on all classes of locomotive on the LMS. It should be noted, however, that by altering the position of the driving link, the oil supply can be increased if necessary.

In addition to the top feed lubrication, the axlebox underkeeps have been provided with ample depth, and a substantial oil pad which is built on a light frame and carried on a centre coil spring is fitted, the pad being made of a mixture of horsehair and wool supplied with worsted feeders which feed the pad from the oil reservoir.

Intermediate Drawgear –

The intermediate drawgear between the engine and tender is controlled by a laminated spring housed in the tender dragbox. The spring has an initial load of six tons.

The main drawbar is directly connected to the spring buckle, and at the engine end the main drawbar pin has only a clearance in the drawbar hole of 1/16 " on diameter.The side buffing spindles have a specially-designed head which ride on inclined planes (case hardened) which are riveted to the hind buffer beam.

The object of this gear is to obtain smooth riding between the engine and tender.

Leading 4-wheeled Bogie – The wheelbase of this bogie is 7' 6", and the diameter of the wheels 3' 0".

Bar frames are provided and a course cross casting which engages the engine bogie pin, also provides the slides. The maximum lateral movement allowed on the bogie centre is 2 7/8" each way, ie a total of 5 ¾ ", and a stop on the engine main frames limits the swivelling movement of the bogie, this being necessary to maintain the necessary clearance of the bogie-wheel tyres and the inside cylinders. The springs for the bogie bearings are of the inverted type with screw adjustments, the materials being similar to the springs for coupled wheels. The journals have a bearing of 6 ½ " diameter by 11" long. The axleboxes are solid gunmetal with a white-metal crown, a sliding underkeep and a similar type of oil pad to those in the coupled wheels is used, but only underkeep lubrication is provided.

Side bolsters transmit the load from the main frames to the bogie. Suitable lubrication is provided for both the bolster and cup and sliding face. The side-check spring arrangement is of a very flexible type, the initial load being 2 tons, and, with the bogie right over the centring, load is 3 tons.

Trailing 2-wheeled Truck – It was decided that this should be of the Bissel type, and the bogie arm is anchored at a point 6' 10" in front of the axle centre to the engine cross stretcher casting immediately in front of the firebox throat plate. The diameter of the wheels is 3' 9" on the tread.

The transmission of the weight from the main frames to the bogie is, in this case also, by means of side bolsters, but

due to the limitation of the design, these are placed inside the bogie wheels. Outside axleboxes are of the solid gunmetal with white- metal crown provided with the laminated springs carried over the boxes. Adjustable screwed links are provided with rubber damper springs. The diameter of the journals is 7 ½ " by 122 long. The lubrication to these boxes is of the underfed type, the oil pad being similar to those in the four-wheeled bogie wheels. The axleboxes being of the outside type, a cover plate provided facilitates the examination of the underfed oil pads.

The lateral movement allowed for the truck is 4 ¼ " each way, ie a total of 8 ½ ", and again in this case, a very flexible bogie side check spring arrangement is provided, the initial load being 1.44 tons, with a maximum centring force of 2.96 tons.

To sum up, the spring gear, bogies, balancing and intermediate drawgear, etc, have been carefully considered with regard to the smooth riding of the locomotive and tender as a whole.

Motion Arrangement – The particulars of the hammer blow, calculated at 5 revs per second, are as follows:

Each pair of coupled wheels: 0.14 tons
Total hammer blow for engine: 0.42 tons

The evolving weights in the crank axle, due to the big-end journals, are balanced by the sweeps being extended at the opposite end.

Drawings Nos D33-12817 and D33-12819 illustrate the inside and outside motion arrangements respectively. The inside motion and cylinders are horizontal, the centre line coinciding with that of the coupled wheels, but the outside cylinders are

Trailing truck as built.
(LMS PR/RH)

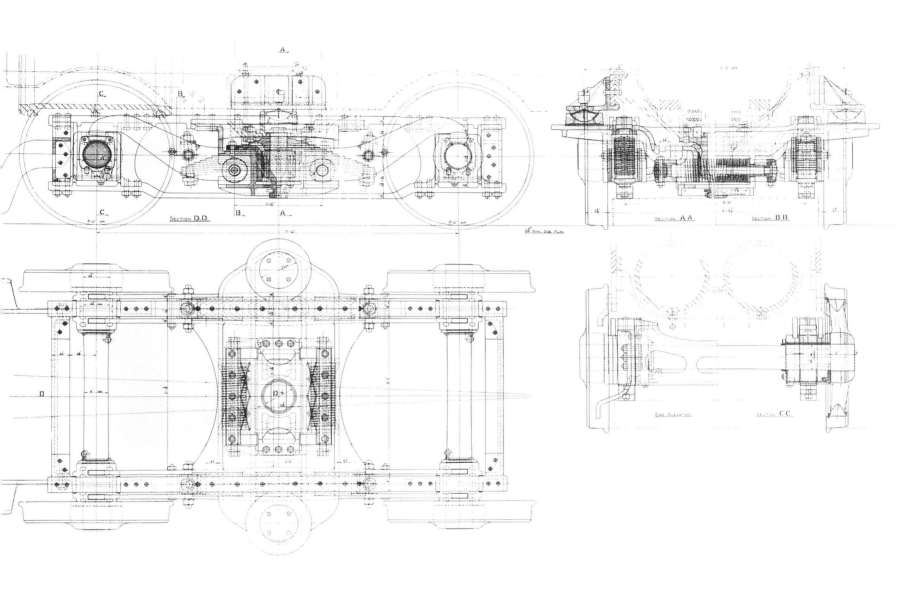

Leading truck
arrangement.

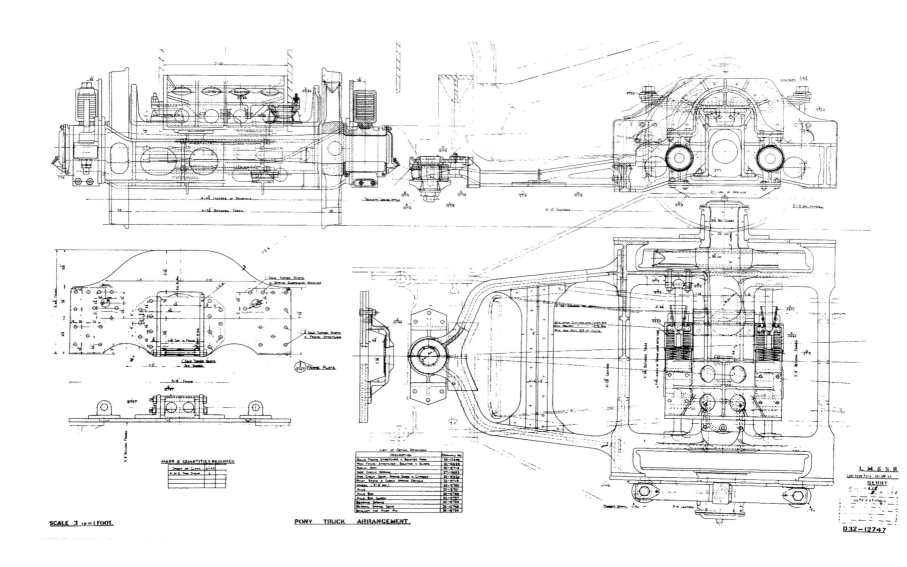

SCALE 3 in = 1 FOOT.

PONY TRUCK ARRANGEMENT.

D32-12747

Trailing truck arrangement.

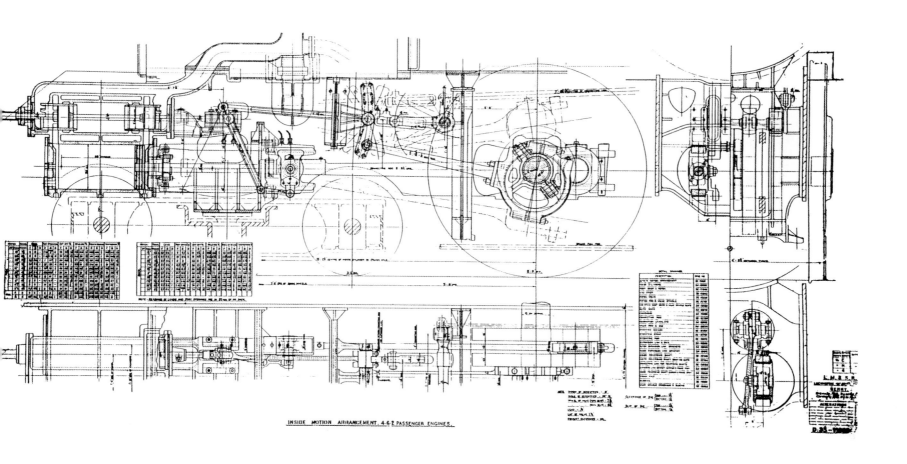

INSIDE MOTION ARRANGEMENT. 4-6-2 PASSENGER ENGINES.

Inside motion.

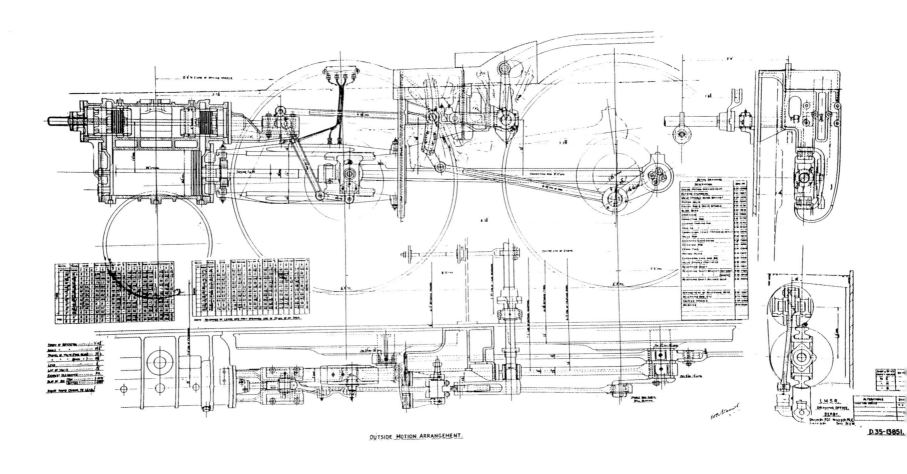

OUTSIDE MOTION ARRANGEMENT.

D.35-13851.

Outside motion.

inclined to the centre of the middle coupled wheels at 1 in 35.

The leading particulars of the motion are as follows:

Throw of Eccentric: 9"

Travel of valve, fore gear: 7.9/32"

Travel of gear, back gear: 7.1/16"

Lead: ¼"

Lap of valve: 1 ¾"

Exhaust clearance: Nil

Slip of die: top 1 3/8", bottom 1 1/16"

Angle of eccentric inside gear: 98 degrees

Angle of eccentric outside gear: 98.1 degrees

Right hand crank to Lead

Coupling and Connecting Rods –

The inside connecting rods have 8' 6 ½ " centres and the outside rods are 9' 0" centres.

The outside connecting rods are fluted, but the inside connecting rods are of a plain rectangular section. The coupling rods are also of a plain section, and these and the connecting rods are of

high manganese molybdenum steel to the following analysis:

Carbon about: 0.25

Manganese about: 1.6

Sulphur below: 0.04

Phosphorus below: 0.04

Molybdenum about: 0.25

The tests to be as follows:
Blooms over 4" diameter or 4" square should be reduced to one of these sections for testing, and shall be

heat treated in this dimension as follows:

To be oil hardened at about 850 degrees, tempered at 600-650 degrees. The test pieces must then give:

Tensile: 40-45 tons per sq inch

Yield: Not below 30 tons per sq inch

Elongation: Not less than 22%

Izod: Not less than 60 ft lbs

The big ends for the outside rods have solid bushes pressed into the butt ends of the rods with white- metal lining. The big end for the inside rods is of the fork type with a glut and cotter fixing, the cotter being driven home without any allowance for draw, and particular care is taken that no draw is allowed on the split brasses. This is a departure from the strap type common to LMS standard locomotives.

The coupling and connecting rods have been provided with bronze lubricating rings, so that side wear on these parts will be reduced to a minimum, and special attention has been given to the lubrication on the motion parts in view of the long through runs that this type of locomotive will be called on to perform.

Piston Valves – *The piston valves are 3 ½ " wide over the rings which are of the narrow type. Six rings, ¼ " wide x 5/16 " deep are provided in each piston valve head.*

It may be remarked that the general adoption of this type of narrow piston valve ring has been given excellent results, the wear having been considerably reduced on the rings themselves, and also the liners, which obviously reflects itself in a more economical steam consumption,

particularly when the engine is getting in a run- down condition.

Piston Rod and Piston Head – *The fixing of the piston rod into the crosshead is by means of a cotter, and when driven home, the rod bottoms into the tapered socket of the crosshead, the taper of the rod end socket being 1 in 18 and requiring a load of 30 tons to assemble. The taper on the cotter is 1 in 48. By this means, it has been possible to restrict the clearance between the ends of the piston heads and cylinder covers to ¼ ", and is great value in keeping down the cylinder clearance volume.*

The piston rod is screwed 3 ¼ " diameter six threads per inch and tapered. The piston head is tapped out with a similar taper, but with an allowance so that when it is finally screwed home on the piston rod it requires a load of 30 tons to assemble.

Piston Heads – *These are of the box type with plain end surfaces, and 3 rings, 5/16 " wide by 9/16 " deep, are fitted.*

Air Relief Valves – *Air valves are fitted to each of the cylinders. This is in accordance with the standard practice, so that, when coasting, the vacuum that is created in the cylinders will lift the valves off the seats and allow air to pass into the steam chest which mixes with the gases drawn from the smokebox, thus reducing the temperature of these gases and preventing the burning of the oil on the cylinder walls, pistons and valves, and so avoiding one of the great troubles of superheated engines, that is, the accumulation of carbonised oil.*

The provision of efficiently atomised lubrication, which has already been described, is also of great assistance in the prevention of carbonisation.

Steam Distribution – *It will be noted that separate 'Walschaert' gear is provided for each piston valve, and there is no doubt that this will ensure a correct steam distribution to each cylinder which avoids any inequalities that are inevitable when one piston valve is controlled by means of a lever from the outside motion or vice versa.*

The valve events quoted on the outside motion arrangement to Drawing D32-12819 cover also the particulars for the inside motion. It will be noted that the vacuum pump is driven from the left-hand outside crosshead, the pump being carried at the front end of the bottom slide bar.

Reversing Gear – *The arrangement of the reversing gear is as shown on D33-12801, and it will be noted that the main reversing shaft which controls the outside motion is coupled through to the reversing screw in the cab by means of a two-throw lever carried in a plummer block. Advantage is taken here to provide the necessary offset for the reversing rod to clear the wide firebox.*

The connection from the main reversing shaft to the inside motion is by means of a connecting rod coupling through suitable levers which are arranged inside the main frames.

The counter-balance arrangement for the motion is of the spring type. This is shown on the outside motion arrange-ment, the spring gear being provided on the main reversing shaft on the centre line of the engine between the frames.

Two sets of the three sets of coupled wheels, the left-hand unit with the shaft for the inside cylinders clearly visible. (LMS PR/RH)

Due to the great width of the firebox, it was necessary to offset the reversing rod between the intermediate reducing lever and the reversing screw bracket in the cab, and to obtain the necessary clearance from the reversing screw handle and the cab side, by introducing gear wheels. A similar arrangement to this, however, has been in use for some time on this Railway Company's 'Garratt' engines.

Slide Bars – *The outside slide bars which are extended at the open end to couple on to the motion plate are of an inverted tee section, and as near as possible to the outer position of the crosshead, clips are fitted between the top and bottom bars. The slide bars attached at the cylinder covers are registered into the covers and a two-bolt fixing is provided at each end of the bars.*

Crosshead – *The crosshead is a steel casting with gunmetal strips provided on the top and bottom bearing surface, so that in the event of heating and the white metal running, there will be no fear of the slide bars being scored due to contact with the steel faces of the crosshead.*

The gudgeon pin has a cast-iron split cone ring washer provided on the outer end with the usual nut and cotter fixing.

Piston Rod Packings – *The standard type of C1 packing is used for each of the piston rods, and is supplied with mechanical lubrication.*

Crank Axle – *The leading crank axle is of the built up type, the portions of the axlebox bearings, big end journals and middle being of steel, with a carbon*

content of 0.3 to 0.35 %, and the sweeps are of steel having a carbon content of 0.4 to 0.45 %.

Coupled Wheels – *The diameter of the coupled wheels on the tread is 6' 6". This is rather smaller than those of the 'Royal Scot' which are 6' 9", but as a means of obtaining maximum power and yet retaining a free running engine, the 6' 6" size was considered a very desirable dimension.*

The coupled-wheel centres are steel castings and the same pattern is used for each of the coupled wheels. The rim is of a triangular section which gives a pleasing appearance, and is at the same time of ample strength. The width of the coupled wheel tyres is a departure compared with the usual practice, the old dimension of 5 ½ " having been increased to 5 ¾ ".

The balance weights are built into the wheels as required, two steel plates being riveted together, the spokes acting as distance pieces and the necessary balance being added after the usual tests are

made in the spinning machine, molten lead to the required amount being poured in between the plates provided.

This section of wheel centre rim is used on all the engine and tender wheels, and the Gibson type of tyre fixing with a retaining ring is adopted.

Coupled Wheel Tyres – *The steel is of the best open hearth acid quality with a maximum sulphur and phosphorus content of 0.40%, the tensile strength 50 to 62 tons per sq inch, with a minimum elongation of 18 to 15%.*

Bogie and Tender Tyres – *The steel is to be of the best open hearth acid quality with a maximum sulphur and phosphorus content of 0.40%, and the tensile strength 56 to 62 tons, with a minimum elongation of 11 to 13%.*

All materials other than those specifically mentioned are to the Railway Company's usual specifications.

Locomotive Cab
A great deal of thought has been given to

the cab arrangements, and it was decided to make a wooden model in the Shops so that various controls could be tried out before positions were finally decided, needless to say this proved a very great help. The overall width of the cab is 8' 10" outside which provides a very roomy interior.

Double-sliding windows are fitted on both sides of the cabs, and on the driver's side on the outside of the cab and between the sliding windows, a small glass screen can be turned into position so that when the engineman is looking outside the cab, it acts as a draught preventer for his eyes. A hinged window giving ample area for lookout is fitted on each side in the front cab plate. In the cab front plate at the top, a number of ½ " holes are provided so that a current of air will pass along the inside of the roof and a sliding ventilator in the cab roof itself should ensure comfort in this direction. Tip-up seats are fixed on both sides of the cab, and to prevent exposure to cold cross winds, gangway doors, spring controlled, are fitted between the engine cab and tender panel plate, rubber extensions are attached at the bottom of the gangway doors.

Sanding Gear

Mechanical sanding is provided and the sandboxes are fabricated from steel plate, and are provided with suitable extensions where necessary so that the filling of the sandboxes is made as easy as possible for the enginemen.

The points sanded are in front of the leading, and in front and behind the intermediate coupled wheels.

In conjunction with the leading sandgear, a water desanding valve is fitted on the left-hand side of the firebox,

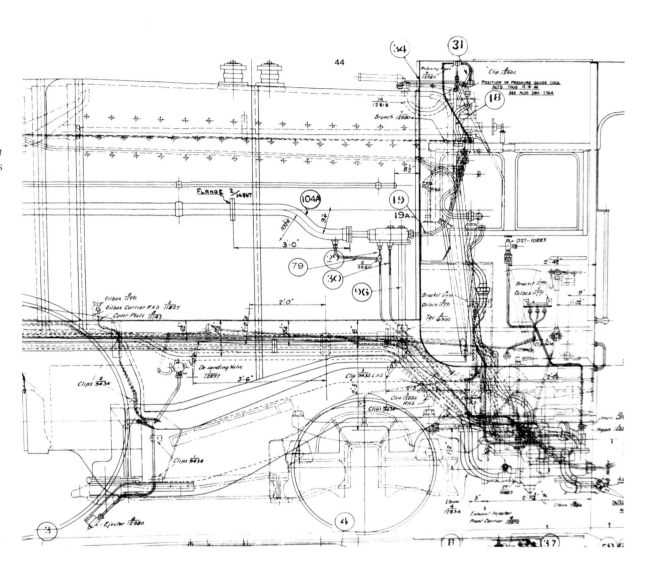

This drawing shows various aspects of the design, including rear bogie, injectors and cab arrangements.

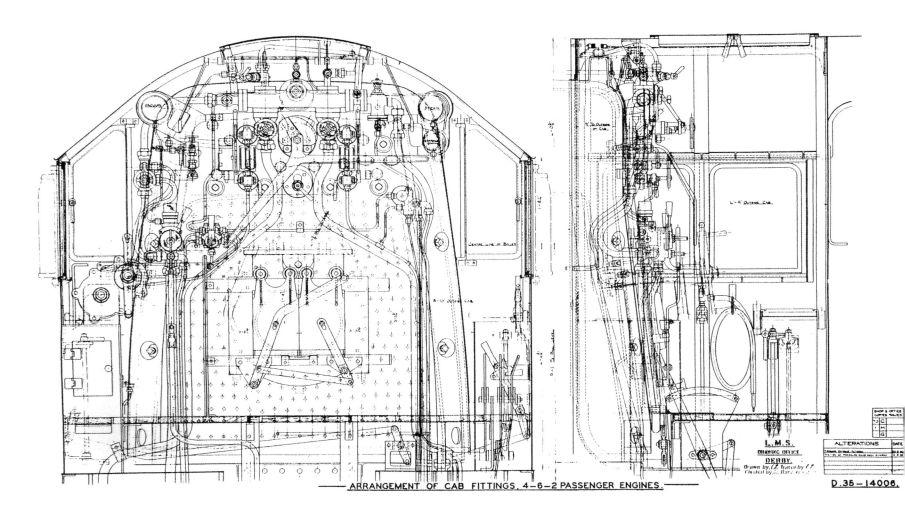

ARRANGEMENT OF CAB FITTINGS, 4–6–2 PASSENGER ENGINES.

D.35–14006.

The cab arrangements –
side and back elevations.

this is coupled to the sanding lever so
that when the leading sand is operated, a
hot-water jet is directed to the rails
which cleans the sand away after the
coupled wheels have passed over, this
with the object of preventing interference
with the track circuiting.

Carriage Warming
*The standard type of carriage warming
is fitted through from the locomotive to*

the hind end of the tender, the working
pressure being set at 50lbs per sq inch.

Grease Lubrication
*Various points on these locomotives
have been fitted with grease lubrication
as follows:*

Bissel truck anchor pin

Top and bottom brake hanger pins, engine and tender

Reversing lever pins and reversing gear in cab

Intermediate side buffer heads

Tank and Coal Bunker – *The tender
arrangement is of a conventional design,
with the exception that the water
capacity is increased to 4,000 gallons,
and the coal capacity to 9 tons.*

*It will be noticed that the only access
into the cab is by means of the tender
front footsteps. This is due to the large
throw over of the engine cab end and
not allowing sufficient clearance at
station platforms.*

6200 completed and ready for duty at Camden Shed in 1934. (LMS PR/RH)

Toolboxes – *Ample toolbox space is provided on the front of the tender and the bunker door admits access to the coal space from the engine footplate.*

Fire-irons – *The fire-iron tools are carried on supports above the top of the coal bunker.*

Water Pick-up and Hand Brake Gear – *The standard type of water pick-up apparatus is provided, but due to the large lateral movement at the engine cab end when taking curves, the vertical-type pillar control handles for both the water pick-up gear and tender hand brake was discarded. The gear is built into the front of the tender tank and the handles are arranged to work in a vertical plane, bevel gear is employed to couple through to the water pick-up*

and hand brake shaft in the usual way. The usual type of water feed valve and control is provided.

Steam Brake – *Steam brake is provided on each of the six tender wheels, and is applied simultaneously with the steam brake on the engine. The brake blocks are fitted behind each wheel. The brake percentage, on the basis of the tender being two thirds loaded with coal and water, is 60%.*

Roller Bearings – *'Timken' roller bearings are provided for all the tender wheels. An oil bath in the bottom of the housing for the roller bearings is provided which should only require occasional attention for filling up with oil.*

Wheelbase – *The wheelbase of the*

tender is 15' 0", and the wheel is the standard diameter of 4' 3" on the tread.

The overall length of the wheelbase of the engine and tender is 63', and provision has been made where necessary for 70 ft turntables to be provided to accommodate this engine.

The first engine to be turned out from Crewe Works, No 6200, is being broken in on light duties, and when fit for regular main-line service will be subjected to the usual thorough testing with the dynamometer car, so that the full engine performance and coal consumption may be obtained, and it is hoped that the results will justify the Railway Company's enterprise in building such a powerful locomotive.

PRINCESS CLASS – OPERATIONAL HISTORIES

6200/46200
Princess Royal.

This information is drawn from Engine History Cards held by the National Railway Museum or in private collections. Towards the end of steam, precise 'book-keeping' could not always be guaranteed, so dates and details should be treated with a little caution for the later years. However, the cards represent the most accurate picture available, with so much having been destroyed during the 1960s. Surviving records owe more to the intervention of concerned individuals than a considered policy of preservation by British Rail in that decade.

6200/46200
Princess Royal
Date Built - 27/6/1933 (Crewe).
Total Mileage - 1,524,631 (up to 12/1960, no details for final months of service).
Date Withdrawn - Week ending 17/11/1962 (at Carlisle Kingmoor).
Date Scrapped - 9/1964 (at J. Connell Ltd of Coatbridge, North Lanarkshire).
Liveries - 1933 – Red, 1947 – LMS Black, 1952 – BR Green, 1958 – BR Red.
Tenders Fitted - 6/33 – 9000, 5/35 – 9065, 11/36 – 9372, 8/55 – 9376,

6/56 – 9066.
Boilers Carried - 5/33 – 6048, 4/35 – 6050, 5/37 – 6049, 8/39 – 6048, 4/42 – 6050, 10/44 – 6048, 8/47 – 6050, 7/48 – 6048, 1/52 – 9106, 9/56 - 9103.

6201/46201
Princess Elizabeth
Date Built - 3/11/1933 (Crewe).
Total Mileage - 1,147,323 (on 20/10/1962).

Date Withdrawn - Week ending 20/10/1962 (at Carlisle Upperby).
Date Scrapped - Sold on 13 September 1962 for preservation.
Liveries - 1933 – Red, 1947 – LMS Black, 1948 – BR Black, 1952 – BR Green.
Tenders Fitted - 11/33 – 9001, 3/35 – 9066, 6/36 – 9065, 11/36 – 9373.
Boilers Carried - 8/33 – 6049, 10/35 – 6048, 9/37 – 6050, 2/40 – 6049,

6201/46201
Princess Elizabeth.

9/42 – 6048, 6/44 – 6049, 11/45 – 6050, 7/46 – 6049, 11/48 – 6050, 5/52 – 9109, 7/54 – 9103, 4/56 – 9235.

6202/46202
Turbomotive/*Princess Anne*

Date Built - 29/6/1935.
Date Rebuilt - 15/8/1952.
Total Mileage - 453,736 (in original and rebuilt forms).
Date Withdrawn - 22/5/1954.
Date Scrapped - Unconfirmed but likely to be June 1954.
Liveries - 1935 – Red, 1947 – LMS Black, 1949 – BR Black, 1952 – BR Green.
Tenders Fitted - 6/35 – 9003, 8/52 – 9003.
Boilers Carried - 6/35 – 9100, 7/36 – 9236.

Date Withdrawn - Week ending 7/10/1961 (Edge Hill).
Date Scrapped - At Crewe Works in 5/62.
Liveries - 1935 – Red, 1952 – BR Green, 1958 – BR Red.

Tenders Fitted - 7/35 – 9125, 12/36 – 9375.
Boilers Carried - 9/35 – 9102, 10/37 – 9105, 9/40 – 9109, 5/44 – 9103, 9/46 – 9108, 8/50 – 9236, 5/52 – 6048, 5/55 – 6049.

6203/46203
Princess Margaret Rose

Date Built - 1/7/1935 (Crewe).
Total Mileage - 1,494,491 (in 12/1961).
Date Withdrawn - Week ending 20/10/1962.
Date Scrapped - Sold in April 1963 to Butlin's Ltd for display and preservation.
Liveries - 1935 – Red, 1947 – LMS Black, 1951 – BR Blue, 1952 – BR Green.
Tenders Fitted - 7/35 – 9124, 1/37 – 9374.
Boilers Carried - 7/35 – 9101, 12/36 – 9100, 11/38 – 9101, 11/41 – 9106, 6/44 – 9102, 10/47 – 9106, 4/51 – 9108, 9/55 – 9101, 6/58 – 9100.

6203/46203
Princess Margaret Rose.

6204/46204
Princess Louise

Date Built - 19/7/1935 (Crewe).
Total Mileage - 1,373,945 (in 10/1961).

6204/46204
Princess Louise.

6205/46205
Princess Victoria.

6206/46206
Princess Marie Louise.

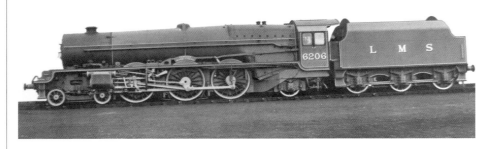

6205/46205
Princess Victoria
Date Built - 24/7/1935 (Crewe).
Total Mileage - 1,446,558 (by 11/1961).
Date Withdrawn - Week ending
25/11/1961 (Willesden).
Date Scrapped - At Crewe Works in
5/62.
Liveries - 1935 – Red, 1948 – BR
Black, 1952 – BR Green.

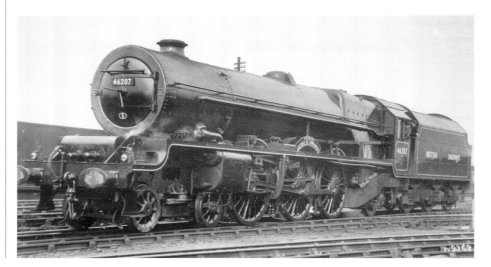

6207/46207
*Princess Arthur of
Connaught.*

Tenders Fitted - 7/35 – 9126, 5/36 –
9344, 7/36 – 9353, 3/37 – 9344.
Boilers Carried - 9/35 – 9103,
1/41 – 9108, 10/42 – 9104, 1/45 – 9109,
9/48 – 9235, 7/52 – 9105, 1/56 – 9107,
8/58 – 9109.

6206/46206
Princess Marie Louise
Date Built - 1/8/1935 (Crewe).
Total Mileage - 1,552,133.
Date Withdrawn - Week ending
3/11/1962 (Camden).
Date Scrapped - At Crewe Works
10/62.
Liveries - 1935 – Red, 1948 – LMS
Black, 1950 – BR Blue, 1953 –
BR Green.
Tenders Fitted - 8/35 – 9127,
10/36 – 9359, 11/46 – 9353,
10/47 – 9359, 10/62 – 9816.
Boilers Carried - 9/35 – 9104,
7/37 – 9235, 6/39 – 9100,
11/42 – 9108, 8/43 – 9235,
7/45 – 9104, 1/48 – 9102, 9/50 – 9101,
2/55 – 9100, 1/58 – 9105.

6207/46207
Princess Arthur of Connaught
Date Built - 9/8/1935 (Crewe).
Total Mileage - 1,502,705 (by 11/1961).
Date Withdrawn - Week ending
25/11/1961 (Willesden).
Date Scrapped - At Crewe Works
5/62.
Liveries - 1935 – Red, 1949 – BR
Black, 1951 – BR Green, 1958 – BR Red.
Tenders Fitted - 1935 – 9128,
1936 – 9376, 12/39 – 9353, 1946 – 9359,
1947 – 9353.
Boilers Carried - 1935 – 9105,
1937 – 9104, 1940 – 9102, 1941 – 9101,
1943 – 9108, 1946 – 9100, 1949 – 9105,
1951 – 9102, 1955 – 9109, 1958 – 9106.

6208/46208
Princess Helena Victoria
Date Built - 16/8/1935 (Crewe).
Total Mileage - 1,449,634 (by 10/62).
Date Withdrawn - Week ending
20/10/62 (Edge Hill).
Date Scrapped - At Crewe Works
11/62.
Liveries - 1935 – Red, 1950 – BR Blue,
1952 – BR Green, 1958 – BR Red.
Tenders Fitted - 8/35 – 9129,
7/36 – 9344, 3/37 – 9353, 6/39 – 9360.
Boilers Carried - 9/35 – 9106,
4/38 – 9109, 4/40 – 9104, 9/42 – 9107,
9/46 – 9235, 3/48 – 9104, 8/50 – 6049,
10/52 – 6050, 2/57 – 9104.

6209/46209
Princess Beatrice
Date Built - 23/8/1935 (Crewe).
Total Mileage - 1,578,045 (by 9/62).
Date Withdrawn - Week ending
29/9/62 (Camden).
Date Scrapped - At Crewe Works
11/62.
Liveries - 1935 – Red, 1948 – BR
Black, 1951 – BR Green.
Tenders Fitted - 10/36 – 9361,
9/46 – 9354.
Boilers Carried - 9/35 – 9107,
2/37 – 9101, 10/38 – 9106, 7/41 – 9103,
11/43 - 9105, 11/45 – 9107,
11/48 – 9109, 8/51 – 9104, 1/56 – 9108.

6210/46210
Lady Patricia
Date Built - 6/9/1935 (Crewe).
Total Mileage - 1,457,814 (by 10/61).
Date Withdrawn - Week ending
7/10/61 (Carlisle Kingmoor).
Date Scrapped - At Crewe Works
5/62.
Liveries - 1935 – Red, 1947 – LMS

6208/46208
Princess Helena Victoria.

6209/46209
Princess Beatrice.

6210/46210
Lady Patricia.

6211/46211
Queen Maud.

Black, 1950 – BR Blue,
1953 – BR Green.
Tenders Fitted - 9/35 – 9131,
9/36 – 9360, 6/39 – 9353, 12/39 – 9376,
8/55 – 9372.
Boilers Carried - 9/35 -9108,
11/40 – 9105, 9/43 – 9236, 8/44 – 9106,
7/47 – 9101, 4/50 – 9103, 1/53 – 9107,
11/55 – 6048, 1/58 – 6050.

6211/46211
Queen Maud
Date Built - 18/9/1935 (Crewe).
Total Mileage - 1,537,215 (by 10/61).
Date Withdrawn - Week ending
7/10/1961 (Crewe North).
Date Scrapped - At Crewe Works
4/62.
Liveries - 1935 – Red, 1947 – LMS
Black, 1950 - BR Blue,
1953 – BR Green.

6212/46212
Duchess of Kent.

Tenders Fitted - 9/35 – 9132,
6/36 – 9345, 9/46 – 9361.
Boilers Carried - 9/35 – 9109,
2/38 – 9102, 11/39 – 9107, 7/42 – 9102,
5/44 – 9101, 1/47 – 9103, 5/49 – 9100,
11/52 – 9235, 1/56 – 9102, 7/58 – 6048.

6212/46212
Duchess of Kent
Date Built - 21/10/1935 (Crewe).
Total Mileage - 1,486,229 (by 1061).

Date Withdrawn - Week ending
7/10/1961 (Crewe North).
Date Scrapped - At Crewe Works
4/62.
Liveries - 1935 – Red, 1949 – BR
Black, 1952 – BR Green.
Tenders Fitted - 10/35 – 9133,
7/36 – 9354, 12/44 – 9345.
Boilers Carried - 10/35 – 9235,
5/37 – 9107, 7/39 – 9235, 6/43 – 9100,
3/49 – 9107, 10/52 – 6049, 1/54 – 9236.

REFERENCES SOURCES

**The National Railway Museum
(Search Engine)**
Records Consulted:
Loco/Expt/1
Test/LMS/21
Test/Expt/1
Tech/LMS/1 to 4
The E.A. Langridge Collection
The E.S. Cox Collection
The R. Riddles Collection

**The National Archives
(On line 'Discovery' programme)**
Various files relating to the work of Frederick Johansen
and streamlining experiments in the NA's Rail series.

The Churchill Archive Centre, Cambridge
The Harold Brewer Hartley Collection.

Other Collections
R.A. Hillier
A.R. Ewer
A. Truckett
T.F. Coleman

Books and Other Publications Consulted
R. Bond – *A Lifetime With Locomotives* (ISBN:0 900404 30 2)
G. Bushell – *LMS Locoman* (ISBN:0 85153 425 2)
H.A.V. Bullied – *Master Builders of Steam* (1965)
J.E. Chacksfield – *Sir William Stanier* (ISBN:0 85361 576 4)
E.S. Cox – *Locomotive Panorama* (two volumes) (1965/66)
L. Earl – *Speeding North With The Royal Scot* (1939)
H. Holcroft – *Locomotive Adventure* (1960)
E.A. Langridge – *Under 10 CMEs* (two volumes)
    (ISBN:978 0 85361 7013)
R. Matheson – *Doing Time Inside* (ISBN:978 07524 5301 9)
O.S. Nock – *William Stanier – An Engineering Biography*
    (1964)

H.C.B. Rogers – *The Last Steam Locomotive Engineer –
    R.A. Riddles* (ISBN:0 04 385053 7)
I. Sixsmith – *The Book of the Princess Royal Pacifics*
    (ISBN:1 903266 01 7)
A. Williams – *Life In A Railway Factory* (1915)
Wild Swan LMS Locomotive Profile No 4 – *The Princess
    Royal Pacifics* (ISBN:1 874103 86 0)
The Journal of the Institution of Locomotive Engineers
    (various editions)
Meccano Magazine (1935–1940)
The Engineer (1935–1940)
Backtrack (various editions)
The Railway Magazine (various issues)
The LMS and GWR in house magazines.

INDEX